Also by Oswald Garrison Villard

John Brown: A Biography Fifty Years After (1910, 1943)
Germany Embattled (1915)
Some Newspapers and Newspaper-men (1923)
Prophets True and False (1928)
The German Phoenix (1933)
Fighting Years: Memoirs of a Liberal Editor (1939)
Our Military Chaos (1939)
Within Germany (1940)

THE DISAPPEARING DAILY

THE
Disappearing
Daily

CHAPTERS IN
AMERICAN NEWSPAPER
EVOLUTION

BY

Oswald Garrison Villard

1944

NEW YORK   *Alfred A Knopf*

FIRST EDITION

T O
WENDELL PHILLIPS GARRISON
Co-Editor and Editor of THE NATION *1865–1906*

DEVOTED UPHOLDER

OF A NOBLE JOURNALISTIC TRADITION

Preface

THIS RECORD of the development of the American press supplements a previous study published in 1923 and republished in a revised edition in 1926. It brings up to date the situation of American journalism in the middle of the greatest of our wars, and illustrates by its study of some of our foremost dailies and press associations the trend of what was once a profession but is now a business, though still vitally affected by a public interest. It would be idle to pretend that the picture as a whole is encouraging, either to journalists or to the public. Coupled with the alarming mortality among our dailies, those tendencies toward chain ownership, consolidations, and monopolies which were pointed out twenty years ago are more obvious than ever, except that the spread of chain ownership has for the moment been checked. A number of historically important journals have disappeared, and the mortality-rate has largely increased since Pearl Harbor. Unfortunately these disturbing developments cannot be offset by the citation of new experiments promising to mitigate the evils inherent in individual ownership of great organs of political opinion. There is no promise today of the sudden rise of new dailies, only the certainty that we shall see a still greater decrease in the number now extant which is already quite too small for this nation, especially as it is embarked upon a world leadership no American could have foreseen. Nor does the radio offer the solution, for that not only is government-controlled, but is itself directly supported by the great business enterprises whose rise and control have more and more dominated the American political and economic scene.

The battle for democracy will not have been won when Germany is beaten. The war itself will produce new dangers to it, both here and abroad. No war heretofore engaged in by the United States has been so secretly conducted as this, as to both military movements and far-reaching governmental actions and policies never submitted to the electorate or the Congress for approval; and these actions and policies have profoundly committed the nation to involvements all over the globe the outcome of which no man can foresee. The trend toward State Socialism will be accentuated in every country, and the specter of totalitarianism will not have been laid by the victorious nations which have resorted to totalitarian methods to defeat the hostile dictators — the friendly ones will survive the struggle. All the more necessary is it, therefore, to focus popular attention upon the fundamental problems of the transmission of factual and correct news, free from selfish business or governmental control, to the peoples of the earth. For without such unbiased information the roads to dictatorship lie open.

The slow disappearance of the American daily is doubly a menace: not only does it tend to deprive the people of vital information, it even threatens, if it continues, to bring nearer governmental supplying and control of news, under which republican institutions could not possibly flourish. It is of the utmost importance, therefore, that every newspaper development be scrutinized and weighed with the greatest care if only because of the danger that our dailies will be more and more controlled by individuals of enormous wealth, committed to the preservation of the *status quo* because of their material prosperity. One can only hope at this hour that out of the present turmoil and struggle, and those which are inevitable in the coming reconstruction period, there will again emerge brave and dauntless spirits to bring about a renaissance of the trade of imparting the news, coupled with the offering of moral and spiritual leadership, as has happened in the past, notably in anti-slavery days.

It remains to repeat what was in part said in the previous volume: While nothing has been set down in malice in this book, the author must admit bias. It is the bias of one who has belonged to the trade for forty-seven years, who cannot witness its rapid decadence without sharp pain. It is also the bias of one who, together with five other members of his family, has had the privilege of serving journalistic ideals for one hundred and twenty-five years, with one exception a longer consecutive newspaper service than that of any other American family.

The studies of a few editors of a bygone generation included in this volume are reprinted in order to supply a historical background of the evolution of our press.

OSWALD GARRISON VILLARD

New York, 1944

Contents

THE DISAPPEARING DAILY

CHAPTER I

The Disappearing Daily

THE OUTSTANDING FACT in any survey of the American press is the steady and alarming decrease in the number of dailies. Consolidation, suppression, and a strong drift toward monopoly are taking their toll. With an increase in population to more than 130,000,000, with world-shaking events of almost daily occurrence and the need for detailed, printed information greater than ever in the battle for human liberty, there are at this writing but 1,754 daily English-language journals in the great American nation as against 2,042 in 1920, and 1,933 in 1930. The decrease has been marked throughout this century. No less than 104 dailies died or were amalgamated between September 30, 1941 and March 31, 1943, although this period, except for the first two months, was distinguished by the attack on Pearl Harbor and the startling developments of our second World War. Not only were the factors making for the decrease of the dailies not offset by these thrilling events in all quarters of the globe, but there was almost no evidence of any desire to start new journals. Moreover, the war added to the difficulties of the weaker dailies through increasing costs, scarcity of labor, lack of paper, and a large decrease in advertising, such as automobile announcements, though others showed striking increases. Today there are no less than 1,103 towns and cities with only one newspaper, and in 159 large towns and cities having more than one daily there is complete ownership of the local press by one man or one group.

It is true that, according to figures compiled by *Editor and Publisher,* English-language daily newspaper circulations increased approximately four per cent during the period from Pearl Harbor to March 31, 1943, the total daily circulation for all the newspapers being 44,392,829 copies. This is the highest figure recorded in the history of the American press, and this despite the loss in the number of newspapers. But this gain in total sales by no means offsets the loss of many organs of public opinion. There are still 11,474 weekly papers (though here, too, there is a marked decrease), and some of these carry considerable weight in their communities by trying to print more news, and in some cases even taking over standard features, such as the work of some of the columnists. In the weekly field there are few signs of vital growth if by that is meant the entrance into the business of vigorous young personalities with a message to impart. The case of the newspaper proprietor in the large towns and small cities also becomes more and more difficult because of those increasing costs of conducting the modern newspaper with its expensive machinery — the New York *Times's* newest press is valued at more than $1,000,000 — and its more and more elaborate means of acquiring and receiving its news. Only in periods of intense financial depression is there any slackening of the mounting costs of producing a daily, whose owners are often at the mercy of the inventor of a labor-saving or time-saving device, however expensive. Finally, in war-time the limitation of the supply of paper comes into the picture. Thus on a single day in October 1943 one of our largest newspapers was forced to omit 125 columns of advertising, and this was not even a Sunday issue.

Few laymen understand that in the smaller communities in particular there is a definite limitation of the possible support to be had for a daily. While there exists, of course, a large volume of what is known as "national advertising," paid for by concerns marketing goods or services in which all communities are more or less interested, the main support of a daily usually comes from the merchants of the place of publication. These sellers of goods not only do not oppose the newspaper trend to monopoly, but encourage it on the ground that if they advertise in only one daily they will save time and labor in the preparation of their announcements and have much less to pay out. What they and the proprietors of newspapers who seek monopolies overlook is that the newspaper business is unlike most others in that it is "affected by a public interest." It is a vital public need that the people in a democracy shall have the news and the opportunity to read all sides of political debates of the hour. As Thomas Jefferson put it, the best way to head off unsound opinion in a democracy is "to give them [the people] full information of their affairs thro' the channels of the public papers and to contrive that these papers should penetrate the whole mass of the people." To establish a press monopoly in a locality is to restrict the field of public information or to narrow its vision, or even perhaps to put an end to the presentation in the remaining dailies of anything but a partisan aspect of the national political or economic situation — and this despite the coming of the radio. Yet every successful publisher is beset by the temptation to increase his power and to make sure of financial profit by eliminating competitors.

From the point of view of economy and avoiding duplication of labor and editorial effort, a case can be made for the realization of the average newspaper publisher's dream of only one morning and one evening newspaper in each large city, and only one daily in all cities having 100,000 or fewer inhabitants. But aside from special influences in the newspaper business, there never was any reason to believe that the newspapers, having changed from a profession open to men of small means into a business requiring millions and therefore possible for only the very wealthy, could escape those economic tendencies which, notably in America, have more or less affected all other large industrial enterprises. Since no one would dream of starting a metropolitan newspaper with less than ten or even fifteen millions in the bank, the daily everywhere takes its place as an important industrial enterprise, a big business whose proprietors are entitled to rank among the foremost mercantile leaders of the community. Their tendency is naturally to think and act as do the members of the economic group to which they belong, and to drift steadily away from the plain people and especially from the workers. Just as the profession of journalism has changed into a business, so there is every temptation for the proprietor to consider all political and economic questions from the point of view of those who have very large economic stakes and to look with alarm upon all proposed social and political reforms. The newspaper owner feels that he belongs in the Chamber of Commerce and the merchants' associations more naturally, perhaps, than anybody else except the heads of the public utilities. His property ranks with those powerful business corporations which in every American community dominate its economic and financial life, whose officials and their wives set the "society" tone and too often control all social progress.

Other important changes in the evolution of the dailies are their increasing standardization, their continuing change from

a purely informative and news-printing medium into an organ
of entertainment as well, and their great loss of political and editorial influence. As for standardization, that is so obvious as to
need no stressing. It is naturally increased by the existence of
chains of dailies under one ownership. When one travels through
the country on a fast train and buys successively the newspapers
of larger cities, one is struck by their similarity. One finds the
same comics, the same special features in almost all, the same
Sunday magazine and financial section, and precisely the same
Associated Press or United Press news. I have looked through
the Sunday editions of nine large Eastern and Midwestern newspapers; a cursory examination of the Philadelphia *Inquirer* revealed twenty features that were also in the other eight newspapers. Today whenever a journal discovers a new feature, there
is a widespread rush to copy it; the competition for a popular
comic strip or its imitation is the clearest testimony on this point.
There is no copyright to bar the adoption of new trade devices if
they are dressed anew.

The newspaper of striking individuality has yielded to the desire to print everything offered by one's rivals. Almost nobody
among present-day journalists sets any store by beauty of type
and originality of appearance. There are still striking exceptions,
like the *Herald Tribune,* the *Christian Science Monitor,* the Cincinnati *Enquirer,* and some Southern newspapers; but with the
coming of mass production of dailies the desire for originality
seemed to pass. Moreover, the columnists and the "canned editorials," the syndicated articles, and even the latest mechanical
developments all make for similarity. When the teletypesetter
came in, Frank Gannett, one of its backers, wrote that it would
"work towards standardization," saying: "It will be necessary
for newspapers that intend to go in a circuit to standardize their
grammatical style, width of column, and the size of type used.
It will also tend to standardize our news services." There are
hundreds of newspapers that receive their editorials from one
source, such as the Newspaper Enterprise Association. I have received as many as sixty clippings from as many small dailies all
over the Union containing editorial comment upon some words
of mine — all alike, all from the same source, the facts and
opinions given being accepted by the editors receiving them
without any critical examination whatever as to their correctness.

Indeed, nowhere is the drift toward standardization more marked than in the editorial pages, unless it be in the first pages, where, in the smaller cities particularly, one often finds slavish copying of the headlines and make-up of the large city dailies. Just as there is no longer any desire to make newspapers distinctive for individuality and for originality in the presentation of news, so many of the proprietors are influenced by this trend not to have striking personalities in charge of their editorial pages. The conservative owner does not want a powerful leader-writer to "ride hobbies or antagonize whole groups of readers," as one of them remarked to me. Curiously enough, he sticks to this although he is often aware of the lack of influence of his editorial page, for he frequently sees no inconsistency in spreading upon the first page of his daily editorials he specially wishes to have read. He even signs them himself in order to win the attention of politicians and public. At the same time he pays large sums to writers of distinction to take over his sports pages or contribute daily columns under their own signatures.

It has not been at all difficult for the dailies to swing over to the amusement side. Indeed, many have been compelled to do so and owe their continued existence to the comics, the illustrations, the puzzles, the fiction, the sports news, and the personal gossip they print. Thus, in order to keep alive, they enter fields of activity which seemed wholly outside of the scope of the newspaper until a few decades ago. Even when empty cupboards have not driven the owners along this road to success, many have realized the tremendous interest of the masses in the amusements which are their escape from their work and the routine of their lives, and, in war-time, from the nerve-racking strains to which most people are subjected. Some dailies, like the New York *Times,* to their infinite credit have refused to yield; but it has not been necessary for their financial welfare to do so. Here, as in so many other cases, we have a world-wide phenomenon.

Sir Philip Gibbs, for example, in discussing the sad plight of the British press, appealed for "less pandering to the gallery of human nature," in addition to his demand for more newspapers to offset the increasing monopolies, and for more responsibility and reliability because the press as a whole has lost its power, because "its word is no longer accepted as gospel." Few newspaper managers care for this loss of standing if they can add to their readership by printing pages and pages of comics, hints to the lovelorn, canned advice to parents, syndicated recipes for the housewife, widely marketed cuts of the coming fashions for women young and old. As long as such features make a popular appeal the modern proprietor does not care in how many other dailies they appear or how trivial and banal or vulgar they may be. He is competing with the movies, with the radio, with the legitimate stage. Hence he is sure that his greatest appeal to his readers is to be found in his "funnies" and his sensational pictures.

The commercial proprietor of this type is, therefore, little affected if he is told that he is not living up to his duty as the mentor and critic of our political and economic life. It is his income that is at stake. He is not worried when he reads a criticism like that of Irving Brant, the head of the editorial page of the St. Louis *Star-Times,* who has declared that: "Taken as a whole, the newspapers of America furnish no driving force for social reform. They are a positive handicap in economic reform. . . . It is impossible to point to one important constructive step in the last eight years which represents either the inventiveness, the initiative, or the supporting activity of the American press." * Mr. Brant, an ardent champion of the New Deal, says that for a few months in 1933 there was an emotional press response to the initiative and leadership of President Roosevelt, but that the metropolitan newspapers have been "substantially regimented against the New Deal" from the day "they were asked to limit the hours of their employees to forty per week and to pay reporters a minimum wage of $25, from the day they were told that the law guaranteed newspaper employees the right to organize for collective bargaining."

Largely because of this changed attitude of the press, it is a fact that its loss of prestige and influence is appalling and overshadows every other development except its decrease in numbers. The newspaper reader pays less and less attention to what the editors are saying and to their advice on the conduct of the nation's affairs. Here the outstanding proof is afforded by the results of the Presidential elections of 1936 and 1940. In both cases the vast bulk of the press opposed the re-election of the

* "The Newspaper in Public Affairs," an address at the University of Colorado College of Journalism on May 8, 1937.

President. Indeed, the opposition was so overwhelming that the election of 1936 was called a vote against the newspapers, a "judgment day for America's daily press." The electorate went to the election booths under the strongest impression not only that the press was mainly Republican, but that it was fighting not for the country as a whole but for its own personal interests. They felt so keenly that it was a hostile force that in Chicago the crowds cheered attacks on their anti-Roosevelt dailies as the returns came in. In 1896 the press threw itself overwhelmingly into the fight against Bryan and stopped at nothing to accomplish its purpose. It showed its power and won. In 1936 and in 1940 it failed.

In an extraordinarily able article after the 1936 election, the editors of the *Christian Century* indicted the press for "its arrogance, its tyranny, its greed, its scorn of fairplay." They declared that every variety of political liberalism, in addition to organized labor and the organized farmer, had definitely come to the point where "they no longer hoped to be given just treatment" in the columns of the newspapers. Undoubtedly the intensity of this feeling, which still persists to a remarkable degree, was due to the opposition of the press to the NRA, and its long-continued refusal to accept a code for itself. Its challenging — and defeating — the child-labor constitutional amendment lest it be deprived of its newsboys, and its hostility to unions among its own workers, were both accepted as further proof that the press had cast aside all pretense that it was governed by devotion to the public welfare. Many a critic besides the *Christian Century* saw in this vote a branding of the press for its "social malfeasance," for its carrying on merely as the property of rich men, as a dangerous enemy in "the ultimate issue in a democracy, wealth versus commonwealth." Whatever the exact delinquency of the press in 1936, it cannot deny that Roosevelt carried the country by a 10,000,000 plurality, polling 27,000,000 votes.

The editors of the *New Republic* made a special study * of fifteen cities in connection with the 1936 Presidential election. Approximately 71 per cent of the total newspaper circulation of the fifteen cities, excepting those newspapers which were for neither Roosevelt nor Landon, was hostile to the Roosevelt candidacy, but in those cities only 31 per cent of the voters cast their

* Issue of March 17, 1937.

ballots for the Republican candidate. In Boston, for example, there was a pro-Landon circulation of 1,158,352, yet there were only 96,418 votes cast for him. In Los Angeles the pro-Roosevelt newspapers sold only 74,252 copies, but there was a Democratic vote of 757,351, which was exactly 400,000 more than the Republican vote. In Detroit not a single newspaper advocated the reelection of Roosevelt, but he carried the city by 404,055 to a Republican vote of 190,732. The *New Republic's* editors felt that the unfairness of some of the newspapers to Roosevelt's candidacy during the campaign showed that the press was getting worse and not better, and that the decay of the editorial page was more and more marked. They charged that the Chicago *Tribune* and the Hearst chain were the worst offenders because they "not only prevaricated editorially, but distorted and discolored news."

Were there any doubt as to the reactionary and selfish character of much of the press, it would be ended by a study of the policies of the American Newspaper Publishers' Association, which speaks largely for it. The Association not only opposed the NRA, the newspaper code, the coming of the newspaper guilds, and the child-labor amendment, but has also attacked the National Labor Relations Act, and stood against the advance of labor all along the line. If many of the individual newspapers allow themselves to be controlled by the Association, then we have here a very grave threat to freedom of the press. As Mr. Brant has said, the objection to such control lies not in the fact that it is conservative, for it would be just as serious if it came from liberals on behalf of a liberal program. It lies in the truth that any attempt at a centralized control of newspaper opinion is an attack upon a fundamental freedom and "weakens the basis of our American democracy."

The loss of influence by the newspapers is also in large measure due to the belief that much of the local reporting is one-sided, biased, and inefficient. Every large community knows how many of its activities go unrecorded, and many of its citizens are aware by personal experience of the too frequent misrepresentation of what does happen. Often the public errs in its judgment of what should and could be reported of a city's life, even by the greatest newspapers. But those citizens who in every municipality are struggling to rectify misgovernment, to apply social curatives, and to improve civic methods know all too well how difficult it is to win and to hold the attention of the dailies. The reformers' programs are usually not sensational and are often not well presented, even when there is a "human interest" side to what they have to offer. When they are told that the lack of space makes it impossible to give room to their activities, yet see columns and columns given to gossip, scandal, and crime, they naturally believe that they have been deceived. They cannot understand it when the editor or publisher tells them he must print discussions of sports, crimes, fiction, "society" and club events, and so on, in order to hold the attention of so diversified a group as any aggregation of newspaper readers.

As one who has been on both sides of the fence, for many years on one side as a reporter and editor, and on the other as a lecturer, author, and protagonist of many causes, I can come to no other conclusion than that there has been a marked deterioration in the character and quality of the average reporting. There are brilliant exceptions — dailies earnestly seeking to be accurate — but in the main the reliability of news accounts is far below what it was years ago, and the chance of misrepresentation through unintentional misquotation as well as carelessness is so great that it is frequently necessary for speakers to safeguard themselves by preserving a copy of their statements, or by preparing in advance a "hand-out" for the reporters. Too often the reporter sent to interview the visitor in town knows nothing about the subject he asks his victim to discuss. Distinguished authors from overseas find themselves cross-examined by high-school graduates who have not the faintest idea of the background or the achievements of the men whom they are undertaking to report and to describe, or just what makes the visitors at that moment "good copy." "Where do you live and how many books have you written?" is hardly the best way to greet a man whose name is known all over the Anglo-Saxon world.

In my small sphere I have encountered reporters who admitted that they did not know whether I was an editor or a hardware merchant or a politician and had no conception of the purpose of their errand. Others could not understand the simplest developments in international affairs and showed their ignorance of outstanding men in American political life. Everyone who has traveled much and attracted the notice of the press will recall his unutterable relief on meeting a reporter who was intelligent, informed, and eager to be accurate. When one has the remarkable experience of having one's remarks recorded with stenographic accuracy and complete understanding, one naturally sends an immediate letter of thanks to the editor and the reporter. I am sure that many besides myself, so far from looking eagerly for the reproduction of an interview, have turned to it only with a wonder as to how bad the misrepresentation would be that time, or have felt relief if no interview was reported at all, or if what appeared was boiled down to a couple of "stickfuls."

On behalf of the reporters it should be said that they are as much sinned against as sinning. It is constantly dinned into their ears that when they go to public meetings or to interviews they must look for something "spicy," something to warrant a smart headline, something unexpectedly sensational or controversial. There must always be a bright, snappy "lead." So happenings of no real importance are constantly "played up" and really valuable statements or actions overlooked. A controversy between two speakers is particularly beloved, or an interruption from the audience. American assemblies and speakers in a joint debate are so unused to heckling and interrogations that when anyone does speak up, it becomes something extraordinary — to be "featured." * So the reporter is trained to look for the bizarre as all-important. If nothing exciting happens and the reporter does not bring out valuable points, or it is a crowded night at the office, his whole report is thrown on the floor. Indeed, what often puzzles the public is to see a group of reporters at a meeting and then to search in vain the next morning for one word of the happenings, or to find only a few skimpy lines. "Why was the reporters' time wasted?" the public asks. "Who called them off?"

One Washington meeting comes to mind, held during midsummer of 1942 to protest against conditions in India and to demand India's freedom. The hall was crowded to suffocation, despite dreadful heat, and hundreds were turned away, even from an overflowing meeting. The speakers were of good stand-

---

* Colonel Henry W. Nevinson, the great English journalist and war correspondent, once said to me, after a meeting in New York at which he had spoken, that he knew he had made a bad speech because no one had interrupted or heckled him!

ing and reputation, one a national figure. The reporters' table was crowded, and the next day — not a word anywhere except a complete misrepresentation of the meeting in an evening newspaper! The speakers had been scrupulously polite to the British, but had any one of them made a violent attack upon Lord Halifax or Winston Churchill, or somebody else, the meeting would have made the front pages. I asked the owner of one of the Washington newspapers why his daily had suppressed the news of so large a meeting on so vitally important a war subject. He said he did not know why, but that he was sure that it was due to the shortage of paper and lack of space and not to any deliberate effort to suppress criticisms of English policy. To the question why, if there was so little space, the newspapers wasted time and money in sending reporters out to do nothing and print nothing, he had no reply.

In the case of this Washington meeting the reporters were obviously not responsible for the failure of their "stories" to appear. The night make-up editor holds the final say, unless overruled by superior authority. Indeed, the modern reporter is blamed frequently for the errors and the stupidities of the copyreaders. There can be no question that there has been a marked deterioration in the technical handling of "copy" and news dispatches. The newspapers of the 1890s and the first two decades of this century prided themselves upon the accuracy of their reports, and were zealous in their efforts to catch blunders, bad English, and inaccurate descriptions. Today a veteran journalist writes me that "sloppiness in product is the outstanding phase of the Manhattan newspapers in 1943. Nobody seems to be concerned about the real meaning of words. The city and copy desks no longer care about blunders. The old zealot pride in Tiffany-grade craftsmanship seems moribund. Showmanship has replaced reportorial accuracy and ability. How can an eager cub develop into an ace when he lacks persistent coaching in the fundamentals of his profession? I have just read this morning's newspapers and gagged over their inexcusable sloppiness." The above cited ignorance of the average reporter as to recent history, political and other personalities, and current events is too often reflected on the copy-desk.

The readiness of the American daily to drop local happenings on any excuse affects not merely meetings and causes, but accounts of notable events. So marked has this been for some time that the late Frank Vanderlip once declared that if he were a younger man he would launch a new-type daily, one that would contain no news dispatches except those from Washington relating directly to the welfare of the city in which the paper was published. Everything else would be news of local affairs. Yet home coverage used to be the groundwork of every newspaper, and notably of the small country weeklies and dailies with their printing of "personal mentions" to take the place of local events of importance when those were not forthcoming. It will be regrettable indeed if after this war the press does not return to its prime duty of reporting the progress, or the retrogression, or the ambitions of its home communities.

One may well wonder if many proprietors and editors have seriously studied the exact division of their daily's space, or really sought to find out if the city's feelings, as indicated by the public's expression of its views, are adequately covered by their publications. Yet there are few things that have done so much to destroy faith in the press as inexact reporting. It is especially dangerous because persons present at events reported testify widely to the failure or the bias of the press. Here again it must be repeated that there are brilliant exceptions. This is, however, one of the many reasons why people no longer say: "I saw it in the newspapers, and so it must be true," but "Oh, you can't believe what you see in the dailies." Yet the former phrase was on the whole well earned by the press during the generations when the reporting — even in the 1850s — was far superior in detail and accuracy to that of the general run of today's. The New York *Herald,* for example, during the anti-slavery struggle, reported an Abolition meeting with stenographic fidelity even when it was entirely opposed to the purposes of the meeting, and, as in the case of one address by Wendell Phillips, had actually hired a mob to break up the meeting; its verbatim report was superior to that of the Abolition *Tribune.* It is true that in those days there was plenty of space and relatively little news. Today the demands on space are tremendous, but the selection of what is to go into it is too one-sided, too often, as said, guided by the search for sensation, by likes and dislikes.

When we turn to the field of labor it is not difficult to understand why the great body of workers believes the newspapers to be their most potent enemy. This is because of their ability, when strikes and other labor troubles occur, to judge newspaper accounts by their own experience and knowledge. Usually the press is against them and presents colored editorial opinions and misleading or false newspaper reports. However in the wrong and unjust the employers may be, or how partisan the conduct of the authorities and the police, it is rare indeed that a newspaper holds the scales even or leans to the labor side. Of late years the New York *Times* and some other strong newspapers have set an admirable example in appointing special labor reporters, like Louis Stark of the *Times,* and have given them free rein to report what is actually going on within the unions and to portray truthfully the labor point of view. But in the main the tendency to take sides with passion and hostility against labor, and particularly any such unpopular labor leader as John L. Lewis, renders any fair reporting out of the question in the bulk of the press or by the press associations.

Certainly no one would allege that the press as a whole has even begun to do its duty in reporting the unfair practices of employers and public authorities such as have recently been brought out by Senator LaFollette's inquiry into them through his special Committee on Civil Liberties in connection with labor troubles. The ordinary tendency is to uphold the police, however lawless and brutal its actions, however ghastly its slaughter of the workers, such as took place in Chicago during the great strike at the Republic Steel Company's works when the police interfered with a murderous brutality surely not exceeded except by Hitler's S.S. Moving-picture films proved the scandalous conduct of the police, and some corrective measures were taken by the authorities. But if anybody should need further proof of how lawless the press and the police can be, he should turn to the trouble in San Francisco in 1934 which took on the character of a general strike. This is one of the very few cases in which the charge of a newspaper conspiracy can be brought against the dailies. The San Francisco newspapers formed the "Newspaper Publishers' Council" so that they could act together. Their first important effort was to prevent the declaration of martial law on the ground that if order was maintained — and therefore the strike was not illegally interfered with — "the announced objective of the general strike" would

have been aided. They were successful in this, and next printed
on their first pages editorials stating that radicals had got control of the unions and "that the general strike was a revolution
against constituted authority," which it was not in the remotest
degree.

Then General Hugh Johnson, the head of the NRA, arrived
in San Francisco. Eager to "grant the request of the general
strike committee that the longshoremen's demands for complete
control of hiring halls be accepted as a condition before any discussion of arbitration should occur," he declared that the ship-
owners were "anti-social," because "labor is inherently entitled
to bargain collectively through leaders of its own choosing," and
because "in the American shipping industry, including the load-
ing and unloading of ships, this right has not been justly ac-
corded." He went on to say that because of this the responsibility
"for anything that may happen here" would be "on the head"
of the shipping managers. Then the Publishers' Council got to
work on him and kept at him until three a.m. When the next
dawn came he announced that the workers whose cause he had
just justified constituted "a threat to the community," planning
"civil war," "bloody insurrection," "a blow at the flag of our
common country." More than that, he declared that if the government did not act, the people would. This was immediately
followed by the appearance of "vigilantes," who, with the police
following and abetting them, were soon smashing private property, entering private premises without warrant, and destroying
the contents of the headquarters of unions, Communists, and
radical newspapers.

The police arrested hundreds of people — again without warrant — and, without the excuse that mob violence was going on,
beat them up and threw them into jail. One San Francisco judge
alone released eighty men against whom, he said, no shadow
of a charge of lawless conduct could be brought. In all of this
the newspapers, always with the admirable exception of the
Scripps-Howard *News* — which was not in the Council — continued to play a despicable part, inciting by their headlines to
public excitement and disorder. They pretended that union men
made the raids, which was not true, for, according to reliable
witnesses, the police themselves were the most lawless and the

most guilty. What can be said of the mentality of those publishers who could not see that offenses by officials under oath to uphold and defend the laws and the rights of the individual constitute vastly more dangerous blows to our American institutions and our Constitution than could the activities of the few really "radical" leaders in San Francisco? Was it any wonder that thereupon the San Francisco unions voted to boycott all the newspapers except the *News*?

It is hardly surprising in the light of this, and any amount of similar evidence, that the workers have no faith whatever in the daily press, that in 1936 and 1940 they loved Mr. Roosevelt for his newspaper enemies. Whatever else may be said of Mr. Roosevelt — and I am entirely opposed to his continuance in office — the workers believed rightly that the New Deal gave them their only hope of the improvement of their social and economic position — until Mr. Roosevelt himself betrayed his creation. The public is buying more newspapers as the quoted figures show, partly, of course, because we are in the greatest of wars. The readers want their comics, they want their sports, they want news of Hollywood, and they want the news of our steady progress in the war. Especially they want the radio timetables that they may hear not only the entertainment features offered by the stations, but important public addresses and "flash" news bulletins. But the people buy the newspapers not for their counsel or their leadership, not for any inspiration, nor in any expectation of finding them championing any far-reaching, fundamental reforms or leading them toward a better era.

Finally, in this survey of the trend of American journalism during the last twenty years, it must be stressed again that the tendencies cited are to be found not merely in the United States, but in other freedom-loving countries. They are part and parcel of the evolution of this capitalistic age, which, through its failure to head off the second World War, has invited its own destruction. In my judgment, the burden of guilt upon the press of the world for the coming of this war is second on the Allied side only to that which rests upon the shoulders of the statesmen of Belgium, of France, of England, for their refusal to see from 1920 on whither the Treaty of Versailles was leading us, their unwillingness to aid the German Republic and the democratic forces supporting it, their failure to prevent the rearming of that country by Hitler, their giving him the right to re-create a navy, and their appeasing of the German dictator.

That a very considerable portion of the press in both England and the United States foresaw what was coming and repeatedly warned against it and encouraged their foreign correspondents to portray what was actually happening, does not mitigate the dreadful failure of the newspapers as a whole to prevent the coming of the greatest catastrophe in human history. But the governments were too shortsighted, composed of men too small mentally or too stupid, too steeped in worn-out diplomatic and power-political conceptions, to heed. And the editors were neither sufficiently united nor powerful enough to arouse a compelling public opinion on their side. It unfortunately cannot be added that the press, both here and abroad, is redeeming itself by its presentation of the war news, or by its editorial leadership in this struggle. Indeed, it is constantly misleading by wrongful emphasis, notably in the headlines, in failure to hold the newsscales evenly and objectively. There seems to be as little statesmanship in the editorial offices as in the chancelleries here or abroad. All of this may be playing its part in the disappearance of the American daily.

CHAPTER II

The Freedom of the Press

IT IS ONE of the bright spots in the current press picture that the newspapers of today are alert to the dangers to their freedom of utterance inherent in the war and in the great concentration of governmental power in Washington during the last few decades. That this awareness has its limitations is true, and so is the criticism that few publishers are as concerned to see that others are also assured of their full liberties under the Constitution, although restriction of the freedom of one group in our national community imperils the liberties of all. Many critics of the press insist that by keeping silent on many wrongs the newspapers deliberately aid the forces of reaction in depriving the disadvantaged of their rights and privileges. As for the existing shackles upon the freedom of expression of the newspapers, no one can deny that many of them are self-assumed because of the profit motive of their owners. Where that motive controls, advertisers become a great danger to a newspaper's freedom. When a newspaper is weak or conscienceless, fear of offending readers and advertisers is a powerful fetter. But however open to censure in this respect the press may be, whenever it does speak out for the preservation of its liberties from public attack it deserves praise. For we live in a totalitarian age, and it cannot be denied that moves to restrict utterances in the press and over the air were evident in Washington, and in some of the individual states, before the coming of the present war.

The attack of the government upon the Associated Press is discussed elsewhere in this volume. The Minnesota gag law which resulted in the suppression of a newspaper active in revealing political corruption is the most striking case of a deliberate effort by an American state to limit the freedom of the printed word. Another serious move during the regime of Huey Long in Louisiana was also thwarted, and various efforts by the courts to enjoin editorial utterances have been repelled. One difficulty in keeping public opinion alert to the danger of suppression lies in the mistaken belief that there can be safe restrictions upon freedom of publication beyond the laws of libel

[19]

and those relating to the printing of obscenity. Few Americans really understand that liberty of the press means *license* and means *abuse* of that liberty. This is the price which must be paid for the enjoyment of freedom; that was realized by all the Founders, and notably by Thomas Jefferson. Yet the tendency is to say "I believe in freedom, but . . ." and then to proceed to urge deadly blows at that freedom because some editors are guilty of bad manners or the use of intemperate language, or otherwise offend. There can and must be no restrictions whatever beyond those of libel and obscenity. The minute anything else is attempted, the way is open to serious infractions of liberty. Hence, whatever their own fallibility, the press owes it to the country to attack every governmental move which even remotely suggests the control or limitation of the radio or of its own activities.

A growing fear of constituted authority is one of the press's weaknesses. Most of our dailies have a seriously mistaken idea of what constitutes their patriotic duty to the government, so that even in peace-time they are often afraid to incur the ill will of officials. They dread denunciation and attack by the government. They recall that the New York *World* was at one time attacked and taken into court by the Theodore Roosevelt Administration because of its revelations of the circumstances surrounding the American government's theft of territory from Colombia to set up the bogus Republic of Panama and to build the Panama Canal. This was a most deliberate governmental move to end freedom of press criticism, which the courts soon quashed. In war-time the dangers to free expression need no stressing. Yet it is at just such a period that the press can perform its greatest service to our democracy. In every war the one safeguard to prevent the civilian and military leaders from endangering the liberties of the people has been the press. If it has often erred in war-time in seeking to dominate military moves and governmental policies, it has none the less earned its characterization as the Fourth Estate by its ability to check and to criticize. We have gone far enough in the present war to prove the very parlous state the people's liberties would be in at the hands of the Roosevelt Administration had the newspapers not been able to ridicule, criticize, denounce the absurdities, the follies, and the blunders of the Roosevelt government on the civilian administrative side.

Curiously enough, the press was itself faithless before we entered the struggle in accepting the so-called voluntary censorship demanded and obtained by the Secretary of the Navy, Frank Knox. This was an unprecedented request, and one that should never have been listened to short of an act of Congress. It is true that we were then on the highroad to war, deliberately put on that road by various governmental actions and laws passed by Congress under the false excuse that those measures would keep the country at peace. Mr. Knox appealed to the editors as patriots. The reply should have been that the primary duty of the press was to uphold freedom of utterance until the highest legislative authority approved war-time limitation. Instead, the newspapers rushed to put on the collar of censorship, which was none the less a censorship because it was voluntarily assumed. By means of that censorship the government successfully concealed from the American people military and naval actions that were little short of acts of war, if not actually such acts. It meant the withholding from the public of vital facts which the people were entitled to have if they were to control the acts of the government and to govern policies. From this point of view the voluntary censorship was an indisputable betrayal of the people's interest and their freedom of action. Since we entered the war the conduct of the newspapers in accepting restrictions has been exemplary. Indeed, it has gone too far; they should have demanded, and could have obtained by united action, the ending of numerous absolutely unnecessary suppressions by both army and navy — suppressions denounced by all the leading military and naval writers. Our government has given the American people far less information about what has been going on than the Churchill administration has vouchsafed to the British public. The English press, be it noted here, has on several occasions, notably as to North Africa, protested against the failure of the American authorities properly to inform it as to American moves while also keeping the American press in the dark.

There is also the grave question whether the press has not erred in this way in allowing too much authority to military and naval officials in other directions than the handling of the news. It has been Mr. Roosevelt's deliberate policy to turn over the conduct of the war almost completely to the generals and admirals, a policy acclaimed by many and held to have been responsible for many of the gratifying successes achieved up to the time of this writing. None the less, the dangers in granting such powers without civilian control, in accordance with what has been the hitherto unbroken American policy, have been well voiced by Wendell Willkie in his charge that the war was being entirely too much engineered by the fighting services, and has been illustrated further by the cruel and morally indefensible, and surely unconstitutional, removal of American citizens of Japanese ancestry from their homes on the Pacific coast by the fiat of the commanding military officer. There is no other safe way for a democracy in war-time than to insist that the military shall be fully subordinated to the civilian authorities. In such matters as what should be our policy for Italy, North Africa, and the other countries we may take over, the press must watch and control day by day the actions of the executive branch of the government.

Alexander Hamilton pointed out in one of his *Federalist* papers that in the end freedom of the press will depend not on any constitutional guarantee, but on public opinion, and, he might have added, on the zealousness of the press itself. As for any constitutional guarantee, he said that it amounted to nothing, using these words: "What signifies a declaration that 'the liberty of the press shall be inviolably preserved'? What is liberty of the press? Who can give any definition which would not leave the utmost latitude for evasion? I hold it to be impracticable; and from this I infer that its security, whatever fine declarations may be inserted in any constitution respecting it, must altogether depend on public opinion, and on the general spirit of the people and of their government. And here, after all . . . must we seek for the only solid basis for all our rights." Since the press to such a considerable degree controls public opinion, it plainly has in its own hands the safeguarding of its liberty.

This applies not merely to the danger of governmental and judicial interference, but also to those other shackles already mentioned, the self-imposed ones, and those that are ingrained in the present economic situation of our dailies. Those newspapers that surrender their right of free opinion to advertisers, or live in terror lest they offend large groups of readers, are playing into the hands of the reactionaries and the totalitarians, if only because they weaken their prestige and the standing of the newspaper business in the eyes of the public. If they blindly accept such reactionary leadership as has been given by the American Newspaper Publishers' Association, they will find it much more difficult to fight for freedom of the press. To safeguard its liberties they must also face squarely the import of the tremendous economic and social revolution in which we find ourselves, a revolution which is threatening to destroy traditional and vitally important educational and political principles and ideals. No press can preserve its power or its liberty if as a group it sets itself deliberately to block political revolution.

Its only hope lies in sympathetically understanding and interpreting this great tidal wave of change which is sweeping us whither no man knoweth, to guide it into wise channels, and to prevent its going beyond wise bounds and thus submerging the rights of the individual. It will lose its usefulness to the public still more, be definitely aligned as an enemy of progress with the worst reactionaries, and find it more and more difficult to maintain an independent economic status if it does not seek leadership, as well as dispense wisdom and tolerance, in the struggle that is going on and the larger struggle still to come. This is vital to the maintenance of American freedom and American institutions — unless leadership is taken over by other means of communication and the newspapers become "as dead as mutton."

As for the outlook, it cannot be said that it is too cheerful. Not only is the daily press vanishing, but other journals of opinion are not showing signs of growth. The weekly political journals do not increase in numbers, do not maintain themselves; and their readership has not been enlarged during the last twenty-five years — the *New Republic,* for example, probably has only about half the subscribers it had in 1917. To float such a weekly journal of opinion calls for hundreds of thousands of dollars; as business propositions they are incapable of success. There are relatively few small publications of protest and propaganda, and their range is extremely limited. The great new weeklies, like *Time* and *Life,* are the creations and the mouthpieces of a man

grown very rich; *Life* from the beginning called for the expend-
iture of millions before achieving its great success, and the most
widely read publication of all, the *Reader's Digest,* influences
public opinion almost wholly by choice of articles from other
publications. There is no strong labor press coming to the front,
and no sign of one — nothing to correspond to the London
Daily Herald, the popular organ of the Labour Party. The ver-
nacular daily Jewish press deteriorates, and in the long run will
have to turn to the use of English.

Only the Negro press has developed by leaps and bounds — a
most remarkable phenomenon, with many of the editors showing great ability and power. Its growth in numbers and in the
extent of its support by members of the race is astounding to
many who have not been aware of the seething currents of dis-
content and anger among our colored millions at the injustices
and the discriminations against them. Born of these bitter passions, the new Negro press speaks with vigor, and far too often
with a violence, that have startled the whites who have suddenly been brought into contact with it. It is not cowed because
this is war-time; it does not tremble before authority. It uses little
or no restraint in discussing the refusal of this government to
grant to our Negroes not only their constitutional privileges, but
full equality in the army and the navy, the right to fight for their
country on equal terms with white citizens. It scorns the pretense
that this country is fighting this war for the Four Freedoms as
long as 13,000,000 people here at home are denied their rights
because of the color of their skins. These militant newspapers
are both creators of the suddenly developed Negro sense of solidarity and themselves an index of a developing race consciousness and unwillingness to remain in a subordinate position, a
helotry in a democracy. It is unfortunately true that many Negro
dailies and weeklies go to censurable excesses and injure their
case by the violence of their unbridled attacks in this extremely
explosive period of our days. The responsibility for this, however,
lies primarily upon those whites who have believed, or pretended
to believe, that this democracy could exist part servile and part
free.

Perhaps this startling evolution of the press of one great group
out of the depth of its feelings as to its own status, its own injustices and wrongs, may be a portent that in the immediate future

the issues confronting the American people, especially after the war, will be so vital, so revolutionary, so all-embracing that the white daily press will similarly catch fire. If H. G. Wells is correct in saying that the only way out of the newspaper impasse is pamphleteering, then conditions may soon be ripe for a return to this medium of expression on this side of the Atlantic. The pamphlet offers a vehicle of protest which one can create and use without being wealthy. Its disadvantages are obvious. The great strength of a daily lies in its power of iteration and reiteration, its ability to drive home its points day after day, to uphold and to portray a cause from its every facet. The pamphleteer must be gifted indeed to win a large audience, as did the brilliant sixteen-year-old Alexander Hamilton in the days leading up to the Revolution, for the author of a tract is at a loss how to advertise the product of his pen unless he can fall back upon the daily press. A new Tom Paine could gain and hold a large audience. What of the lesser lights? And how should we check the too frequent tendency to compose long documents, too long for the overburdened modern to read and digest? Surely there would have to be great political excitement for tracts to reach large numbers of readers in an audience of more than a hundred million. Yet it is one of the few possible remedies for a failing press.

When the editors of the *New Republic* made their already cited study, "The Press and the Public," they admitted at once that "it is always easier to draw up an indictment than to suggest practicable methods of reform. One thing, however, is certain: the press will not reform itself." They turned to the old stale suggestion of endowed newspapers seeking only enough money "to cover their operating expenses," and "conducted primarily for the good of the community." But the *New Republic* itself has long been an endowed journal, and has certainly never made both ends meet. Who would control the board of trustees of an endowed newspaper? Would not the very trusteeship involved in the handling of a great endowment and of safeguarding it inevitably ensure an ultra-conservative management no more inclined to progressive leadership than is the New York *Times*? Next these editors thought of a ten-cent newspaper without advertising, and discarded it. So they fell back upon that glittering old generality that the readers themselves can control a newspaper and make it conform to their wishes. Even this position is untenable. The simple fact is that when a conscientious, progressive owner finds that he cannot carry on his paper, it ceases publication or passes into other hands. If another type of newspaper cannot make both ends meet, it, too, dies or is amalgamated. I do not know of a single case in which public opinion has compelled any radical alteration in the mental attitude and policies of a daily journal. The *New Republic's* final hope that labor might perhaps come to be a dominating factor and crack the whip which is to make the whole press free, honest, progressive, and sympathetic with the masses, is as idle as its other suggestions.

As for other means of offsetting the commercialization of the press, if there were more journals like the *Christian Science Monitor,* which is without the profit motive because of its being sponsored by a religious organization, and if there could be experimentation with English-language dailies along the line of the non-profit-making Jewish *Forward,* there would be a marked advance. Twenty years ago there was in existence the Minnesota *Daily Star,* the "newspaper with six thousand owners," described by me in an earlier volume. Unfortunately, it soon failed needlessly, because of unskilled and inefficient business management, and so we learned nothing from this co-operative venture to establish group ownership of a daily and thus escape the evils of one-man control. Still another interesting experiment, Marshall Field's *PM,* "the daily without advertising," has also unfortunately got off to a very bad start and, as set forth in another chapter, may not live to demonstrate whether a well-run and honest daily of this type can be made to pay without advertisements. This is a misfortune because information on this point would be extremely valuable. There are no other experiments which offer any promise of an amelioration of the parlous conditions of the press or an offset to its steady decrease in numbers.

There remains the coming of the radio, as to the value of which in the formation of intelligent public opinion there can be no question whatever. When it first came upon the scene, the newspapers mistakenly looked upon it as an enemy and did everything in their power to prevent the broadcasting of news, fearing that that would cost them many readers. They recognized that their competitors on the air had possession of a weapon more potent than theirs. In time, however, the newspapers learned that this competitor not only did not destroy their circulations but in all probability helped them, since it is a human characteristic to wish to see in print, if possible, what one has seen with one's own eyes or has heard. It seems ridiculous now to read that in 1936 the chairman of the radio committee of the American Newspaper Publishers' Association declared that "the sale of news to any broadcasting station or to any advertiser for sponsorship over the air is just as unsound as if the newspapers sold news to their advertisers and then permitted them to commingle this news in their advertising copy. How long would the newspapers hold the confidence of the public as media for the dissemination of information if they adopted such a policy?" They adopted it soon thereafter.

Like the newspapers, radio is "an instrument that can enslave or free." It is in even greater danger from censorship because of the constant and dangerous supervision of the Federal Communications Commission, which leads the broadcasters to supervise and edit any statement or manuscript of a controversial nature. Ruth Brindisi in her study of broadcasting has pointed out that news is now hourly interpreted by men who receive their weekly pay checks from the business rulers of America. It is probably a cause for congratulation that there are few charges that news is mishandled, but it would be impossible to assert that it is always free from color, especially as it is so easy in speaking to slur over some things and to stress and emphasize others and because radio is the happiest vehicle for propagandists. But every allegation of this kind brought against the radio can, of course, be paralleled by similar charges against the dailies.

After the first period of hostility to the radio passed, many newspapers themselves entered the field and purchased or set up stations of their own. Undoubtedly in some few cases there is a considerable advantage in this, but Hearst has sold some of his stations, and the move in this direction seems checked. The New York *Times* could, of course, have entered this field immediately, but refused to do so. It now hires time from a New York City station to give out hourly news bulletins, something that would have seemed treason to the press ten years ago. It is beyond question a service to the public, notably in war-time, and an excellent advertisement for the *Times*. Whether in due course the government will not demand a separation of the newspapers from the radio stations is an open question. There are parallels in other fields pointing this way. In the main, however, it must be stressed again that the coming of the radio has been a great boon to the American democracy, and radio will remain its chief source of news since it penetrates into millions of homes, many of which cannot obtain a daily newspaper. If the press continues to decrease in numbers and influence, the necessity of the radio for informing the people will hourly become more apparent.

Today perhaps the only hope for the press is, as has been suggested, such a development of the affairs of the world and of the present world-wide revolution as will again bring to the editorial chairs men of fire and passion, with programs to further and vital, stirring causes to lead. They will find their tasks even more difficult than those which confront the editor of today. As has been said, "the world has become a vast sounding board of conflicting voices." Everything is in flux, in conflict, and there is not the slightest sign that after this global war is over, business will be as usual in any market-place in the world. The present-day editor is overwhelmed by the magnitude of the problems with which he is confronted, for the solution of which he is supposed to give leadership. But the task cannot be shirked if the press is to survive as a leader. After all, there are principles of human life and human conduct long tested and beyond question, just as the tenets of democracy are proving in this struggle that they are surviving, while the new totalitarian doctrines are largely going down to defeat. It is by the principles of liberty that free editors must be guided in their fight, not only for the Four Freedoms, but for all of them.

The editor will always have a great advantage over his competitors for leadership on the platform, in the senates, over the air, for the printed word *is* superior to the spoken. It is far less perishable. If it has beauty, as has been written by a veteran editorial writer of the *Herald Tribune,* Roscoe C. E. Brown, that beauty is far more certain to survive. If it has wisdom, it is at least temporarily "engraved upon tablets" and capable of enlightening men's minds and stirring men's emotions, even when the last of those who heard the spoken word have perished from the human scene. The editor's is the power to write day by day with unyielding emphasis. If he is a free man and his soul is his own, he is among the most fortunate of men, for the spiritual fight to better human conditions brings more joy and balm to the soul than any other. No one who has ever had the power to fight unceasingly in a printed page, with absolute freedom, for the oppressed, the disadvantaged, the victims of human greed, can ever be willing cheerfully to give up the opportunity to battle on. There may be times when he will recall Isaiah's saying: "The voice said, Cry. And he said, What shall I cry?" But if he is true to his ideals he will always know what to say, and whatever the obstacles he will find a medium in which to say it.

CHAPTER III

The Press and the President

WHEN THE PRESIDENT was asked at his press conference on June 29, 1943 for his comment on the sharp attack by Vice President Wallace upon the Secretary of Commerce, Jesse Jones, he returned to what his former close friend and aid Raymond Moley calls his "oldest grudge" — he attacked the press. He admitted that the newspapers had not started up the controversy between Mr. Wallace and Mr. Jones, but he insisted that the press was encouraging such controversies in the government, and then reverted to his old charge that correspondents and reporters write colored accounts of what is happening in the government under orders from their employers, the newspaper-owners. On being asked by some of the correspondents to be specific and give exact examples of cases in which pressmen had inspired governmental quarrels, the President replied that there were flocks of them and suggested the reading of the articles written by almost any of the columnists. When the President in turn asked who was encouraging the belief that there were intergovernmental disputes, one of his auditors replied: "Everybody." Finally the President insisted that there were a number of men in front of him who had to write under orders or lose their jobs.

That the President's attitude is strongly resented by the newspapers and the great majority of the correspondents is certain. Indeed, it is impossible to deny that the relations between Mr. Roosevelt and the dailies have become steadily worse as time has passed. It is the more remarkable because no President ever had a better press at the beginning of his Administration when his rescue of the country by national bank-closing received such wide acclaim on every hand. His colorful personality, his nose for news, his flair for the sensational, his striking phrases and epigrams, many of which have become permanent parts of the English language, all helped to carry everything before him. But, as with other Presidents, the early happy relations have steadily waned; now only a minority of the 150 correspondents who attend the biweekly conferences are thick-and-thin admirers and supporters of the President. The majority are becoming more and more hostile.

Many of these still laugh at the President's display of wit and his sharp repartee, but the thoughtful ones have turned against him, shocked by his levity in discussing vitally important matters, his frequent flippancy, his striving for effect, his constant lapses from the exact truth, and his growing tendency to petty antagonisms and dislikes. Of the latter the most striking case is that of John O'Donnell of the Chicago *Tribune* and the New York *Daily News,* whom the President publicly denounced through his secretary, Mr. Early, as a falsifier of news. The President so far forgot himself as to bring into the conference on one occasion a German Iron Cross, which he asked a correspondent to present to Mr. O'Donnell, who was present, presumably as something earned by him. The whole corps was shocked by the proceeding, yet it did not move as a whole.

In fact, the group has never acted as one in opposing any of the President's actions, though a number signed a protest when the President made his first trip around the country inspecting war industries without permitting adequate press representation. As Frank Kent has pointed out, the often humiliating position in which the representatives of the press now find themselves is their own fault. He avers that if their respect for their profession and for their own intellectual integrity were as high as it should be, they could bring about a change in their relationship to the holder of the Presidential office. As he puts it:

The plain fact is that unless there develops a fixed determination among the correspondents as a whole to assert and insist upon their professional rights and aggressively resent personal disparagement — and unless their newspapers back them up — their rights will continue to shrink and their personal standing diminish. . . . But the fact remains that, as a result of what is being done, newspapers and newspapermen are losing ground now they may not be able to regain. That is serious for the press, but, despite their lack of understanding and concern, it is also serious for the people.

Doubtless many of the men would not be sustained in any revolt against the President's methods; the owners of the newspapers, some of whom are above all else concerned with keeping in the good books of the White House, would probably be against any joint move. Moreover, there is a new argument at work — that the President is now the Commander in Chief and therefore must not be criticized, lest the enemy be encouraged thereby.

As for the President's own attitude and the question of his veracity and fair dealing, it may be pointed out on his behalf that this is war-time and that the President is justified in stretching the truth or dodging issues, or in forgetting certain aspects of a subject in order not to betray public secrets. The charge is made, however, that this was his policy long before war came, and that his attitude has never been motivated by anything else than his desire to have his achievements and those of his administrative heads portrayed in the press as he thinks they should be — something that can truthfully be said of every President. An example of what the correspondents complain of occurred at the same press conference on June 29, 1943, and is therefore worth citing here.

Mr. Roosevelt at the beginning of that historic meeting asserted that he had not denied at his conference on June 25 that Chester C. Davis had submitted his resignation as War Food Administrator. The resignation was then in his possession, dated June 16. Mr. Roosevelt picked up the official transcript of the June 25 conference, which showed that when his attention was called to newspaper reports that Mr. Davis was resigning and was asked if he had any comment, he had said: "No." The President added from the record his additional statement that the last time he had seen Mr. Davis that gentleman had answered: "God forbid!" to Mr. Roosevelt's question whether he wanted to run the Office of Price Administration. It appeared, therefore, as if the President had a clean slate, but he failed to read the rest of the record, which included his further statement that that "God forbid" utterance was the last thing that he had heard about the matter — when actually the resignation of Mr. Davis was in his hands. In other words, he technically told the truth, but concealed for his own reasons the vital fact that Mr. Davis was resigning. Yet it was this that he was asked to confirm or deny.

The late J. Fred Essary, for years a representative of the Baltimore *Sun,* gave the best picture of Mr. Roosevelt's attitude at his conferences. It runs thus:

He dodges often. Oftener still, he parries. His fencing is good natured, as a rule, and skilful, but he fences nevertheless. Sometimes we suspect him of dissembling. Many of the questions put to him are searching. They go straight to the core of some matters which he does not propose to answer, or cannot. "But I have not read the bill," he will answer, a bill perhaps written by his own Attorney-General. Or: "This is the first I have heard of it." Or, (and this has happened many times): "Really I don't know what you are talking about." "I cannot discuss with you any matter that is pending in Congress" — when in fact, he did discuss with us at some length the World Court issue while it was pending before the Senate. "All I know about the $4,800,000,000 Work Relief Bill is what I get from a casual reading of the papers . . ." he said one day, although on the same day Senator Glass, in charge of the bill, said he conferred with Mr. Roosevelt regarding it the night before.

How steadily the President has lost faith in the press was best instanced by his refusal to permit the newspapermen to have free access to the noteworthy International Food Conference held at Hot Springs, Virginia, in May and June 1943. There never appeared to be any possible military reason for suppressing the news of this gathering, and, in the opinion of many, there were most excellent propaganda reasons for letting its remarkable proceedings be known to the Axis countries as proof that the United Nations not only were holding together, but were so confident of victory as to be planning a complete reorganization of the world with the purpose of doing away with all famines and having a satisfactory supply of food on hand at all times. But the President insisted on secrecy, and at a press conference scornfully inquired of the correspondents where their desire to pry into government affairs would cease, and whether they would not soon be demanding the right to watch him in his bath. Actually, as was to have been expected, the effort to gag the press at Hot Springs did not succeed. There was entirely adequate reporting of what went on. But the newspapers were doubly unhappy about it because they felt that the President's increasing hostility to them might lead him similarly to shut them out of future conferences, and especially the future peace conference, if there is any.

No one must assume that all the right is on one side in this question of the relation of the press to the President. It is difficult for a man holding the highest office in the world to submit himself to cross-examination by a large group of persons about whom he has very mixed feelings. Possessed of many facts that they cannot have, he finds it harder and harder to be cross-examined as if he were a pupil and not the master. He not unnaturally resents questions which are at times plainly inspired by hostility, or by a desire to put him in a hole and make him contradict himself. On the other hand, the correspondents are at a great disadvantage because the meetings are largely one-sided. Though they have the right to put questions and do often voice daring ones, they are not on equal terms with the President and never can be. He has them more or less at his mercy because of the power to withhold facts and his right to refuse to answer at all. All of this is proof that the arrangement is not an ideal one, however valuable it may and should be.

Mr. Roosevelt has developed with great subtlety the "off the record" procedure in which he tells his listeners things that are to be kept in absolute confidence. On its face this would appear to be a helpful and generous method of sharing confidences with the pressmen and giving them important backgrounds to aid them in correctly portraying what is going on, even when the President himself cannot be quoted. It is none the less resented by the more responsible correspondents. The reason for this is the belief that this procedure can become a clever device for imposing a censorship and bringing about a suppression of the facts that the Chief Executive does not wish to have brought out, which he fears might leak out in some other way and he feels must not be given to the public. In other words, this custom may make it impossible to inform the public about important developments by telling the reporters about them in Presidential confidence, which cannot be violated. All the writers who hear them from the President's lips are silenced, even though they may have received the same information previously from a member of the Cabinet, or an important senator or high officeholder, or perhaps a foreign ambassador. Obviously this puts these men who have legitimately acquired this information in a hole, and makes it easy for the President either in peace-time or in war-time to suppress facts which are not *ipso facto* war secrets, but matters he wishes suppressed for his own personal or political reasons. It must not be forgotten in connection with these conferences that the man the correspondents talk with is not only the President of the United States but the leader of his party, and invariably he is desirous of succeeding himself in the Presidential office.

The more one studies the history of the relationship of the modern Presidents with the press, the more difficult it is to suggest a perfect arrangement unless all contacts are restricted to receiving from the President formal statements and an accompanying background — so much depends upon the personality of the President. Cleveland was cold and unapproachable; the country was small and almost wholly aloof from international affairs, and very little news originated in the White House. The correspondents found William McKinley weak and colorless, but the office grew under him because of our war with Spain and the Filipinos, our first plunge into war across the globe and into imperialism. Then came Theodore Roosevelt, who proved to be a godsend to the correspondents, and they made the most of him. The glamour and the fascination of his vivid, virile personality carried the correspondents off their feet. However opposed politically one might be, it was impossible not to yield to his personal charm and the extraordinary stimulus which came from association with him. The writers rose to him because he made their work far more vital and important than it had been. And he was himself wonderful "copy." He flattered them not a little by confiding freely in some of them and consulting them on matters of state, and he appointed some of them to important offices.

Personally most eager for publicity, it was he who first used the correspondents to send up trial balloons, which he unhesitatingly disavowed if the public reaction was unfavorable. There is a story that he once gave to a group of correspondents an announcement with one hand, while in the other he held a denial to be released the next day — the correspondents served him as he wished. Theodore Roosevelt went so far as to demand of certain newspaper managers that they withdraw reporters whom he did not like, or whom he accused of falsification, or who refused to worship at his shrine. Most of them did worship, and created the legendary Theodore Roosevelt. In their admiration for his personality, they lost the power to discriminate as to his political and executive deeds. Sometimes, it is true, he wanted to shake them off and would not let them go along, as, for example, when he made his amazing ride on horseback of 104 miles from Washington to Warrenton and return in a single day in order to prove to the army and the navy that the equestrian test he had instituted to determine the physical fitness of their officers was not excessive. Again, when he went to Africa he wanted to be free of them, and Archie Butt, his military secretary, quoted him as humorously declaring his willingness to subvention native African chiefs to kill off certain correspondents if they should follow him, fixing the price of $100 for a New York *World* reporter, $300 for a Hearst emissary, and $500 for a correspondent of the New York *Evening Post* — his special hate.

As for Woodrow Wilson, I was present when Wilson received the correspondents for the first time. He greeted them most charmingly and cordially and said that he intended to use them as his "wireless antennæ" who would keep him informed as to just what the people in their home communities were thinking and saying of his Administration and what they wanted. But what Wilson promised never came to pass; he did not, and because of his cold nature he could not, maintain warm relations with the newspapermen. From the very beginning of his political career he was afraid of them; he distrusted them, when he was not timid and shy in their presence. Moreover, he could not brook being questioned by men whose business he did not like, who were, he was certain, intellectually altogether his inferiors — his intellectual arrogance and snobbishness were two of his greatest weaknesses. Gradually the press conferences became more irregular and took place at greater intervals. When 1914 came and the first World War, he had the latter as his excuse for abandoning the conferences, just as the meetings of his Cabinet similarly decreased in frequency, lost their character of a free and open give-and-take, and became merely a meeting at which the President conveyed to his constitutional advisers the decisions he had arrived at without having previously consulted with them. The result was that the pressmen were forced to fall back upon their very satisfactory relations with Joseph P. Tumulty, Wilson's private secretary, whom all the newspapermen liked and trusted.

President Harding got on well with the journalists because he had himself been a small-town newspaper-owner and because he had an open, likable nature, with weaknesses that appealed to the average man. He was cordial and genial, warm and friendly, and had an extraordinary knowledge of what the average American was thinking about — the "feel" of the successful politician. Though the correspondents were under no illusion as to Harding's Administration, on the whole he fared well with the press; probably no President will ever be more generously protected than he was. Such press troubles as he had were due to his lack of background and fitness to deal with many of the vital questions with which he was confronted. He at first essayed to answer spontaneous questions of the correspondents at his conferences, but he was compelled to abandon this procedure by a bad blunder he made during the Conference on the Limitation of Armaments. The press had been told by the Secretary of State, Charles Evans Hughes, and some of the foreign delegates that the Four-Power Treaty called for the protection of the main Japanese islands, although the fact was cleverly concealed in the treaty itself. One of the ablest correspondents asked Harding at the conference whether he understood that the main islands were to be protected, and he replied emphatically that they were not. The news that he had said this brought Hughes to the White House on the run and Harding was compelled to agree that thereafter he would answer no questions except those submitted in writing in advance. It was, of course, a great humiliation, but it was necessary to prevent the President's going off half-cocked when unexpected questions were suddenly fired at him.

President Coolidge was a good deal of a problem to the correspondents, who often found it extremely difficult to interpret what he had to say, to know just what his meaning was. Coolidge was wedded to the fiction of the "White House spokesman" and regularly hid behind this subterfuge. On one occasion he "took a stand upon no less than ten public questions without once speaking for quotation or permitting the correspondents to reveal the true source of these statements," although many of them dealt with vitally important issues about which the public had the right to be informed. He also followed the Harding rule of answering only written questions, and so did Herbert Hoover. The device of the White House spokesman Coolidge found useful because he could later freely disavow any statement if the effect of it on the public was unsatisfactory. In one such case two of the Washington correspondents, Arthur J. Sinnott and Henry Suydam, struck when he did this, believing that their professional honor and their reputation for accuracy had been placed in jeopardy by the President's action. They published the truth and revealed that Coolidge was the spokesman. Curiously enough, the incident was passed over and the two correspondents were neither disciplined nor expelled from the biweekly conferences.

What happened was this: On December 22, 1924 the French Ambassador, the distinguished Jules Jusserand, then about to retire from his Washington post, made a speech containing the familiar French plea for debt abatement, asking particularly for a moratorium, on the ground that France had suffered most from the war. Twenty-four hours later the Washington correspondents asked Coolidge what he thought of the Ambassador's speech. Coolidge showed sharp irritation, saying that the government would pay no attention to a moratorium since Jusserand had made a public appeal instead of going to the Debt Funding Commission, the proper authority, where he could have gone long before. According to Mr. Sinnott, the President said that "such problems could not be settled if every move were to be heralded to the public by ambassadorial speeches which had a propaganda flavor." The spokesman device did not hide the fact that this was the worst rebuke to an ambassador ever given by an American Chief Executive. Jusserand besought Secretary Hughes for help, properly referring to the approaching end of his long and honorable career, and insisting that his was an unprecedented humiliation. Hughes responded sympathetically and went over to the White House. Immediately an official press statement was issued declaring that the Ambassador had not been criticized by that mysterious somebody, the one "high in power," that there had been nothing new in his speech, and otherwise contradicting the original statement. The official stenographic notes bore out Sinnott and Suydam. But what of it? Jusserand was appeased, his record cleared, and Hughes was satisfied. The incident remains a vivid example of the continuing fact — down to this hour — that the ordinary rules of morality and truth-telling do not hold in the White House when it is inconvenient to obey them.

President Hoover, too, was not easy to deal with. The correspondents soon found that even the scientific mind when injected into high politics is controlled by clear ideas as to how its possessor should be treated by the press, and how far it is removed from the ordinary canons of conduct that govern human relations. On one occasion he drove J. Fred Essary temporarily out of the press conference by viciously attacking Essary's paper, the Baltimore *Sun,* for publishing the name of Hoover's son in the list of the officers of a company which was seeking an air-mail subsidy. The *Sun's* facts were correct, but Hoover insisted that his family should not be "dragged into the news."

Franklin Roosevelt has been so satisfied with his own record in these conferences that for the first time the stenographic notes have been printed and published. They make an extraordinary record both of the President himself, of his mental attitude, and of this curious institution, which is hardly duplicated anywhere else. It could be very interesting if Winston Churchill's frank reaction to this manner of dealing with the press could be brought out. He has been a guest on at least two such occasions. For the present the White House conferences will undoubtedly continue to constitute as much of an acid test of the character and integrity of both sides as it has been thus far. It is to be hoped that Roosevelt's successor, whoever he may be, and whenever he may take office, will try a different and more straightforward policy of simply telling the whole truth in clear-cut statements, duly written in advance and followed up by informal elucidation and explanation. It is certainly much to be desired that any future occupant of the White House take a different viewpoint from that of the Hoover regime. One of Hoover's private secretaries, Theodore G. Joslin, frankly and freely admitted in his book on the Hoover Administration that the White House suppressed important news developments and even defended the "necessity" of cold-blooded falsehood in some cases.

CHAPTER IV

The Associated Press I

NO MORE THAN a river can the stream of news rise higher than its source. For the Associated Press its sources within the United States are its members, except where it has established its own bureaus with special reporting staffs. Thus in all places where it cannot maintain its own correspondents it calls upon each member newspaper for all the local news which that member has gathered, which it is compelled to supply to the Associated Press alone. It cannot sell its news to any other news service. The stream of the Associated Press's news must, therefore, reflect the intelligence, the taste, the integrity, the news and business standards of its members, as well as their prejudices and class feelings — it cannot rise any higher. Its directors are elected by the membership from their own number and so again reflect the news-gathering ideals of at least the majority of the membership. If the standards of the greatest of news-gathering organizations have sunk seriously in the last forty years, it must be in response to the changing methods and efforts of its approximately 1,246 members.

The best feature of the Associated Press is that it is a co-operative, non-profit-making enterprise and not a concern to make money, being incorporated as a membership society under the laws of New York State. But it is a curious fact that its strength is also its weakness, for as a co-operative organization it is at the mercy of the mass psychology of its members. Since it has become one of the most powerful engines for the creation of public opinion in the world, it is of the utmost importance for the safety of our democracy that its standards, its integrity, and its leadership should be of the very finest. If the service is biased or unfair or unduly influenced by fear of the government, or by the prejudices of its membership, it is obvious that tremendous damage can be done. It has been done in the past — again and again, often without its officers or members realizing what was happening, but sometimes with deliberation. It has insisted that its purpose, to use the words of Melville Stone, who was one of its founders and for many years its able general manager, "was to tell the truth about the world's happenings — perhaps not the whole truth — but nothing but the truth. . . . Newspapers have but one common demand upon the organization: that it shall furnish news and not views; that as nearly as possible, considering the frailties of human nature, its service shall be free from bias or deduction or opinion. And the only tie that binds any member newspaper to it is the confidence of the newspaper member in its integrity and impartiality!"

That reads extremely well, is quite idealistic and high-minded — and has never been lived up to. The words "perhaps not the whole truth," which Stone inserted, obviously cover a multitude of sins. Undoubtedly an argument can be made that no one can tell the whole truth. Yet if the Associated Press could be run by high-grade men in an entirely independent management position, conscious of their tremendous responsibility to the public and so situated as to be indifferent to those bearing the cost of their services, there would be a vast improvement in their reporting. Whether the Associated Press could long survive such a management is more than dubious since our newspapers are what they are. They do demand objective reporting of the Associated Press, but their, and the AP management's, definitions of reporting are often far from what they ought to be. What news the Associated Press receives from its members is too often tinged by the conventional herd viewpoint; that coming from local newspapers is subjected to every local prejudice and pressure, either from advertisers or from readers. Its constant omissions of news are among its deadliest sins, but, curiously enough, the Associated Press is rarely aware of those omissions. In consequence the activities of great groups of our citizens are reported not at all or with extreme bias.

It usually takes no account of grim social situations until they result in violence or some sensational happening. It is quite rightly not concerned with essays on given problems or situations, nor can it be expected to be bent on reforming unhappy American conditions. Theoretically, it exists to report spot news and not to take sides in social conflicts; actually, it has constantly done so and still does. It is not concerned with the terrible plight of the sharecropper, or the migratory workers, or with the Negro situation, or with the special problems of labor and capital. It has no love for handling hot pokers, and that it serves capitalistic-minded masters (with distinguished exceptions) is never for a moment forgotten by its reporters, consciously or unconsciously. Just because of its organizational character it reflects usually the prevailing popular opinion, the middle-class point of view of the bulk of its membership, and this whether in peace or in war. Hence it can never live up to Stone's boast that it handles all the news with impartiality. It has not only not held the scales even in class and social conflicts; it has all too frequently chosen reporters through whom it could not possibly receive unbiased and impartial news, as will be shown later.

One of its besetting sins is that it has always bowed down before authority and rarely ever stood up to the government in any controversy until its decision to fight the government's suit against it. It is the first to take orders from Washington, for it desires above all else to stand well with every administration, if only to make sure that it gets the news. That reverence for authority was the special weakness of Frank B. Noyes, who was the president of the Associated Press from 1900 to 1938, and of Adolph S. Ochs of the New York *Times,* long the most influential member of the board of directors. It seemed impossible for them, or anyone else on the board, to realize that it owed a higher duty — to the freedom of the press and to the American people — than it did to any administration.

By that is not meant, of course, that the Associated Press should be unpatriotic, or play into the hands of our enemies, or take an anti-governmental attitude. Far from it. It does mean that it should refuse to be the tool of any administration or to allow itself to be used for propaganda purposes, and that it should always endeavor to be above and beyond the prevailing public currents or passions, and especially that it should be unafraid of and independent of any governmental authority. Surrounded as it is in Washington by governmental activity and subject to all sorts of official pressure, it is naturally easy for the service to find opponents of the Administration's policy much less interesting than its defenders. The assaying of the value of a news event to see whether it is worth reporting, and if so how much space it is worth, often depends on whether the creators of the news are on the popular or the unpopular side. All minority groups are apt to chide the newspapers and the Associated Press for their failure to give them the space they think they deserve.

They are obviously not the best judges of that, yet there is too often truth in their contentions; reformers and representatives of new or unpopular causes cannot get their opinions, their resolutions, or their actions before the public as can representatives of conservative and influential bodies, or persons of high social or political standing.

Perhaps the worst case on record of the Associated Press's being willing to act as the tool of the Federal government goes back to 1926, when on November 16 the then Assistant Secretary of State, Robert E. Olds, induced the Associated Press to carry "a lurid tale of Russia plotting against America, with Mexico as a base, and the Panama Canal in danger of occupation by enemies." He said he felt that this picture should be presented to the American people, that it could not be proved, but that "we are morally certain that a warm bond of sympathy, if not an actual understanding, exists between Mexico City and Moscow. . . ." The next day the Associated Press sent out a most sensational dispatch beginning: "The spectre of a Mexico-fostered, Bolshevist hegemony intervening between the United States and the Panama Canal, has thrust itself into American-Mexican relations, already strained. . . ." The Hearst news service and the United Press refused to carry the story, which gave no facts and mentioned no authority. As George Seldes has written, it was purely "State Department propaganda, concocted by officials, for the purpose of creating hatred and an atmosphere of war." Extraordinary as it seems, President Noyes always defended this outrageous imposition of a falsehood upon the American people. When the facts were brought out by Paul Y. Anderson of the St. Louis *Post-Dispatch,* the Department was denounced by every liberal newspaper. But Mr. Noyes held that the fact that it was given out by the State Department, even though the Department refused to let itself be named as the authority for it, warranted the Associated Press's handling it. This is the clearest example of what remains a grave weakness of the Associated Press. Though no such flagrant cases are being revealed just at this moment, that crass misrepresentations can and do appear is shown by what happened when President Roosevelt visited the Ford bomber factory at Willow Run. The Associated Press report said that the President when at the factory "saw sheet aluminum going into one end of quarter-mile-long assembly lines and four-motored B-24 bombers ready to fly away at the other." The President actually passed this dispatch and permitted its publication, but told his press conference that Willow Run was not yet in production, although nearly so. It is hard to say whose conduct was more reprehensible in putting over this lie, the President's or that of the Detroit office of the Associated Press.

It was amazing that Mr. Noyes in 1926, and the board of directors of the Associated Press latterly, were not able to see that this subservience makes the Associated Press merely an agent of the Administration in Washington and that nothing could possibly damage it more than to have the American public come to think that this is the case. It is undoubtedly this un-American attitude of truckling to government officials which is in part responsible for the failure of the Associated Press to reveal corruption and wrongdoing at the centers of government. Its officials feel that muckraking or exposing misconduct in high office is no part of their business. The result is that when such revelations occur they are the work of individual newspapers and their representatives. For example, it was, again, Paul Y. Anderson of the St. Louis *Post-Dispatch* who made the initial revelation that revealed the Teapot Dome scandals and crimes, which the Associated Press was only too happy to follow up and report at length after the ball had been set rolling by Mr. Anderson. I should hate to think what would happen to a reporter of the Associated Press who would venture to bring in proof of a misdemeanor on the part of a high official. I once had the privilege of driving out of the public life of New York the acting Lieutenant Governor of the state. The representatives of the Associated Press at that time were just as aware as I of what was happening in Albany, but not in one hundred years would the Associated Press ever have revealed what it was my good fortune to print. For the rest of that session of the legislature, however, the Associated Press had little to report from Albany except the impeachment trial of Senator Allds.

To cite up-to-date examples, the Associated Press must have known long before we got into this second World War that actions leading us into war were being taken by the government without the knowledge of the American people, and directly contrary to the statements made by the government itself. But

once more the Associated Press felt that its first loyalty was not
to the American people, but to the government, and it cheerfully
accepted the voluntary censorship the government asked the
newspapers to impose, and thereby established a precedent
fraught with grave danger to the freedom of the American
press. To give a less important example, during March and April
1943 the legislatures of the most powerful Middle Western
states, Indiana, Illinois, Michigan, Missouri, and Iowa, passed a
resolution calling for an amendment to the Constitution so that
no President of the United States could hold office more than
two terms. Were this to be backed by thirty-six states it would
automatically prevent the election of Mr. Roosevelt to a fourth
term and it was therefore of sensational importance, particularly
as this method of amending the Constitution by votes of the
legislatures had never been attempted in the whole history of
the Republic. But the Associated Press could at first see no news
significance in this. Other examples of this kind could be cited.

Again, the Associated Press has been derelict in utilizing biased correspondents. During our occupation of some Caribbean
lands it on occasion used as correspondents Marine Corps officers or men affiliated with the business interests involved in the
interventions. That, of course, ensured that all the news that
came out was highly favorable to the government and invariably
represented the Nicaraguan or Haitian patriots as "bandits,"
when they were doing against us exactly what we have praised
the Norwegians, the Dutch, the Belgians, the French, and other
conquered peoples for doing against their German conquerors.
Indeed, this failure of the Associated Press to report the truth, or
even part of it, about those imperialistic aggressions of this country in the Caribbean — finally terminated by Franklin Roosevelt to his everlasting honor — made it a part of the governmental conspiracy which at that time hid from the American
people the truth about our brutal conquest of several countries.
For example, the Commandant of the Marine Corps officially
stated that in one year more than *five thousand Haitians* were
killed by our marines — many, he said, quite unnecessarily from
the military point of view. Yet little or anything of this was reported by the Associated Press. Its readers occasionally learned
that American troops were victorious over the "bandits."

Major General Smedley Butler of the Marines, who played a

prominent part in the Haitian and other conquests, once stated in my presence to an audience of 6,000 persons that the *Nation* under my editorship was the only publication to tell the whole sad truth about the invasions in which he, General Butler, had participated. Why should it have been the only one? And would it have been if the Associated Press had lived up to its obvious obligations and employed its own reporters in Haiti with instructions to get out the truth despite the Marine Corps censorship, for which there was no authority in law? Had its correspondents then been expelled by the Marines, the lid would have come off the whole shocking aggression, and the Associated Press would have ended in the case of Haiti the agony of an innocent people, not one of whom had ever lifted a finger against the government of the United States until we tore down its government on the plea that we had thus to prevent the establishment of German submarine bases. But the Associated Press was satisfied to let Marine officers send out the news it received.

The greatest weakness of the Associated Press comes, however, from its reliance upon its members for reports of local happenings. Many of the worst injustices perpetrated by it are due to this fact. Here my clearest example is the reporting of matters affecting the colored people, notably in the South, where the members of the Associated Press do not employ any colored men, are served by reporters imbued with every local prejudice and bent, consciously or unconsciously, on always presenting the white man's side of any race trouble in the most favorable light. There is no such thing as a square press deal for the Negro citizen in the South, although there are differences in the attitudes of the white journals. There are some papers, like the Louisville *Courier-Journal,* that are really trying to bring about fair play for the Negro. But in the main the above statement is correct. Usually a Negro makes the first page of a newspaper only if he commits a heinous crime. It is true that a handful of Southern newspapers have of late years found that they can increase their circulations by devoting some space to happenings among the colored people. But for generations the press has followed the color line religiously and ignored or misrepresented happenings among the Negroes. The colored people say with reason that many injustices and many terrible events are suppressed or ignored because of the dependence of the Associated Press upon its Southern members for its news. The AP is not even certain that its own reporters in the South can be trusted to tell the truth in racial matters. A terrible example of misrepresentation was an Associated Press report dealing with the murder by white men of some Florida Negroes whose sole crime was that they tried to vote. It utterly failed to tell its readers that American *men, women, and children* were *burned alive* by the white mob in this election trouble. Had the situation been reversed, had a number of Negroes thrown white women and children on the pyre, the story would have reached the front pages of every newspaper served by the Associated Press. When called to account for its dereliction, it correctly blamed its local reporters for its not only failing to report the truth that Melville Stone promised, but for its being made the means of a complete misrepresentation of what actually happened.

One more case must be cited in this connection. During the first World War the Associated Press was the medium of wholesale lying and crass misrepresentation in reporting a race conflict in Phillips County, Arkansas. This it portrayed to the American people — in war-time — as a "Negro rebellion," "of more than a local nature, possibly planned for the entire South." Now, the truth was that a group of white landlords deliberately attacked a meeting of colored tenant farmers held, under the guidance of a white attorney, to formulate the innocent demand that they receive written settlements of their accounts from the white landlords who were systematically plundering them by refusing ever to render a written statement of their business relations. This is as far from a Negro rebellion as anything could possibly be. Yet that reflection upon the patriotism and loyalty of the colored people, which have never been exceeded by those of the white people, was spread all over the United States. Fortunately the facts were later established in the Supreme Court of the United States, which saved from hanging some of the innocent Negro victims of that landlord conspiracy to keep black sharecroppers in complete subjection. But the Associated Press, despite my and other protests at the time, never apologized for the wrong it had done, or sought to rectify its misrepresentation, or even to print the whole story when the vindication by the highest court in the land occurred.

Is it any wonder that no thoughtful Negro expects any justice

at the hands of the Associated Press? Or thinks that there will
be the slightest effort on the AP's part correctly to report and
interpret the tremendous upsurge among our Negro fellow citizens, than which there is no more extraordinary development in
this most extraordinary of wars? At this writing the Associated
Press does not employ a single colored reporter. Yet there are
13,000,000 colored Americans, constituting perhaps the gravest
domestic problem under the American flag, who are becoming
more and more determined, as they grow in means, influence,
and political power, to insist upon having their constitutional
rights. There is plenty of spot news developing every day among
these people, but it does not find its way into print through the
service of the Associated Press, whose Southern bureaus, I repeat, conform absolutely to local prejudices, so that, for example, on its Southern wire Negroes are never designated as Mr.
and Mrs. but only by their full names.

It has also long been the case with the reporting of labor events
that the Associated Press is at the mercy of the local reporters —
unless it sends its own men to cover some sensational development. For years the "anti-labor policies" of the Associated Press
were regarded in labor and social-reform circles as being as self-
evident as a statement that the sun rises and sets. For example,
in one West Virginia strike the AP's correspondent was the pro-
vost marshal of the strike district into which troops had been
moved! It was so obvious that he could not supply an unbiased,
objective account of what was happening that it was impossible
to understand how the AP could have appointed him. Now, it
is perfectly true that it is never easy to hold the scales even in a
labor dispute; that when deep passions are aroused in a strike,
with violence resulting, it is very difficult to get at the truth and
to send out a report which will not be attacked as biased by one
side or the other. But there was certainly no excuse for the Associated Press's taking strike news from the Tennessee coal fields
sent by a correspondent employed by the local newspaper which
was owned by a coal company. In other words, he was an employee of the coal operators. In the case of the lockout of its
Guild workers by the Lorain, Ohio, *Journal,* the Associated
Press received its news from a strike-breaker.

Undoubtedly the AP officials in New York mean to do the
right thing and never consciously take sides in labor disputes. Yet

there have been many times when false pictures were given or vital news suppressed. It is a pleasure to add that of late years there have not been so many complaints of poor reporting of labor troubles, which is doubtless in part due to the absence of any highly exciting strikes — beyond the sensational Pacific coast labor news — and to the desire of the present general manager, Kent Cooper, to keep the service clean. But just as long as the AP is compelled to rely upon its local members and their employees for its news of labor difficulties it must expect to be misled, or deceived, in many instances.

The Associated Press has often been accused of dealing very lightly with persons of influence and position in the business world. One concrete example was the curious reporting of an address to Boston lawyers by the former Attorney General of the United States, Robert H. Jackson, who held that office when he delivered the address. In the course of it he denounced as enemies of democracy a number of prominent persons, among them H. W. Prentiss, Jr., then head of the National Association of Manufacturers, Merwin K. Hart of the New York State Economic Council, and the editors of the *Saturday Evening Post*. That both the United Press and the Associated Press omitted these names may, of course, have been purely accidental. None the less, the tendency to "go easy" when men in high positions are involved is an ever present danger with the news associations and the daily newspapers. The AP has also at times been extremely wary of antagonizing and disciplining any of its members, even when there was good reason for doing so.

Thus, on one occasion the head of an AP newspaper in Pennsylvania paid $300 to a New York City reporter in the expectation of getting a "more accurate" report by the Associated Press of the government's proceedings against the Standard Oil, despite the fact that the reporter in question was not connected with the Associated Press. That this editor should promptly have been expelled from the Associated Press goes without saying. Instead he went unscathed, after making an apology. Far more important was the case of William Randolph Hearst, fully described in the chapter devoted to him in this volume. Never was a man more clearly convicted on every count of the indictment brought against him by the Associated Press. But after taking the case to the Supreme Court and winning it, the AP allowed the offender to remain a member of the group he had cheated and robbed of news.

Indubitably no press association anywhere else undertakes to censor the journalistic morals of its patrons. But the Associated Press does impose certain standards of conduct upon its members, besides refusing to permit them to sell the news delivered to them or the local news which they originate. Thus, it holds them rigidly responsible for releasing at the proper time matter sent to them in advance, and it fines them for any violations of instructions. They may be suspended or expelled for violation of the by-laws, though the latter step may be taken only if it is approved by four fifths of the membership. Moreover, the Associated Press does not hesitate to punish its critics among its members. It fined the editor of the Philadelphia *North American* $300 for saying that an AP cablegram had in all probability been written "in New York or Washington, and never was near an ocean cable." Later the Lancaster *Intelligencer* was made to apologize for charging falsely that the Associated Press was "scooped" by another news service. If it can set up regulations and standards of conduct in cases like these, it certainly seems incomprehensible that it should have permitted a man to remain a member who had struck at its integrity and had not hesitated to use any means, however corrupt or contemptible, to gain his ends. It is the simple truth that a small newspaper doing these things would have been expelled; its directors apparently were afraid of Mr. Hearst's power and of the number of memberships in the Associated Press held by him.

CHAPTER V

The Associated Press II

IN THE LAST ANALYSIS any organization is what the men in it make it. What of the men in the Associated Press? It is a great pleasure to record the fact that, despite the usually inadequate salaries paid, the Associated Press has generally been served by a most loyal, devoted, and honest group of men and women, a credit to themselves and to the service. For its reporters and correspondents in the field there is no eight-hour and no twelve-hour day. They must be first into any disease-ridden, or calamity-scourged town, and of course they are not afraid of the firing line — that has been again proved by the magnificent services of men in the present war, in which several have lost their lives. Men of a very fine type are drawn to the service by the extraordinary fascination of all newspaper work and by its excitement. They often feel that they are in a degree public servants, and the interest of the "game" compensates for the small salaries and exacting hours. Sometimes they exercise a profound influence upon the progress of political events, becoming guides, philosophers, and friends to men in high office. Rarely is any charge of manipulating the news for personal profit brought against an employee. Indeed, I have never heard it alleged that anybody in the Associated Press was using his position in order to make money, although there must have been plenty of opportunities if only because of the custody of important public documents in advance of publication. Where irregularities have occurred in this connection, as in the matter of misreading a Supreme Court opinion, it has almost invariably appeared that the error was accidental.

I was myself at one time chairman of a committee of the Associated Press which had *carte blanche* to make the most careful inquiry into charges of corruption, mismanagement, and favoritism in the presentation of news. After months of inquiry we found nothing which in any way affected the integrity of the service, and we were able to dispose in short order of the libelous charge brought against Melville E. Stone by Frank B. Kellogg, one time Ambassador to England and Secretary of State, that Stone had "completely sold out" to the Standard Oil Company during the trial of the suit brought against it by the United States Government, with Kellogg as prosecutor. This was a typical case of the way in which the layman often comes to unwarranted conclusions as to the handling of a given news story. Kellogg thought that the suit and his leading part in it should be on the first page of the newspapers, or be elsewhere reported every day with full details. It appeared that the Associated Press had adequately reported the sessions, but after the suit had dragged on for weeks, the newspapers had relegated the matter to unimportant places and cut down the accounts. There is nothing in the by-laws of the Associated Press to compel any newspaper to print all that it sends; indeed, no newspaper could do this. As Kellogg came from the Northwest, and his home state newspapers, those of Minnesota, were little interested in the case and gave it the minimum of space, he decided that he and the government were being discriminated against.

Stone promptly brought Kellogg to book and gave him a very short time in which to retract his statements or face a suit for libel. Kellogg retracted. It was Stone himself, for so many years the general manager of the Associated Press, who created the spirit of loyalty and devotion to the service among its employees of which any organization might well be proud. Being human, Stone had his weaknesses and made his mistakes. He was far too remote from the life of the masses of the people, and he erred in accepting decorations from foreign governments and being too friendly with people in the seats of the mighty, both in politics and in business, but there was no sacrifice that he would not make for the Associated Press. Within the limits of his vision he rendered notable services and he was able in his contacts with the heads of governments and of nations. His own example of complete devotion to the AP was bound to be followed by his subordinates, whose good work he was never chary of recognizing.

Taking the Associated Press as a whole, its story is plainly that of the growth and development of journalism in America. It has grown as the profession has grown and turned into an industry. But during all the years of its existence it has never been without men who felt that service with it was a public trust to be respected at any cost. It has kept the avenues of promotion open and usually reserved the high places for its own men of merit. The present general manager, Kent Cooper, is a product of the service, having risen not from the news-gathering side but by way of the communications branch, in which he speedily made himself an authority. Unassuming, never in search of public recognition, Mr. Cooper has devoted himself chiefly to a magnificent crusade to free the Associated Press, and all the other American news-gathering agencies, from having to receive news from the government-controlled or influenced news bureaus, or private news monopolies, abroad. These bureaus not only had complete control of foreign news but undertook to say just how much should reach the United States and with what coloring. By an extraordinary contract, arrived at early in the history of the Associated Press, it was restricted to North America; on no other terms would the foreign news agencies do business with it. Truly, under Mr. Cooper's leadership the Associated Press, to use his own words, "waged a struggle not only for its freedom, but for the principle of freedom of international news exchange by all those who were under restrictions in any country." That battle lasted until 1942, when the Associated Press won a complete victory and freed the American press as a whole from domination by the foreign agencies, which were usually the tools of their governments, instruments of selfish national policies, to which all considerations of truth, justice, and fair play in news-gathering were entirely subordinated.

The story of this extraordinary achievement Mr. Cooper has set forth in his book *Barriers Down.** In my judgment it is impossible to exaggerate the value of this service to the government and to the people of the United States, and it was the irony of fate that, after having conducted so splendid a fight against press monopolies the world over, the Associated Press should itself have been charged with conspiracy to restrain the trade in news at home. There was still another phase of this crusade which should never be forgotten, and that is that because of it a clean stream of informative news goes from the United States to the rest of the world, whereas for generations the press of Europe contented itself with portraying only the bizarre and sensational aspects of American life, the incidents being selected by representatives of the foreign news associations in the United

* Published by Farrar & Rinehart, New York, 1942.

States. For what he accomplished by rigidly sticking to this crusade, year in, year out, Mr. Cooper would have received high honors in other countries. Here even most of the reviewers of his book failed to understand the vital importance to the nation of this liberation of the American press from foreign domination.

If henceforth the news from abroad in peace-time should prove not to be truthful, accurate, and without bias applied in the country of its origin, it will be possible to hold the Associated Press strictly accountable, as it could not wholly have been under the old system. In war-time, of course, lies, misrepresentations, and half-truths have the right of way, with censorships at home and abroad doing their utmost to color or pervert or suppress, to which end the plea of military necessity can be made to cover every possible sin. Since the United States is destined as a result of its intervention in the second World War to play the leading role among the nations, the vital importance of a free two-way news service with all foreign countries must be plain to everybody. There is no more creditable chapter in the history of the Associated Press than this achievement of one of its own men.

It would be gratifying if it were possible to add that similar great gains have been made in the domestic news service of the Associated Press during Mr. Cooper's headship of the organization. This is not the case. There have come to pass changes in the point of view and the activities of the association, some of which must have made Melville Stone turn in his grave. There has been a distinct lowering in the tone of the service as well as in its character. Under Stone the accent of the Associated Press was on straight news. Whether the incentive to a change came from Mr. Cooper and the board of directors or originated with the individual members, the fact is that it has followed the general trend of the American press in the direction of amusement and entertainment features, including many light and "spicy" items of dubious value, intended to offset the criticism that the Associated Press dispatches are always heavy and deadly factual. Items like "the best story of the day" and odd anecdotes play their part in filling small spaces. More than that, ill-written, banal, and even vulgar items have found and find their way into the news report. It is a pleasure to recall that Adolph S. Ochs, long the most powerful director of the association, voted against every proposal to lower the standards and to introduce comic strips and cheap, worthless anecdotes. From straight news the Associated Press has gone to "comics, comment, cookery," and other features.

Even Frank Knox, not usually considered a stickler for style, once protested in an editorial in his Chicago *Daily News,* which he wrote himself, saying: "Since Melville Stone's death the organization has been experimenting, not always to the benefit of its own reputation. However, to those who knew and admired the AP tradition, it comes as a shock to learn that the management is now offering to members a new Washington column of such doubtful ethical quality that the AP is not even willing to take public responsibility for it. . . . A gossip column . . . the lowest form of journalism! . . ." The reference was to the daily feature written by one Preston Grover, who was supposed to send "spice, humor and harmless speculation" and to shun scandal. The editors were asked not to add to this column the designation "AP" which heads all of its news stories, because "in the interests of providing a livelier Washington column than would be possible under strict adherence to the rules of Associated Press reporting, Preston Grover is being given a latitude of expression which makes it mandatory that the AP logotype be omitted from his copy." In other words, the creator of this remarkable column sought to hide its paternity. Yet it was so proud of Mr. Grover's column that the AP advertised it as "a credit to American journalism . . . logotype or no logotype."

Other fields into which the AP has entered where Melville Stone would never have led are a wire-photo picture service which sends its pictures "to member papers with telegraphic speed over a circuit 16,000 miles long." In addition, in its own words, it supplies its members "with a complete feature budget, comprising news feature stories with and without illustrations, news cartoons, comic strips, and a full budget of departmental features" — all a long cry from straight news of world events. Thus the AP from having been a specialty news shop has become a full-fledged department store. It is an interesting fact that the acquisition by the AP of the stock of Wide World Photos, Inc., was attacked by the United States government as being in violation of the anti-trust acts of 1890 and 1914. It also used against the AP its boasts that its feature budget is "the only feature service with full facilities for coverage — pictures, stories, columns, backgrounds — in every State and in foreign countries. . . . The only complete feature service available in whole or in part," as another reason for its being declared a violator of the anti-trust statutes. It is needless to point out the danger of coloring the news when the AP sends out news cartoons.

While thus willing to be "open-minded" and to yield to the "modern trend" in newspaper publishing by taking on entertainment features, the Associated Press under Mr. Cooper refused to recognize the movement which became strong in the 1930s for the organization of newspaper writers and editors into newspaper guilds. For years it took the position that the Associated Press "has no labor relations" and dismissed operators and editors who affiliated themselves with labor-union movements. Thus, on one occasion it discharged nine traffic-department employees for union activities. It threatened discharge, demotion, and transfer to other cities in the case of other union employees, and was even charged with circulating anti-union petitions and propaganda among its workers, interfering with union meetings by the use of spies, and other tricks, all for the purpose of intimidating employees. In the case of Morris Watson, a staff writer who was dismissed for his activities as vice-president of the American Newspaper Guild, it was necessary to take the case to the Supreme Court of the United States, which on April 12, 1937 upheld the Watson side, ordered his reinstatement, and awarded him back pay.

It is only fair to add that after this Mr. Cooper's attitude changed materially. He frankly acknowledged this in a hearing before the National Labor Relations Board when he recognized that the desire of the workers for collective security was overwhelmingly great and arose from a deep-seated need; and he stated that he admired the achievements of the Newspaper Guild. He engagingly added that he had learned "a great deal." Prior to this event there were many charges in the labor and liberal press that the AP was only printing news unfavorable to the labor movement and laying stress upon court decisions making against the new Roosevelt labor laws. The relations of the Associated Press with its employees now appear to be entirely satisfactory to both sides.

It seems to me, as an outsider, that Mr. Cooper has failed to take adequate note of the widespread criticisms of the Associated Press service in both the foreign and the domestic field, and that they suggest the best opportunities for improving the service. The greatest effort should be made to impress upon the AP's employees the absolute need of objectivity. It may seem strange that this must be stressed when the AP is so certain that it does not take sides; but it does so constantly, usually unwittingly, I believe, because its employees and those of its member newspapers, from whom it draws so much of its news, are greatly influenced by prevailing taboos and so easily and readily drift with the currents of public opinion. It is, of course, absurd to say that the Associated Press has been "one hundred percent wrong in its selection and coloring the news in every international crisis since 1919," as has been charged by Professor William Orton of Smith College. This critic was correct, however, in dwelling on the dangers that lie in selecting for transmission only facts favorable to some specific policy or purpose, thus indirectly coloring the news and creating false impressions in the minds of the readers. He was also correct in picking out the AP's handling of the Russian news in the years immediately after the first World War as beyond belief, false, inaccurate, and tendentious.

For years the Associated Press could see no more good in the Bolsheviks than could the New York *Times,* and it made every possible error in the handling of the news, particularly in its assumption that the Bolshevik regime would soon collapse. Professor Orton also cited the case of the Arabs who were in rebellion in Syria in 1924-5. They were in revolt against the tyrannical administration of the French, the cruelties and wrongs to which they were subjected, and the failure of the French and the Allied nations to give any relief. Just as in the case of our own lawless invasion of Nicaragua, Haiti, and Santo Domingo, the Associated Press characterized the revolutionists as "rebels." That, of course, they were, but the Associated Press usually gives the impression in a case like this that they are rebels against a worthy established order and never seems to be able to represent the revolters as true aspirants for the Four Freedoms for which, Mr. Roosevelt claims, we are fighting the second World War. Similarly among the criticisms heard of most of the Associated Press and its reporting of domestic news is one that it never takes the side of the underdog or, better, never appreciates that the underdog very often has sound reasons for rising against the existing social order. Hence the numerous allegations that it is still unfair to organized labor, that it shows favoritism in dealing with leaders of big business and industry, even to the suppression of names of offenders among them. Undoubtedly there is exaggeration in this, yet the feeling persists.

There was one unsettling fact in connection with the United Mine Workers strike under John Lewis's leadership in May and June 1943. Suddenly there appeared dispatches quoting American soldiers and sailors at the various fronts as denouncing the miners for asking more pay when the former were risking their lives abroad. It was impossible for me, as a former member of the Associated Press for a period of twenty-one years, to believe that in India and Africa and the Southwest Pacific private soldiers rushed to the Associated Press representatives and simultaneously demanded that their views be cabled to all the Associated Press newspapers. If that was not in response to a tip to various AP correspondents sent out by the home office, it was certainly one of the most remarkable of news happenings. Again, those soldiers could have had no idea of the real facts behind the strike, or the exact conditions confronting the miners, or the acts of the War Labor Board. Yet the Associated Press gladly spent large sums in cable tolls to reproduce their views within the United States. One naturally wonders whether if these soldiers had expressed sympathy with the miners their views would similarly have been cabled from abroad. There could be no clearer instance of the danger which confronts a news-gathering agency in a time of national excitement, when its officers and workers should make doubly sure that they are not merely circulating an expression of popular passion.

Here again we come back to the fact that the Associated Press is made up of and controlled by more than 1,200 American newspapers, and that it naturally reacts to the prejudices of the majority of its members. Sometimes those members, as in the case of the re-election of Mr. Roosevelt in 1936 and 1940, have been proved to be quite at variance with the opinion of the majority of the American people. All of this puts the greatest responsibility upon Mr. Cooper and his entire organization to lean over backward if necessary in being absolutely objective — even *be-*

yond and above the prejudices of the public or of the AP members. The nearer the Associated Press can come to achieving this ideal detachment from the emotions and passions of any one moment, the greater the service it can render to the country and the fewer will be the criticisms of its world-wide reports.

CHAPTER VI

The Associated Press and the Government

WHEN THE ROOSEVELT ADMINISTRATION brought suit against the Associated Press in 1942 on the ground that denial of its service to certain newspaper applicants for its news was in violation of the anti-trust law, the directors of the AP promptly decided to go to court and face the might of the United States government to ascertain if ever since the organization of the present AP, on May 22, 1900, it had been violating a law surely never intended to control a news-gathering association co-operative in nature and entirely non-profit-making. Only once before had the Department of Justice been interested in the actions of the AP. On March 12, 1915 the then Attorney General, T. W. Gregory, decided that a complaint made against the AP by a non-member newspaper was without merit. The Attorney General pointed out, however, that one of its by-laws could be interpreted as forbidding members to buy the service of competitive press associations organized for profit. This by-law had never been enforced, but in accordance with Gregory's advice it was immediately abrogated.

What were the grounds which led the Roosevelt Administration to move against the AP on behalf of Marshall Field's Chicago *Sun* and Mrs. Patterson's Washington *Times-Herald*? It was primarily because of a by-law which gave to members of the AP in any one locality the right to protest against the admission of another daily publishing in their territory, whether it was newly established, like the Chicago *Sun,* or an old journal. If the members exercised their right of protest the applicant was barred unless he took his case to the entire membership of the AP and four fifths of those present voted in favor of his being admitted. In view of the government's stand, at the annual meeting in April 1942 the members amended the by-laws to eliminate right of protest and substitute a majority vote for the four fifths previously required in case of the appeal of a candidate. The original purpose of this so-called protest by-law was not to create news monopolies, but, as it seemed necessary, in order to protect the members in their legitimate rights. Its adoption must

[60]

be regarded in the light of the almost chaotic conditions in news-gathering at the time when the predecessor of the present Associated Press was organized in 1893. Then the newspapers were threatened by what the present management of the AP terms "a sinister domination by private interests of the news services, both American and foreign," in that there was danger of the AP being taken over by three men who controlled the United Press of that time.* Of those three men, only one was a journalist; one was a bank president, and one associated with the United Press. Had these men acquired control of the AP as well as the UP, there would have been complete domination of American news-collecting by three mercenary individuals not qualified to bear such a tremendous responsibility or to wield the power which would have been theirs had they established a complete news monopoly. As Melville Stone put it, "there could be no really free press in these circumstances. A press to be free must be one which should gather the news for itself."

At once newspapers of the highest ethical standing, like the Chicago *Daily News,* the *Evening Post* of Edwin L. Godkin and Horace White, the Springfield *Republican* of Samuel Bowles, the New York *Times,* and many others, acted with lightning speed to head off that menace. They sought neither to violate the Sherman Act nor to create monopolies. On the contrary they wished to prevent a monopoly and were concerned with building an organization able to protect itself and its clients against raids by the members of another body which had shown a hostile spirit and boded no good for the press. Had anybody suggested to those veteran editors that the process of exchanging news through the Associated Press and receiving that which it collected was an illegal and unmoral proceeding, and that in banding themselves together as members of the association they became a public utility, they would have met the assertion with uncomprehending amazement.

It must also be remembered that at that time the trend toward local newspaper monopolies had hardly begun, that most cities and towns had plenty of newspapers, and some, like Chicago, too many. There was a warranted fear that newspapers might be founded in communities already served adequately, in which

* This must not be confused with the United Press founded by the Scripps brothers.

newcomers could not be profitable enterprises and, as sometimes happened, were deliberately founded to be bought out at high figures because they jeopardized the profits or the existence of the established dailies. That this protest by-law did, on the other hand, make it possible for a member to keep out a rival because of spite or of fear of worthy and proper competition is true, but there was always the possibility of appealing to the sense of justice of the entire membership. It has not been claimed that there were many cases of genuine hardship as a result of this veto right.

The government has naturally not specifically stated that it aimed to have the Associated Press declared a public utility, and therefore compelled to give its service to anyone asking for it, whatever his motive, character, or standing; but that would have been the effect had it won its contention. It could not maintain that the Associated Press was a monopoly, because it admitted that there are two competitors, the United Press and the Hearst International News Service. It asserted, however, that the Associated Press is so superior to the others in its news-gathering and in its coverage of the world that a newspaper without its service is gravely disadvantaged. It even declared in its complaint that "access to the service of a news service is therefore essential to the survival of any newspaper." Newspapers must, it contended, be "unhampered by any artificial or unnecessary restraints, public or private, upon their choice of, and free competitive access to the various sources of news, including agencies engaged in assembling and transmitting daily news reports of world events." Thus the government adopted the position that the best is none too good for the newspapers; that if they can only obtain a less efficient news service than that of the Associated Press they are disadvantaged and restrained in their business of trading in the news, and the Associated Press is guilty of restraint of trade. Actually a number of newspapers have become strong and prosperous without having had the Associated Press news, and some newspapers have deliberately dropped the Associated Press after utilizing it for years.

Yet the government's complaint asserted that "many newspaper readers prefer or demand AP news," and that therefore a newspaper denied it is "deprived of freedom in determining the character of its publications and freedom in determining those elements of the newspaper-reading public to which it will particularly address itself." In my twenty-one years of daily journalism I never heard of any reader giving up a newspaper because it did not have the Associated Press news; in 999 cases out of 1,000 the reader neither knows nor cares where his favorite newspaper gets its news. By the same reasoning cartoonists and creators of comic strips could be forbidden to sell their products to only one paper in a given territory on the ground that their failure to sell them to all the others was a restraint of trade and an interference with the freedom of the newspaper publisher to buy whatever he wished in order to determine "those elements of the newspaper-reading public" to which he particularly desired to address his appeal.

After the preliminary documents had been filed in the case of the government against the Associated Press in the United States District Court for the Southern District of New York, the Attorney General suddenly moved for a summary judgment without formal trial. The court appointed three of its judges, all men of highest repute, Learned Hand, Augustus N. Hand, and Thomas W. Swan, to constitute a special bench to expedite the decision. In giving its judgment the court was divided, the two Judges Hand upholding three of the government's contentions, rejecting the others, and ordering certain changes in the AP's by-laws, while Judge Swan entirely supported the Associated Press's position. But the majority opinion made it quite clear that the two judges entertained unusual doubt as to the correctness of their decision, and desired the appeal to the Supreme Court which is now pending. The court found that the AP does not monopolize or dominate the furnishing of news or news pictures and features, or access to the original sources of news, nor monopolize or dominate transmission facilities for the gathering or distribution of news, pictures, or features. These findings are of the utmost importance because they end forever the far-reaching assertion that the AP is a monopoly and a combination in restraint of trade, trying to control the news field. Both the majority and minority decisions stressed the fact that the competitive services are able and well conducted and can be utilized satisfactorily by those newspapers which do not have the AP service.

The majority ordered that the members of the AP in voting upon the admission of an applicant for membership shall be bound by a new by-law forbidding them in the consideration of such an application to regard the effect that the admission of the new member would have upon those members already in his field. In other words, the court undertook to specify the state of mind in which the members of the AP should enter the meeting-room to vote upon the desirability of the candidate for membership. This is plainly going amazingly far for a court, and the two Judges Hand revealed the peculiarity of this ruling in their next paragraph, in which they said: "It is of course true that the members may disregard the last provision in practice; but that is not to be assumed. At any rate, we think that the plaintiff is entitled to that much positive assurance in the organic law; and it is as far as we can go." But since the most important questions in connection with applications for membership have always been the effect the admission would have upon the members in the same territory, and whether the applicant was actuated by a desire to injure or displace the existing dailies, whether or not it was a purely "strike" or blackmailing venture, the court demanded a great deal in asking each member in voting to eliminate from his mind the hitherto vital points.

Apparently the government here won its demand not only that the protest right be finally done away with, but that the membership of the Associated Press be open to everybody. Not at all. While enjoining "the defendant from continuing to enforce the by-laws regulating the admission of members in their present form," the court went out of its way to say that it left it open to the AP "to adopt substitutes which will restrict admission." The government promptly claimed a great victory, despite the fact that the court thus blew hot and cold and the AP is now apparently free to say that it will not admit members whose opinions it does not like, whose clothing does not appeal to it, or whose manners cause irritation. They may even forbid admission in all communities of 100,000 people. It is no wonder that in view of this confusion of thought the two Judges Hand expressed their hope that the Supreme Court would finally clear the situation up.

The sharpest disagreement between Judge Swan and his associates in the whole controversy came on the latter's far-reaching opinion that the anti-trust laws compel the Associated Press to give its entire news report to all comers who may ask for it, without regard for any local conditions whatever or the circumstances of the applicant for admission. Judge Swan emphatically declared that this contention was based on a complete misinterpretation of the previous decisions cited by it as precedents. He said: "To my mind the nature of a news report, which is the intellectual product of him who makes it, points to the conclusion that he may choose to whom he will disclose it, rather than to the conclusion that he is under a duty to disclose it to all applicants." In other words, he grants the right of an originator of news to say that only the AP shall have it or someone else shall have it. It has never been easy to see why the special news stories created by the special correspondents of a newspaper must be turned over to anybody who asks for them. That would destroy all incentive to newspapermen to exceed their competitors in their service to the public.

The majority decision declared that the purchase by the AP of a picture service known as Wide World Photos from the New York *Times* did not violate the anti-trust laws, as charged by the government, and that the exclusive news-exchange contract with the Canadian Press would not be a violation of law if the by-laws were changed. But the extraordinary fact remains, as has been pointed out by the honorary president of the AP, Frank B. Noyes, that the majority decision declares that although the AP "neither has nor seeks a monopoly and does not seek to impede competition, it nevertheless is in violation of the anti-trust acts." He then continues: "The vital question is whether the members of the association may use their own judgment in election or denial freely, or whether they can be properly coerced to vote against what they regard as the best interests of the organization itself." The board of directors appealed to the Supreme Court because: "The court found the Associated Press was not a monopoly. It found that it was not a common carrier. Yet the decision, if not appealed and overthrown, would impose a method of doing business upon the Associated Press which would hamper its efficiency and weaken its cooperative structure."

The appeal was well taken. Had the government been entirely upheld and the AP been classified as a public utility, it would have been quite possible, as the lawyers for the Chicago *Tribune* contended, for members to go into a court to ask it to determine whether the rates of the AP were fair and reasonable, or the news service discriminatory, or whether its budget was too high or too low. In other words, as in the case of all public utilities, there would have been government regulation. And government regulation in this case would have been a long step toward the control of the news. The government in its complaint against the AP admitted that a free press is essential to democracy, yet had it won a complete victory a serious blow to press freedom in this country might have been struck. So the government's contention that if the old order continued in the AP the newspaper industry would "grow increasingly stagnant, increasingly conservative, and increasingly out of touch with public opinion" was never well founded. The trend to stagnation and to monopoly and the decrease in the number of journals have in nowise come from the conditions in the Associated Press to which the government objected. They would have come had the United Press and the International News Service been governed by precisely the same by-laws, for they arise from those trends in our entire economic life already stressed.

Never was the government's charge justified that if the Associated Press were to continue in its former methods, "freedom of the press would be changed from a public right to a vested interest." That obviously assumed that there was no other press than the daily press, that the freedom of the entire daily press would be a possession of the AP, and that nothing could be done about it. This ignored not only the existence of the UP and the Hearst service, but the fact that there are thousands of weeklies published in this country which have nothing to do with the AP, magazines of all kinds, and small publications of every possible variety which have freedom of the printed word and will continue to have it, no matter what happens to the AP. It also ignored the fact that there has arisen a great new competitor for all newspapers — the radio. While it does not print its words, its spoken words do constitute an offset to some of the failures and delinquencies of the daily press, and assure the giving of news and opinions to the entire American people subject only to governmental restrictions.

Unfortunately the radio *is* controlled by the government in some degree, in both peace-time and war-time. Indeed, the mere existence of the Federal Communications Commission constitutes a censorship by the government. It is doubtful if there is a single radio station in the country which does not live in fear of hostile action by the government; there are few if any stations that do not always have in mind, in judging an offering or the contents of an address, the possibility that through the Commission it may bring reprisals from whatever administration is in power. There could be no clearer example of the fact that regulation by a government agency invariably means conscious or unconscious, direct or indirect control of those regulated, and no clearer indication of the necessity of preventing any approach to government control of the press. In writing this the excellent attitude taken by Chairman Fly of the Commission in urging the stations to permit outspoken criticisms of the government even in war-time is not overlooked. It will not be sufficient in itself, however, to relieve the stations of that dread of Washington authority which had been so manifest long before the second World War came.

Had the co-operative principle in news-gathering been destroyed by the judges in the AP case, that would have been extremely regrettable. While it is impossible to agree with the AP that its management has been wholly above commercial considerations, there is no doubt that if the co-operative principle were abandoned commercial considerations would more and more control. Rightly or wrongly, the directors of the AP are satisfied that, with the service thrown open to everybody, "the incentive of each member to contribute his time, effort and money to the upbuilding of an organization for the mutual benefit of himself and others making a like contribution would disappear." Even if the directors are mistaken as to this, the destruction of the co-operative principle would, in my judgment, be a serious blow to the efficiency of the Associated Press, and probably have a deleterious effect upon the quality of the news.

Since the government has stressed the size and importance of the Associated Press it is right to add here some facts as to its present activities. In 250 cities of the world it has offices of its own, and it maintains 94 news bureaus within the United States, of which seven have staffs of fifty or more full-time employees. It has 2,500 correspondents located in foreign countries; of its domestic staff of 7,200 employees, 1,940 give their full time to the organization. The government declares that approximately 100,000 persons contribute directly or indirectly to its news service and that its Washington office comprises 150 reporters, while 200 writers, editors, and statisticians are assigned to the financial news service. It leases a transatlantic cable and uses a network of telegraph wires in the United States connecting fully 727 cities. Every twenty-four hours it sends out news reports of at least one million words, with supplementary reports and services. In Chicago the morning newspapers receive daily 273,000 words and the evening papers 246,000 words; the reports in Washington comprise 276,000 words for both morning and evening newspaper members. It paid out in 1941 about $12,000,000 to gather and distribute the news, of which $8,450,000 were expended in the United States alone. All of this was paid for almost wholly out of the weekly assessments levied upon its members.

As for its influence outside of the country, the government in its brief quotes the Associated Press as saying this: "Through facilities which it has created, the news of America collected by the Associated Press appears in virtually every newspaper in the world outside the United States." This vast, world-wide supplying of the Associated Press reports, whatever their faults, to foreign newspapers on such a large scale has been an inestimable service not only to the government but to the people of the United States. Since we are in a global war, it is not necessary to stress the enormous importance to the carrying out of our national policies of supplying to the press of our allies and of the neutral countries a true and correct picture of what is happening here — true and correct so far as the censorship and government control permit. Anyone who has traveled abroad during the last fifty years knows well how shameful and utterly misleading was the American news which appeared in foreign newspapers during most of that period — usually merely a record of sensational crimes or freakish events and of disasters, with the result that in every country, even including England, there was a totally false picture of American life, progress, ambitions, and aims.

As an American I profoundly regret having to add my belief that the Department of Justice would never have brought suit against the Associated Press had it not been that the Chicago

Sun, one of the newspapers whose applications for membership in the Associated Press were denied, is an organ largely created to advance the fortunes of Franklin Roosevelt and the Democratic Party. Had it been founded to promulgate beliefs similar to those of the Chicago *Tribune,* which successfully protested the *Sun's* admittance to the Associated Press, and been equally opposed to our entry into the war and to the New Deal, it is unthinkable that the Department of Justice under Mr. Biddle's direction would have found time to espouse the cause of this hostile newcomer.

CHAPTER VII

The Columnists

THE GRADUAL DYING-OFF of the great metropolitan editors and the ending of the individual journalism of the nineteenth century and the first decade of this one for a time made it appear as if all personality were to be eliminated from our dailies. Adolph Ochs was long determined to make his *Times* a great institution — great as such and not because there shone through its columns the soul and the spirit of its chief leader-writer. When he appointed Rollo Ogden editor-in-chief he made no public announcement of the fact, which became public only when a brief item appeared to the effect that among the speakers at an unimportant dinner was "Rollo Ogden, editor of the *Times.*" Ochs refused to allow himself or the members of his family to be puffed in the *Times* and rarely permitted the publication of his own name.* He wanted the New York *Times* to be as much and as impersonal an American national institution as the London *Times* was an important part of the machinery of the British Empire.

But a new trend soon developed in American journalism to which Mr. Ochs himself had finally to yield. This was the rise of the star columnists, the cartoonists, and the outstanding reporters and correspondents, who were allowed to sign their own names when the owners suddenly discovered that those signatures had a large circulation and money revenue value. When for some months in 1915–16 I became the Washington correspondent of my own daily, the New York *Evening Post,* after the sinking of the *Lusitania,* and signed my daily dispatches with my initials, I found myself the target of considerable criticism by some of the Washington correspondents. They held that this was a sort of exhibitionism unworthy of the professional journalist, to be left severely to the "trained seals" or "sob-sisters" who were hired by the more sensational dailies to report conventions or important murder trials or other emotional events. In other words, a "by-line" was something to be shunned. To this belief Ochs and other owners clung as long as possible.

* When he died, the *Times* naturally gave much space to tributes to his career.

But yield they did, even if they did not seek for distinguished editors to lure readers by their personalities and their individual editorial thunderings. Among the first columnists were the sports writers, who often carried with them many thousands of readers when they switched from one daily to another and who received enormous salaries, far beyond those ever earned by a Bowles, a Godkin, a Greeley, a Raymond, or a Watterson. Thus the proprietors and editors made the old, old discovery that their readers were more interested in personalities, whether of editors or writers, or Hollywood stars, or jazz and swing kings, or jitterbug saxophone idols, than in any purely depersonalized publishing institution. Gradually the "by-line" crept into every daily, and those journalists who had scoffed at its use were among the most eager to "sign their stuff." Out of all this there gradually emerged the columnist, whose personal appeal to the public was far more direct and individual than that of the editor whose unsigned diatribes readers sometimes picked out of an editorial page because of peculiarities of style or vigor of attack.

Soon there were literary columnists, humorous columnists, political columnists, foreign-affairs columnists, philosophical columnists, big-business columnists, financial columnists, military columnists, and, finally, pundit columnists, who took all human activity for their special cue, and lectured the whole world daily as to what it should do and how it should behave. The sex line was promptly crossed by some really able commentators — and then by Mrs. Roosevelt's incredibly banal, mawkish, and disingenuous diary, the great popularity of which can be cited as proof by those who assert that Americans are the worst fawners upon the rich and powerful to be found on earth. So far has the swing to the "by-line" gone that one could almost say that American journalism is today a compilation of private opinion, a conglomeration of individual views upon current events in every field of activity, a foisting of personality upon a public not only willing but incapable of satiation. It is almost the glorification of the gossip of the small town and the village. It is stimulated by the fact that the financial rewards of the successful columnist are enormous, exceeded, perhaps, only by the leading radio commentators hired by somebody's toothpaste or by some watchmaker. The income of a Lippmann or a Thompson soars into the many thousands, and the President's wife out-coins them all by virtue of her husband's office. Their thousand words or less go to multitudes of readers.

Here is one of the worst phases of the columnist epidemic: they contribute enormously to that standardization of the press referred to elsewhere. They encourage the newspaper editor with a weak and inefficient editorial page to continue to refuse honest and able guidance to his readers. Why hire a first-class leader-writer when one can obtain a well-known columnist for relatively few dollars and yet not be responsible for his views, which are marketed by some syndicate or press agent? If there is danger of the columnists' antagonizing business readers, or labor, or the conservative defenders of the existing order, why, it is easy enough to label them each day with a stereotype heading: "Mr. Blank's views are his own and do not necessarily represent those of the editors of this newspaper." That makes it possible for a paper to assume a broad-mindedness, or at least to pretend to present different opinions and points of view, even though it may be among the most hidebound and reactionary journals.

However, it thus does present different aspects, even if it shirks its own duty as a leader of public opinion, and exposes its readership to varying ideas, be they sound or unsound. It gives the columnists, if it employs several, the opportunity to make converts — if they can — to their theses. How far they carry their readers with them no one knows. The difficulty is that everybody turns to the columnist who most often portrays the reader's own ideas. Thus, big business reads its own ex-Socialist Walter Lippmann, and the labor-haters Westbrook Pegler, the informed students of European affairs their own Anne O'Hare McCormick, the Thompsonites their own Dorothy, and the followers of Sokolsky and David Lawrence their columns. Just so the radio listeners tune in on their pet narrator, be he a Swing, or a Fulton Lewis, or a Kaltenborn ($365,000 a year, the highest annual sum, he insists, paid to a brain-worker in the United States). One can at least believe that because of these numerous and diverse opinions of the public commentators Americans are becoming more and more aware of what is going on in the rest of the world, of the enormously widespread and conflicting economic and political trends, of the coming of the vast new revolution in which the globe finds itself. Whether the result of this is to be anything else than awareness remains to be seen, but the American people have been divorced from their habit, so ingrained prior to the first World War, and so slowly discarded, of never thinking of foreign events and of never considering American political problems except during the three months of the Presidential campaigns.

I do not deny that the columnists often enable a newspaper of modest means to give an interpretation of the news that it would be itself incapable of forming, or to vary its own interpretation. No one can question the value of the specialized writer on finance, foreign affairs, and so on, to the small-town newspaper. The danger comes when the editor sits back and lets the columnist do the thinking that he should do. Sometimes an editor deliberately employs columnists to attack those whom he is himself afraid to criticize for political or other reasons. This has been especially true of a portion of the Southern press. Compelled by hoary political tradition to give lip-service to President Roosevelt, these dailies use Kent, Lawrence, Sokolsky, and other critics of the New Deal and the Administration to pound the President, whom they would gladly see put out of the White House but are unable openly to oppose because of the sectional necessity of supporting the Democratic Party. The wisest editors are those of the newspapers which still value their own editorial pages, who do not feel committed to use every article submitted by each columnist, and often take issue with a columnist even when they print his or her column. This helps to preserve, of course, the dominance of the editorial page.

The numbers and diversity of the columnists, and the wide range of their surveys of national and international events, constitute their greatest safeguard from criticism and attack. Here comes into play not merely the extraordinarily short memory of the American newspaper public, but the lack of time available to the average reader to balance and counterbalance the opinions offered to him by the commentators. It is a terrific drudgery to plod through the back files of newspapers and read hundreds of columns each year to obtain a full estimate of the consistency or inconsistency, of the fallibility or infallibility, of the folly or the sanity of a columnist. Few of them could stand the results of such scrutiny. Many of them, like Mr. Lippmann, have boxed the compass of political opinion. Hardly one of them could escape deadly paralleling of their diverse and contradictory statements. Yet they go on unscathed and undaunted. Take the case of one of our leading military commentators, who over the radio one month before Pearl Harbor declared that it would be easy to dispose of Japan through a "full blockade" by the American, British, and Dutch naval and air forces, which Japan "could not long endure" and could not break. As for the Japanese air force, said he: "It is almost non-existent" — veterans of Pearl Harbor, Midway, and Guadalcanal please take notice! Yet this prophet still sails serenely on, giving his views every day undeterred by the fact that at this writing the Vice Commander in Chief of our navy has just announced that it is planning for the war with Japan to last until 1949, perhaps eight years after Pearl Harbor!

The truth is that there are very few persons indeed who have the background, the knowledge, the deep human experience needed to hold forth daily in all-wise fashion over their own signatures. Every other day should be the limit. In a world of such extraordinarily varied and shifting values there are still fewer whose thinking is so governed by fundamental principles as to enable them to chart their courses in advance, year in and year out, and to hold their helms steady. The temptation to snap judgments, to superficiality, too often overcomes the fear of inviting unfavorable judgments, of which there are far too few. It would seem as if the anonymous leader-writers had perhaps a better chance of doing well, day in and day out, than does the columnist who signs his name. The former is perhaps freer from self-consciousness, freer to write quietly and sanely than his contemporary who signs and is aware that his personal reputation is at stake, or feels that he must do something bold and startling, or restrict himself to playing safe. There are compensations, of course. A writer does get a thrill and stimulus in putting his name or his initials to a completed job. But the temptation to opportunism, to follow the party code, the line of least resistance, or to play to the crowd and write in accord with the public current, faces many a columnist, consciously or unconsciously.

Certainly few columnists are capable of the extreme objectivity of Hanson Baldwin, to whom a tribute has been paid elsewhere in this volume, and few can write so thoughtfully and painstakingly as Anne O'Hare McCormick. But these two are specialists by their own choice. It is when a writer undertakes to furnish a complete political survey of the rest of the world, in addition to daily laying down the law as to what should or should not be done in every field of our own national endeavor, that the pitfalls loom. It is then that the thoughtful reader is compelled to ask: "Well, who told her — or him — that?" or "Where did he run across that idea?" It is much safer to be a Westbrook Pegler and harp day after day upon just a few strings than to be one of the all-knowing who can tell us exactly what Stalin is really thinking and why the State Department has failed or succeeded in dealing with North African political problems. The truth is that our very greatest American editors of the past never pretended to the universal knowledge of a Lippmann or a Kaltenborn or a David Lawrence. They were to a degree limited in their range, if only because the American scene of their day was so constricted. None except Godkin was an expert in foreign affairs. They were specialists in the national political field and usually left economics and finance to members of their staffs hired for their knowledge of those fields. They were undoubtedly accused of seeking to be pundits, but how unfairly when one regards some of our all-knowing ones of today!

That some of these columnists do profoundly affect public opinion, at least at times, is quite true, and they reach a far vaster audience than ever did a Pulitzer, or a Bowles, or a Joseph Medill, or a Horace Greeley, or even a demagogue like Hearst. Mr. Lippmann was for long the "white-haired boy" of all big-business men; one could not continue to be a cashier or a vice-president of any first national bank without reading Walter prior to reaching one's desk. That phase has passed with him, like numerous other phases in his career. As for Westbrook Pegler, he has for years been the *bête noire* of all those devoted followers of labor who refuse to admit that there is the slightest ground for criticizing anyone or anything in the labor movement, and is the adored of all the opponents of union labor, especially those Americans who once so ardently worshipped Benito Mussolini because he made Italian labor "come to time." No one can deny the tremendous blows Pegler has struck at the large number of corrupt or criminal labor leaders, and at those unsound and unjust union practices which work such injustice to the individual worker and tend to close the avenues of entry and advancement to those who will not pay up. No American writer has stirred deeper passions or invited more bitter personal attacks, especially from those who insist that the unions must not be regulated by Congress, and must be permitted to clean their own house, however laggard they may be in doing so. Whether Pegler is right or wrong, no one can question his moral and physical courage or his desire to serve his countrymen. Violent attack upon something or someone appears to be his stock in trade, without which he would shrivel.

As mentioned elsewhere, the Scripps-Howard columnists — Simms, Denny, Edson, Ernie Pyle, Pegler, and others — give the main strength to those journals. Were they suddenly to disappear, those newspapers would have an extremely limited bill of fare to offer to their readers. Often their work is not sufficiently co-ordinated; hence they sometimes overlap and duplicate. Some of them face the charge of being given assignments abroad without adequate preparation for their tasks. A case of this was the sending of Raymond Clapper to India, whence his reports bordered on the naïve until he began to orient himself and to acquire background and experience. But that has long been a fault of American newspapers, much criticized by the editors of other countries who have picked their foreign representatives from men especially competent in the fields for which they were selected. The American managing editor has too frequently been ready to send any bright young reporter to Italy, Germany, France, China, or Japan, whether he knew anything about those countries and their languages and history or not.

As for the gossip and scandal columnists, they are excrescences of journalism who do no credit to the profession or to their employers. It is astounding that some of the newspapers which patronize Winchell and pride themselves on their high standards continue to do so. Indeed, nothing affords clearer proof that the age when the horsewhipping of editors was a familiar custom has disappeared than do some of these men. Drew Pearson, a different type, sometimes renders valuable service by publishing inside Washington information the public is entitled to have. He and Winchell are declared in Washington to be instruments used at times by some of the New Deal inner circle to initiate attacks upon political enemies or rivals. The percentage of error in Pearson's work is great. He is said to rejoice in more libel suits than any other columnist, and is plainly ready to sacrifice accuracy to the scoring of a point or the creating of an interesting story. But he did not deserve Mr. Roosevelt's denunciation of him as a liar, the unfairness of which, and the impropriety of the President's attack, reacted strongly in Mr. Pearson's favor, even among journalists who dislike him and his methods. Among the Washington commentators who do useful service because of their independence are Paul Mallon and Ray Tucker, while Mark Sullivan is as much a part of the Washington scenery as the Lincoln Memorial, with his unvarying appeal to the conservatives and the defenders of the *status quo,* and his ability to find more destroyers of the present order under the bed than anyone else except Martin Dies. It is only fair to add, however, that Mr. Roosevelt has several times indicated that he does not consider Mr. Sullivan an antagonist to be ignored.

By and large, the columnists are as varied as there are shades of opinion in America. There are goods for every customer. It cannot be said of the columnists what Mr. Roosevelt has repeatedly charged against the Washington correspondents, that they write not what they believe, but what they are told, for in the main the columnist is a completely free agent. Whatever his faults of vision, of presentation, they are his own and are not imposed upon him by an employer or some counting-room. But even with their variety and their different points of view, the fact remains that they do contribute to the standardization of the press and to the decrease of the personality and originality of many dailies.

CHAPTER VIII

The New York TIMES and Adolph S. Ochs

1. *The* TIMES *Today*

IN THE YEARS that have elapsed since the death of Adolph S. Ochs in 1935, the New York *Times* has more than ever established itself as the foremost daily of the world. As an institution it outshines the London *Times,* which no longer thunders. In America no other journal approaches it in the volume of news and coverage of the world. No important journalist can possibly do without it, and it has literally made itself indispensable to anyone who desires to be thoroughly informed as to what is happening on this globe. To miss even an issue is a detriment to all who deal with foreign affairs. There is little exaggeration in the statement that anyone who subscribes for the Sunday *Times* and reads it carefully will be able to take his part in any discussion of national or international affairs. As a whole it is a much better and fairer journal than it was in the days of Adolph Ochs, which period of its existence is set forth later in this chapter. Today the *Times* seems less biased both in its news stories and in its editorials. It takes a broader view of many problems, appears less of a group organ, and is much less inclined to bait the "Reds," or attack persons for their opinions. It still kowtows to wealth, power, and authority, and has of course some of the conventional faults of the ordinary daily, which drifts, as Frederick Lewis Allen has put it, "before the winds of circumstance, timidity, and self-interest." But the *Times* is not as timid as it was, and is, I believe, freer from fear of its advertisers. It has mellowed with the years, while improving its news, both foreign and domestic.

For these advances Ochs's heirs and successors, Arthur Hays Sulzberger and General Julius Ochs Adler, and the present staff deserve full credit. They have faithfully carried on Ochs's creation and have continued to justify his belief in the sales value of news as such. As is explained below, he purchased the *Times* on a shoestring when it was very nearly perishing, and for some very hard and dangerous years he stuck to his belief that by assembling and printing every day a great amount of news from all over the world he could achieve financial success. No more

[78]

than anyone else could he have visualized how great that success would be, especially as he had the courage and character to refuse to cheapen his paper. To this day it maintains itself without resorting to comic strips or cheap Sunday supplements, or other appeals to those who buy newspapers solely in order to be entertained on a low intellectual level. Moreover, the present owners continue to plow back into the paper a large portion of its earnings. They have much improved the standards of their special dispatches from all over the world and the quality of the men sending them. They also take excellent care of their employees in sickness, in health, and in old age.

It is still not possible to say that the *Times's* handling of the news is perfect or free from bias. It is better than in the days of Ochs, under whom much perverted and false news, notably in regard to Russia, appeared. The Russian news was so scandalous that the record was finally exposed in a special supplement of the *New Republic,* one of the compilers of that indictment being Charles Merz, now the editor-in-chief of the *Times.* It is not possible to say of the *Times* that it has reached the editorial standards of the *Manchester Guardian;* it is in the volume of its news and, in the main, the trustworthiness of its special reports that the *Times* triumphs. It was misled and grievously misrepresented by its correspondent William P. Carney during the revolution in Spain, and it was much too long served in Rome by Arnaldo Cortesi, who clearly showed his inability to be objective. Against these and other lapses must be put the work of a large number of extraordinarily brave, fair-minded, and devoted men who have risked their lives again and again in their eagerness to give to the readers of the *Times* the real truth. It may be invidious to single out a few, but it is impossible to withhold the fullest praise from Herbert L. Matthews, as one example, with his brilliant record in Ethiopia, in Italy, and in Spain, on the war fronts, and in India, where he showed himself remarkably impervious to British propaganda and presented the Indian case with rare intelligence and justice.

I have no means of knowing if it is true that Mr. Matthews's copy has often been edited and changed in the office of the *Times;* whether, for example, during the war in Spain, a night managing editor substituted the words "insurgent troops" wherever Mr. Matthews used "Italian troops." It was charged by

Better Times, the extraordinary and critical paper for a time published secretly by Communist members of the *Times* staff and frequently containing office secrets, that in a dispatch sent by Mr. Matthews to prove that Mussolini was intervening in the Spanish war, the words "these troops were Italians and nothing but Italians" was altered to read: "these troops were insurgents and nothing but insurgents," which of course made no sense whatever. A newspaper that alters dispatches sent by its correspondents in order to give them a different slant is highly censurable, and no first-class correspondent should allow his dispatches to be twisted or take orders as to what he is to send. It is a fact, however, that reporters, as well as editors, take the color of their employers unconsciously when they do not do so consciously.*

Only a few can maintain complete independence, as did Walter Duranty of the *Times* for years in his Russian correspondence, which the *Times* printed although it must have hated to do so on many occasions, especially as he frequently contradicted its reports about Russia from other countries. On the other hand, a newspaper may quite innocently be the victim of its correspondents' errors or bias or prejudices. It has been an unhappy fact that many of the foremost foreign correspondents of late years became deeply embittered by what they witnessed of the describable and indescribable horrors and brutalities of the Nazi criminals. A number of them returned to the United States and went upon the lecture platform as bitter propagandists. That is quite understandable; to see at close range the dreadful wrongs inflicted upon the invaded countries and to remain objective was probably asking too much. Yet never was there a greater responsibility upon newspapers and newspapermen to hold the scales even than in the years prior to our entrance into the war. If that ideal was not obtainable, it was none the less the duty of the newspapers which really wished to serve humanity to approximate as nearly as possible the ideal of unbiased reporting. The deserved plaudits won by Anne O'Hare McCormick of the

---

* ". . . Editors and reporters find out that what pays is to write the sort of news-stories which pleases the men at the top. In rare cases, of course, there may be actual corruption; but more often what puts bias into the news is merely the permeation of the staff by a sense of expediency. They put their jobs first and the truth second. . . ." — Frederick Lewis Allen: "Newspapers and the Truth," *Atlantic Monthly,* January 1922.

Times, and the prizes bestowed upon her for her distinguished foreign correspondence and her comments upon foreign developments after her return to the United States, were surely earned not merely by her knowledge, but by the restraint and the usually judicious quality of her writing.

It is also impossible to omit mention of Hanson W. Baldwin's unequaled military and naval commentaries. No one else approximates his standards of military reporting and analyzing, or even approaches him in the detachment with which he discusses the progress of the war, or the frankness of his criticisms of our army and navy. Carefully avoiding the prophesying which has so injured the standing of others who rank as experts, Mr. Baldwin has refused to allow his patriotism to sway him or to make him don rose-colored glasses. Unlike most of his countrymen, while certain of final victory, he has not deluded himself when we have achieved minor victories into believing that there was an easy path ahead. In consequence his work has been criticized for its alleged somberness and pessimism. Except regarding Russia — as to which everyone erred — it has stood the test of events remarkably, notably in his accounts of the fighting in the Solomon Islands and his criticism of some of the leadership there after his trip to the scene. The caution he displayed in commenting upon our North African venture was also wholly sustained by what happened, and he steadily dwelt upon the submarine menace when those in high positions were complacently satisfied or ignorant. His realism is enhanced by his frequent visits to the fleet, to our troops, and abroad. This is the place to add that the *Times,* besides giving Mr. Baldwin complete freedom, also merits high praise for its display of much of its war news, but not all. Its headlines are generally conservative, are more nearly in accord with the real facts underneath the sensationalism and partisan press-service accounts than most, and are correctly informative. If it undervalues enemy reports, the responsibility for that rests with the government rather than with the *Times.* Editorially its discussions of military and naval happenings and policies are of the very best, for which it is probably again necessary in part to thank Mr. Baldwin.

In the field of domestic correspondence the *Times* has given the world some of the finest reporting from Washington and the most voluminous ever printed. Arthur Krock, its chief representative, is detested by the New Deal and by all those adorers of President Roosevelt who think that he can do no wrong. As one who was himself a Washington correspondent and has been for more than forty years a commentator upon Washington events, I cannot withhold high praise from Mr. Krock. To me — I am by no means always in accord with his judgments — he seeks plainly to be objective. It is his calm statement of the facts upon which he bases his reasoning and the absence of emotion in his deductions that make his letters so effective as to have earned for him the bitter dislike of the occupant of the White House. If there were to be a criticism of the *Times* news service not only from Washington, but in general, it would be that it is often overwritten, that the same story is several times repeated — in the headlines, in the introduction, in the narrative of the special dispatch, and in the retelling of it in the Associated Press account, and, a few times, in the United Press report as well. If this procedure is due solely to a desire to present different points of view, it is commendable. But much space and paper could be saved with more and better copy-editing; on the other hand, to "carry" the great volume of the *Times's* advertising there must be supplied many columns of reading matter, and this the *Times* draws from all directions. Few other newspapers approximate its huge annual cable tolls or specialize in so many fields.

As for its editorial page, there has been a great improvement in it since the death of Rollo Ogden and the accession of Charles Merz as chief editor, together with the addition to the staff of some younger men of liberal viewpoint, such as Robert L. Duffus and Henry Hazlitt. Occasionally there appears an editorial of surpassing merit, such as "Twilight on the Don" in the issue of February 5, 1943, which is certainly one of the greatest editorials to appear anywhere in recent years. Yet the weaknesses of the page continue. The *Times* still does not *lead*. It rarely maps out policies or hammers them home in issue after issue. As under Adolph Ochs, one feels that all too often the *Times* withholds its fire, not in order to see the whites of the enemy's eyes, but to observe the whereabouts of the largest battalions. If this is too severe, one certainly gets the impression that it is an editorial page under severe restraint. Perhaps this is due to the reported presence of Mr. Sulzberger at every editorial conference, for Mr.

Sulzberger is quoted by George Seldes as saying that he is opposed to a very vigorous editorial page lest the correspondents at home and abroad take their color from it. He should certainly know that, whether an editorial page is weak or strong, unless the owner is himself a working editorial contributor, his presence at an editorial conference is bound to have a repressive effect and is certain to weaken the spontaneity and the sense of freedom of the editorial writers. The editorial staff, by the way, consists of ten writers, and the page includes contributions from "a large number of men and women in other departments of the paper" who have specialized knowledge. In one year, 1941, the *Times's* editorials were contributed by no less than fifty-three members of its staff.

The *Times's* policy has been to make its columnists regular members of the staff, writing exclusively for it, and it has gained and not lost thereby. None the less, the able personalities of the editorial staff should have full play for their talents in order to develop that outstanding leadership which the *Times* ought to give and is in a most strategic position to furnish to a country beset by the greatest problems. I should of course like to see the page as distinguished for its liberalism as has been for so many years that of the *Manchester Guardian*. But I should much prefer to have it a strong, ultra-conservative page than one which so often takes a safe, middle-of-the-road policy. Of course the *Times* does print strong opinions and take clear-cut positions, and if these were listed, it might well be that they would seem to refute the points just made. Yet it is an undeniable fact that most readers of the *Times* feel that the editorial page, despite its improvement, does not yet measure up to the standards of other departments, while some denounce it warmly.

Mr. Sulzberger is also quoted as saying once that he deemed himself fortunate in not having to take sides in so vital a conflict as the revolution in Spain. But how could anyone fail to take sides in such a struggle, in the prelude to the second World War, during which curtain-raiser the Fascist nations all but destroyed an innocent, republican people because of the deliberate connivance, if not approval, of the governments of democratic France and England? A newspaper which could not speak out against a crime like this must certainly be lacking in conscience, or be without vision or true understanding. Certainly the function of a great American daily is to take sides whenever democracy is crucified — if only in defense of our own democratic life. But the example of Adolph Ochs appears still effective in the *Times* office; he was naturally a very timid man, kindly, well-meaning, but above all else anxious not to get into personal controversies and not to offend many readers, and anyone who defended the republican government against the Franco insurgents brought down upon himself the full hostility of the Catholic Church in the United States.

While the *Times* seems less subservient to wealth than it was, it is still profoundly tender to the House of Morgan and other influential businesses. It remains the organ of a section of the community rather than the mouthpiece of progress, of social advance, or of the aspirations of the masses of the plain people. It is not a tribune of the people. Its democracy still has a strongly capitalistic tinge. It still, as the Europeans say, "has a tendency" — and that is to take the side of the *status quo*. When this is changed, I believe that its circulation, which now averages 484,-687 copies and reaches over 790,000 on Sundays, will rapidly increase. As it is, its influence stretches far beyond the city in which it is published, and not only because of its indispensability to newspapermen. It is read by thoughtful people in every town and city of the United States. One feature that contributes to this is its admirable reporting of labor happenings and its assigning to this field so capable a correspondent as Louis Stark, something not offset by its less satisfactory handling of broad labor trends.

The greatest opportunity for betterment in the *Times,* aside from the editorial page, lies in its attitude toward certain domestic events. Its natural conservatism in the past explains its blind eye for unpopular radical causes, but I agree with Mr. Seldes that it is hard to understand why so great a newspaper should constantly have opposed Congressional inquiries, and should have failed to understand or to reveal much brought out by those investigations. Thus it steadily deprecated and sneered at the Daugherty and Teapot Dome inquests. It declared that the Senators making them behaved "like men who at heart are enemies of lawful and orderly government," in order "to paralyze the Administration, to terrorize members of the Cabinet, to break down the efficiency of the government." They were "scandalmongers and assassins of character." Senators T. J. Walsh and B. K. Wheeler were called "the Montana mud-gunners." * It is proper to point out that this shocking misrepresentation, of what turned out to be probably the most useful and remedial Congressional inquiry in our history, and saved a great oil reserve for the navy, which now needs it so badly, besides sending one Cabinet member to prison, took place a number of years ago. But it is unfortunately true that since then the *Times* has also misrepresented investigations of great moment, like the Nye munitions inquiry, and, more recently still, that of Senator LaFollette's committee upon labor espionage and the abuse of civil liberties in labor troubles. It severely criticized the LaFollette report because it questioned its findings in eight cases and proved one to have been mistaken. But there were fourteen volumes of documentary evidence in addition to all the unchallenged cases — nearly 1,500 — and so important and sincerely written a report deserved far better treatment.

It is an old complaint that newspapers of this type ignore proceedings which do not commend themselves to the big business interests. It is of course impossible for the *Times* to report everything and every inquiry in detail. One wishes none the less that its correspondents were able to dig up and to reveal some of the wrongdoings in Washington with the same fine zeal and determination to bring out the truth at any cost which has distinguished the work of the Washington office of the St. Louis *Post-Dispatch*, which initiated the Teapot Dome disclosures. Naturally the proponents of new or lost causes will never see eye to eye with newspaper editors as to the amount of space which should be given to them. It is within the power of the *Times* to set a higher standard in this respect than is yet to be found in the United States. For example, it should always report hearings accurately and without partisan bias. It did not do so when universal military conscription was voted by Congress. Mr. Sulzberger and General Adler were outstanding backers of this measure, and Mr. Sulzberger is credited with a considerable subscription to the fund raised to put conscription over. In this case the Washington office is charged by opponents of the measure with both biased and unfair reporting of their activities and testi-

---

* Later when Senator Walsh died full of honors, after being selected for the Cabinet, the *Times* praised this "mud-gunner" very highly.

mony. Some of the sharpest critics of the *Times* assert that it still suppresses, or prints most inconspicuously, news unfavorable to large advertisers or to the privileged groups. There appear to be occasional instances in which the judgment of the *Times* copy-readers is certainly open to question if there is no ulterior motive in the placing of some news.

Another unfortunate trait of the *Times* of today which has come down from Ochs's management is its handling of matters relating to the Jews. The only possible explanation of this is fear that its Jewish ownership will be held against it more frequently if it becomes a vigorous defender of the horribly ill-treated Jewish people. Whatever the exact reason, its attitude is highly regrettable. Not long ago five hundred Christian ministers and laymen met in conference in New York City and passed resolutions denouncing the systematic Nazi destruction of the Jewish people. It was news, and it was eminently fit to print, but it was given only a few lines by the *Times* and buried inconspicuously on page seven. A similar happening was carefully interred on page seventeen. Actually one hears it often said that the *Times* is both anti-Semitic and pro-Catholic! If there ever was a case where the *Times* should have risen superior to fear of consequences it is this. For never were human beings more entitled to be defended and championed by a great organ of public opinion; certainly never have men and women anywhere been tortured and slaughtered in such numbers with less reason.

When a newspaper prints such an enormous volume of news as the *Times* does, mistakes of policy are bound to occur and errors certain to creep in. Since it is a human institution, it will never be perfect. It is a case, however, where the spirit at the top counts profoundly. Mr. Sulzberger is convinced that the *Times* is a liberal newspaper; his definition is not at all that of the liberal section of his community. While, as I have said, the *Times* is in most respects steadily improving, it is difficult to prophesy that it will go much further under its present ownership or free itself from its tendency to take the conventional, popular side — which is again evidence of its lack of a desire to lead. But it would be wrong for any critic not to recognize and to praise wholeheartedly the *Times's* enormous achievements and the tremendous service that, despite its faults, it renders not only to the United States, but to the whole world, and to the profession to which it belongs. It has created a news standard in this country which, I believe, has been more or less imitated by the whole press. Its pages, and the *Times Index* of its issues, are invaluable, for there exists nowhere else so full and accessible a record of the day-by-day life of America, with all the most important American and foreign documents given in full. To it the historians and statesmen of the future will turn as long as the pages of its admirable special edition on rag paper hold together.

11. *Adolph Ochs's Achievement*

The twenty-fifth anniversary, on August 18, 1921, of his control of the New York *Times* gave Adolph S. Ochs an opportunity to review the period of his ownership and to set forth the journalistic success he had achieved, which he continued to achieve until his death in 1935. The *Times* was a decrepit, losing proposition when he took hold of it, running behind $1,000 a day, and having a circulation of only 18,900. On that anniversary its circulation was 352,528; its advertising had increased from 2,227,196 lines to 23,447,395 yearly. It then did an annual gross business of $20,000,000 and Ochs was especially proud that of its annual gross income only five per cent had gone to the owners, the rest having been put back into the property for its betterment. For 1922 its net profits were reported to be $2,500,000, and despite depressions and wars it has continued to be highly profitable. Regarded simply as a business venture it was an extraordinary achievement, comparing most favorably with similar feats in purely mercantile lines, all the more so because, on account of his lack of funds, Ochs had to carry it largely with borrowed money until the property became profitable. He had a clear vision of what he wanted to achieve and the faith to stick to it against great odds.

Ochs's frankness on that occasion in 1921 was not limited to statistics of circulation and advertising. He laid bare once more the details of the ownership, with a view, doubtless, to ending forever the whispered charges that there was British capital in the *Times*. There were — and are — only American owners, and he and his family held sixty-four per cent of the paper's stock. Nobody in journalistic circles ever believed this gossip as to foreign control. In the first place, the *Times* is naturally so pro-English that the British would never have had to pay money to it had its owner been venal, and Ochs's honesty was beyond question; in the second place, during the first World War hysteria it was the fashion to charge any newspaper whose views one did not like with being in the pay of the other side. It is true that some rich Wall Street men helped Ochs at times, notably in the matter of the bonds of the *Times* Building. But it was false to deduce from that certain characteristics of his paper; it would have taken precisely the course it followed had Ochs never needed to borrow a penny from anybody. No journalist has ever questioned the fact that it was Ochs's paper, or that it bore the stamp of his personality.

During those twenty-five years the *Times* had been clean and enterprising, able and shrewd. Not that it had always lived up to its slogan of publishing only the news fit to print, nor had it printed all the news. It had simply purveyed all the news which especially interested its owners and editors and, by preference, that which supported its editorial viewpoint, but it had rendered a genuine public service in increasing the volume of news and especially foreign news. Newspapermen are like sheep; if one hits upon a rotogravure supplement, or a comic "ribbon," or a Sunday comic section, or a humorous column on the editorial page, and it is successful, everybody else tries to follow suit. Hearst's financial success had by 1898 deluded a good part of the American press into imitating him and his methods; Ochs's increase in the volume of his news and the number of his news departments, notably in the commercial field, had a beneficial influence upon the whole press, and led many thousands to read the *Times* to whom its editorial opinions were anathema. It was under Ochs's guidance, too, that the paper began its policy of cabling and printing important speeches and documents in full, even when extensive summaries were carried by the Associated Press.

Full credit must also be given to Ochs for having kept his advertising columns clean and for the excellence of his auxiliary publications. His rotogravure supplements were long the best, while his Sunday magazine is in a class by itself. Moreover, Ochs's refusal to stoop to a comic supplement when it would indubitably have largely increased the paper's circulation during its critical days ought long to be remembered to his credit. If all journalists are to be measured simply by the outward aspect of their daily and by the yardstick of business success, there can be no question that Ochs earned a prominent place in any journalistic hall of fame.

But as men cannot live by bread alone, so no newspaper can or should be finally judged by the amount either of its revenues or of the number of its advertising lines or of the yards of news it prints every day, or by the multitude of its readers. If these were the sole tests, Hearst would rank high on at least two counts. There are fortunately other tests, especially the ethical one, which any definite, worth-while survey of the rise and fall of American journalism must apply above all others. It should ask last of all what were the returns of the counting-room, but should inquire first what ideals a given journal upheld, what moral aims it pursued, what national and international policies it championed, what was the spirit of fair play and justice which actuated it, and, above all, on whose side and under whose banner it fought. The minute one begins to measure and to value the *Times* of Ochs's management from these points of view, the whole picture he drew of his own achievements changes for the worse.

Adolph Ochs no doubt sincerely believed that when he said that his was an "independent newspaper" that tolerated "no tampering with the news, no coloring, no deception," and that it had attained a high reputation "for the fullness, trustworthiness, and impartiality of its news service," he painted a just picture of his daily. It would have been pleasant to agree with him, but the truth lay elsewhere. The *Times* was neither independent then nor swayed by a desire to be just. It was a class paper, pure and simple, as much so as any labor journal. Its news could not stand up under a qualitative test, for no journal had exceeded it in disseminating falsehood and misrepresentations during the unparalleled era of wholesale lying in which the whole world lived during and after the first World War. In a sense all newspapers at that time were the victims of their lying governments, but few made any real effort to print only the truth.

So far as its treatment of Russian news under Ochs is concerned, efforts were made to excuse it by placing the responsibility upon the Associated Press. But many of the worst fabri-

cations which appeared in the *Times* came from special correspondents; in the second place, no newspaper is compelled to
print the Associated Press news it receives, and it is supposed to
employ editors for the express purpose of reading and correct-
ing or discarding any dispatches which seem to it without adequate foundation. In the third place, Ochs was, without question, the most influential director of the Associated Press and, if
he had tried to do so, could have stopped the kind of reporting
which made his newspaper inform its public within a comparatively brief period that Petrograd had fallen six times, been on
the verge of capture three times more, been burned to the ground
twice, been in absolute panic twice, and in complete revolt
against the Bolsheviks on six different occasions — all without
the slightest foundation in fact. Only in the columns of Hearst
could one have found a record surpassing this.

As for the careers of Yudenich and Kolchak, the White Russian generals, in the columns of the *Times,* they must ever stand
as the high-water mark of false propaganda and misrepresentation intended to mislead the American public. This record alone
should have prevented Ochs's referring to the "trustworthiness
and impartiality" of the news in the *Times.* Surely if any rulers
were ever justified in excluding correspondents from their country, Lenin and Trotsky were in shutting out those of the *Times*
during this period. Its special correspondents were primarily
propagandists, to defend a point of view and that organization
of society by which the *Times* stood and stands. And the *Times*
has always found it hard to apologize when it commits an editorial wrong. Take the case of Jane Addams, one of the noblest
of our American women. The *Times* denounced her because she
told the simple truth that Allied troops in the first World War
were often given liquor or drugs before they were called upon
to charge across no man's land. Yet when the facts came out at
the hands of Sir Philip Gibbs and others, not one word of apol-
ogy was forthcoming.

Never did any reputable newspaper print a more inexcusable
editorial than that of the *Times* of October 10, 1917, commenting upon the resignation of Professor Charles A. Beard from
Columbia because of his refusal to be muzzled in war-time and
his just criticism of the violations of academic freedom by the
president and the trustees of the university. It was not only based

upon absolute untruths; it was filled with venom and spite. It declared that Columbia was "better" for the resignation of this distinguished scholar and outstanding historian, whom it charged with falsifying history and with seeking the "overthrow of our institutions and the reorganization of society by the apostles of radicalism"! The trustees, it declared, had the right to "dispense with poisonous teaching" and must be ever mindful of the fact that "sane public opinion," and the alumni, would hold them accountable for "errors of indulgence to the teachers of false doctrines sheltering themselves behind the shibboleth of academic freedom." In this editorial alone is the answer to Ochs's assertion that his newspaper tolerated "no coloring, no deception," as well as the complete proof of its utterly conservative and reactionary character at that time, which made Rollo Ogden say then that nothing would induce him to take service under Ochs — an opinion later radically changed in Ochs's favor.

Not even the dead were safe in its hands — as witness the case of Robert G. Ingersoll, whose memory the *Times* would not clear even after the truth was presented to its heads. It never did justice to the elder Senator Robert M. LaFollette, who was for years a victim of a deliberate Associated Press misrepresentation of a speech of his which made him say the exact opposite of what he did say. Happily it has far more sympathy with the underdog today, and its present editorial writers would never think of saying as their predecessors under Ochs did, with callous heartlessness, that "a certain degree of unemployment is curative of many social disorders. It is the argument of the stomach which becomes necessary when the appeal to reason and industrial morality fails" — let the dogs of workers eat cake if they have no bread! But how it bleated if Congress or the tax-gatherers squeezed the rich every older reader will recall. Standing up for the privileged was part of Ochs's philosophy, a great secret of his business success — that and his unending devotion to the god of things as they are.

At his door knocked in vain for help those who sought fundamentally to better the world, woman suffragists, land reformers, tax reformers, the toiling masses, many who strove internationally for peace and goodwill on earth, anybody remotely suspected of endangering the existing order. As for its treatment of the Jews, Ochs's own race, it refused to print the British report of the Polish pogroms against the Jews except as paid advertising. Ochs could not deny that the *Times* printed a false Associated Press summary of Sir Stuart Samuel's report of those Polish pogroms which made him acquit the Polish government when he actually held that government guilty. Or that the *Times* refused both to print either the Associated Press's correction of its error or the full text of the report when it arrived — save as an advertisement paid for by some of his coreligionists. That it has been uninterested in, when not deeply prejudiced against, the Negro is likewise true. Witness its denunciation of a group of decent persons for meeting at dinner with some Negroes to discuss the plight of their race in New York City, which today, more than thirty years later, is still an utter disgrace to the metropolis. As a teacher of race hatred the New York *Times* was long unsurpassed; Ochs could not divest himself of the colorphobia he brought north with him from Chattanooga.

So no one could declare that under Adolph Ochs his great newspaper was a champion of popular rights, a journalistic John Bright, an incessant pleader for the lowly and the oppressed, an invariable and ardent defender of all who seek to rise, a never failing protagonist of the true spirit of American equality and liberty. Nor was Ochs the spokesman of the America of Lowell and Wendell Phillips, of Sumner, Emerson, and Abraham Lincoln. He was a remarkable newspaper manager, in some respects the most successful in the whole history of American journalism. As such he created our foremost daily, which will never lose its commanding position if its directors but realize their responsibilities and their duties to this country and all of its people, and rise to them.

CHAPTER IX

The HERALD TRIBUNE

IN THE WHOLE GAMUT of journalism there is no more tempting subject for the historical commentator than the New York *Herald Tribune*. Founded as the *Tribune* in 1841 by Horace Greeley, it began its career as a radical weekly newspaper — radical in that it denounced slavery, recognized in that issue an irrepressible conflict, and represented the limited social conscience of that day. Its great success was the achievement of a simple but ardent and fearless leader, often visionary, often tempted by dubious remedies, not infrequently mistaken, but steeped in sound principles, and a passionate advocate of liberty. Greeley was as deeply rooted in the American soil and as truly representative of the middle-class Eastern Americans of conscience and with a sense of social responsibility as any editor who ever presided over an editorial page. His earnestness and courage appealed so much that he built up a personal following exceeded by few, if by any, in the history of our journalism. The influence of the weekly *Tribune* was unequaled for decades after the institution of the daily, and a rare tribute to the man who wielded it.*

The *Tribune* survived Greeley's ill-fated contest for the Presidency in 1872, and his death on November 29 of that year in consequence of his campaigning, without losing its prestige. From then on, its development is the exact story of the sorrowful evolution of the Republican Party from the party of idealism and freedom, the savior of the Republic, supported by the conscience and devotion of the finest elements in the North, into the protagonist of the subsequent period of dire reaction and crass materialism. So the *Tribune* in due course became the mouthpiece of the most conservative possessing classes, the spokesman of the wealthy, the chief advocate of the tariff barons, the protected manufacturers, who bought election after election and then received their swag in the shape of the higher tariff schedules by which the deluded American public was more and

---

* According to Charles Merz, editor of the *Times,* Greeley's editorials consisted of much rhetoric and invective. He says: "It is a fair statement that the reason why Horace Greeleys are not writing editorials today is not the scarcity of Horace Greeleys, but the difficulty of finding people who would read them."

more mulcted. It had nothing to say against the rapid exploitation of the country's resources in the interest of the few at the
cost of the many. It championed at all times the rottenest and
most corrupt elements in the Republican Party, supporting in
1884 the candidacy of the tainted James G. Blaine with a passion,
a bitter intolerance of opposition, which made it the outstanding
American daily of its brand. It was long "the greatest organ of
its party."

In that era of personal and partisan journalism, marked by
intense narrowness, bitter prejudices, and usually a refusal to
print the other fellow's views, the *Tribune* was guided by Whitelaw Reid, who had nothing in his training or his extremely fortunate situation in life to make him espouse popular causes or
emancipate himself from thralldom to the very rich, with whom
in his later years he lived and worked. He was a fair journalist,
and a prominent reporter at the front during the Civil War, and
he kept his paper as clean and as dignified in its appearance as
it was nasty to its opponents. Reid, too, developed political ambitions, becoming first Minister to France, then an unsuccessful
candidate for the Vice-Presidency, and later, by appointment of
Theodore Roosevelt, Ambassador to the Court of St. James's.
Cold and uninspiring, he was in most respects the antithesis of
Horace Greeley, and was the never failing bulwark of all the
ultra-conservative forces. He does not rank as one of the great
American editors.

But Reid had the satisfaction of seeing many of the causes and
ideas he championed through the *Tribune* adopted by his country. He was one of the first to advocate the building of a great
fleet, the annexation of Hawaii, and the establishment of a colo-
nial system for the United States. When in 1895 President Cleveland suddenly asserted the right of the United States to settle the
boundary disputes between Great Britain and Venezuela and
threatened to go to war if necessary to obtain our wishes, the
Tribune was delighted. It declared that President Cleveland
"could hardly have adopted the *Tribune's* view more completely,
or have expressed it more exactly, if he had copied one of our
editorials as part of his message." But Reid, who was sojourning
in Arizona, soon heard that his friends, the very rich men, among
them Morgan, Lanier, and Sturges, were very much opposed,
fearing a financial panic. So Reid found Cleveland's message

"needlessly offensive," turned the *Tribune's* policy around, urged the country to "Keep Cool," and continued to assail the President's manners and language while generally supporting his aim. Reid enthusiastically approved the war with Spain and was appointed one of the commissioners to settle the terms of peace with the Spanish government, and in that capacity he helped to obtain in Paris all the territories the *Tribune* had demanded from Spain. He warmly upheld Theodore Roosevelt's "taking" of the Panama Canal, and was consistently for a strongly militaristic and imperialistic policy.

The *Tribune* has never departed from these lines. It favored our entry into the first World War, and called for a second war with Germany fully a year and more before Pearl Harbor. It denounced Woodrow Wilson for his slowness in getting into the first war and for his original pacifist policy. At first it praised the Fourteen Peace Points, but before the armistice it definitely broke with the Wilson program. As for the League of Nations, the *Tribune* protested that the terms of the Covenant were too vague and supported the Hughes amendments. It strongly advocated the ratification of the treaty by the Senate, although some of its warmest friends, like Henry Cabot Lodge, opposed doing so. The reason for its support of the treaty was a curious one — that it was as severe upon the defeated as it should have been! The paper had feared that it would not be so because of the "youthful radicals and dangerous advisers" with whom President Wilson had surrounded himself. It of course favors severe punishments for the Germans today, their disarmament for all time, and some kind of world organization to prevent the recurrence of another world war.

With Reid's death in 1912 the *Tribune* passed to his son, Ogden Reid, who, with his wife, Helen Rogers Reid, breathed new life into the historic paper. While Ogden Reid has not stood out as the proprietor and editor, he is unquestionably entitled to a good deal of the credit for the transformation which has taken place in his daily. He and his wife have picked good men, taken their advice, co-operated well with them, and let them go ahead. Here especial credit must be given to the late Clinton W. Gilbert, from 1913 to 1918 the associate editor. It was he who selected, with Reid's approval, the new staff and directed the drastic changes which took place. I shall be abused in certain liberal circles for saying that the *Herald Tribune* has in considerable degree been liberalized, but it is a fact. It is still a conservative daily, beloved by the dyed-in-the-wool, old-line Republicans, but it has found that it can print views and speeches from the other political camp and gain thereby. It has even on occasions refused to support Republican nominees, something that never could have happened under the previous managements. As its mail attests, it is read by many who disagree with most of its editorial views, but prefer its presentation of the news and its editorial page to those of the *Times*. It has gained in dignity as it has in presentation of its news, and is today probably a better newspaper than at any time in the past. It is still being charged, as by Irving Brant some years ago, with coloring the news, and it does reveal its bias in its news reports. It was probably no more capable of presenting with complete fairness the viewpoint of the so-called isolationists prior to our entry into the war than were any number of other pro-war publications. But it must be said in its defense that even the most liberal of publications is bound to write and to record events from the viewpoint of its directing spirits. The New York *Evening Post* under my management naturally reflected my political bent and supported my social crusades.

How slowly unfair reporting has disappeared from the American newspaper scene can be illustrated by two experiences of mine with the *Tribune*. In testifying in 1919 before the New York State Reconstruction Commission on my return from the Paris Peace Conference, I made the surely harmless statement that there was much of very great interest in the Soviet experiment, and that we should watch it, study it, and profit by it if we could. At one point I looked up from my carefully prepared manuscript, turned to the reporters, and said: "I repeat I am not a Communist nor an advocate of Communism." As we walked away after the hearing, a friend said to me: "I am sorry for you. There were two reporters from the *Tribune* present sent to get you, and you will catch it tomorrow." On the first page the next day was a column report announcing that I had "advocated a Soviet form of government for the United States," and this was followed the next day by an editorial, despite the receipt by the editors of a letter of protest from me. A few lines from my letter were carefully hidden in a place where letters to the editor seldom appeared. This episode led to my denunciation by newspapers all the way across the continent, the Portland *Oregonian* speaking of my "disordered intellect." Some later apologized, but the deliberately offending *Tribune* never did.

Later when London reported that the Bolsheviks had been making substantial financial contributions to certain American journals, a *Tribune* reporter appeared in my office and said that editors of the paper wished him to find out how much money I had received from Moscow. It seems incredible now that any self-respecting journalist could have been found to convey such a message to a fellow journalist of standing and of years. It is not surprising that, if these things could happen to the editor of the *Nation,* there were plenty of others to doubt the fairness not only of the *Tribune,* but of the press in general. I do not believe that anything like this could happen with the *Herald Tribune* today, but the American press has made a large part of the public believe that it is not safe to rely upon any newspaper reporting because of just such incidents as the above.

It is true that the revolution in the *Tribune* effected by Mr. and Mrs. Reid is due in considerable part to the sea-change in the whole journalistic situation, as a result of which the day of narrow partisanship, personal vituperation, and limited range has so completely disappeared that few indeed of the newspaper audiences of today are aware that it ever existed. Whether one likes the *Herald Tribune* or not, whether one still believes it to be merely the mouthpiece of the privileged or not, there can be no doubt that its evolution and broadening under its present owners could never have taken place if they had not had a high journalistic ideal. The *Tribune's* absorption of the *Herald* in the course of that evolution was one of the most dramatic events in modern newspaper history, the more striking because of the intense antagonism and rivalry which existed between the elder James Gordon Bennett and Horace Greeley in the days when the former shocked the whole publishing world and seemed to staid New York a journalistic fiend incarnate and, as the Civil War came on, a traitor to the Union. It was as if some inheritance of the Bennetts' news-gathering abilities passed into the *Tribune,* if only because, contrary to the general rule, it held the bulk of the circulation which it had purchased with the *Herald.*

In Mrs. Reid the *Herald Tribune* found a keen and able journalist with a creative mind, quick to act and to judge. To her belongs the honor of having developed the *Herald Tribune's* remarkable Forum, originated by the late Mrs. William Brown Meloney, so long the editor of the supplement "This Week." The Forum has become an annual event of genuine political and social importance. I am convinced that both Mr. and Mrs. Reid are actuated by a high public spirit in carrying on their newspaper, for it has often had lean, very lean, years as well as prosperous ones. If financial rewards had been their only aim, they would have long since sold out and invested their money in other and less risky enterprises and relieved themselves of a great care and a telling responsibility. Instead they have held on and made at times great sacrifices, not merely because of the family tradition, but because of their sincere belief that in this time of dire national stress they can serve the Republic well by presenting their political, economic, and social views, whether sound or otherwise, through the medium to which they are devoted, in which their sons are also deeply interested. It must be noted, too, that they have not sought political or social preferment by means of their daily.

It is a constant charge against the *Herald Tribune* that it is as much an English journal as if it were published in London, and it is customary to lay this in part to the fact that Mr. Reid's sister married an Englishman of title, and that the family's connections with England have been close ever since Whitelaw Reid's service as Ambassador to London. It is not necessary to say that Mr. and Mrs. Reid are Americans to the core, but it is a fact that, historically speaking, the *Tribune* and *Herald Tribune* have had an English bias. The former's long-distinguished London correspondent, George W. Smalley, was thoroughly pro-British, and Whitelaw Reid had strong admirations for England, as have had the very rich and influential people with whom Whitelaw Reid's lot was thrown. Its imperialistic policies have naturally made it drift strongly in the English direction. It has always felt keenly the kinship of the Anglo-American family, even when it supported President Cleveland's threatening attack upon England during the Venezuelan dispute.

While it cannot be said that the *Herald Tribune's* editorial page is the ablest in this country, it is marked by a fine style, ability, vigor, and news sense. It seems as if its editors held before them Horace Greeley's statement that journalism is "a public responsibility and a public trust." Its writing staff is headed by Geoffrey Parsons, a man of high ideals, fine integrity, keen intelligence, beloved by his friends. His editorials dealing with the war situation won him a Pulitzer prize in 1942, an award that was not criticized. It does not detract from Mr. Parsons's achievement to say that had his editorials championed the other side of the great debate as to whether the United States should or should not enter the war, he would not have been awarded a prize, however able his "leaders." Given his point of view, there can be no question of the ability of his presentation of it. It is a curious and ironic fact that another member of the staff who desired an early American entry into this war is Walter Millis, the author of two remarkable historical works, one telling the true story of our utterly uncalled for, morally indefensible, and imperialistic war upon Spain. The other showed how America was led into the first World War by propaganda and sensational journalism which played up many German atrocities that, as has since been freely admitted by high English authorities, never occurred. No other books ever made a deeper impression upon the American public as to how countries blunder or are misled or betrayed into war. Yet in this struggle Mr. Millis, like many another, changed over and became an advocate of our trying to save democracy by mass murder.

While I find myself among those who disagree with the basic policies of the *Herald Tribune,* I am naturally not of those who would like to see all of our journalism devoted to their own points of view, for that would make for dull newspapers and against the intellectual growth of the nation. The clashing of honest opinion should be the breath of life for any healthy journalism, as it is essential to the progress of any democracy. A conservative newspaper has a necessary place in any country in which there is a free give-and-take of opinion, if only to check unwise experiments and perhaps undue ardor on the other side. It is not necessary to say that such a conservative daily is far more worth while than a newspaper of more liberal tendencies which changes its opinion at the behest of its owners or solely for financial reasons. If anything should happen to the *Herald Tribune* it would be a great loss to the metropolis. It has earned its place, just as has the *Wall Street Journal,* which, also under new and vigorous management, has become one of the outstanding American newspapers. Frank and honest in its viewpoint, extremely well edited, it is entirely comprehensive in its field, so that no intelligent person, whether a New Dealer or a rock-ribbed Republican, who wishes to know financial developments and obtain also excellent reporting, perhaps the best summary of the progress of the war, and the most enlightening financial correspondence to be found anywhere, can afford to do without it. Similarly the *Herald Tribune* has won a high place on its merits.

The *Herald Tribune's* chief rival is, of course, the *Times,* and the former is open to the charge that it has lost some originality by imitating its rival's news policies so closely. It followed Adolph Ochs's lead by printing a large volume of news and increasing its Washington staff and its foreign correspondence. The similarity in style and contents of the two papers is most marked on Sundays. Both then print a weekly summary of the world's news and a considerable number of cabled articles from their correspondents abroad. Both have their real-estate, financial, society, and sports sections, their tabloid book and magazine sections, and usually publish on the same day special supplements as lures to their advertisers. Both print much political news from Washington, and some — but not enough — from the rest of the United States. Both still have that insularity which seems inseparable from the business of publishing a daily on Manhattan Island; the Hudson River has long been a greater news-gathering obstacle than the Atlantic Ocean! It is hard not to say that the *Herald Tribune* is a lesser Republican *Times,* though its staff would resent this. Both are obviously front-rank news dailies, with the *Herald Tribune* often excelling in its editorials, in the "copy-reading" and the office handling of its news, and frequently presenting it better. Especially does it avoid the *Times's* constant overwriting and overprinting; as remarked elsewhere, it is sometimes possible for the *Times* buyer to read the gist of a single dispatch four or five times — in the full headlines, in the opening paragraph, which by a hoary newspaper custom tells the whole story, and elsewhere. Both dailies have taken to the trying custom of interrupting their narratives by inserting correlated items from other sources.

While the *Herald Tribune* method of editing the news is far better and saves time, money, and paper, it suffers in comparison with the *Times* because of the latter's greater bulk and larger coverage. Newspapermen feel that the *Times* is indispensable — the *Herald Tribune* is their second choice. Both these newspapers think very highly of their book supplements, much too highly if one regards them by the standards of Dana's *Sun* and Godkin's *Nation*. They are mistakenly believed to be influenced by the book advertisers; actually the best publishers are not enthusiastic about the reviews their books receive. The just complaint is that there is a lack of able and expert reviewing, too much revealing of the critic's own opinions, and not enough helpful criticism by writers who really know the subject they are treating. Every author who is at home in his field knows this to be true. Since some publishers are careless or reckless in accepting works which have not been verified, it is all the more the duty of the important book sections or magazines to choose the most competent reviewers wherever available. Finally, both the *Times* and the *Herald Tribune* risk hasty and inferior reviews because of their eagerness to notice each book the day it appears or as soon thereafter as possible.

Both have excellent financial departments, both have much the same lack of vision and, as they put it, lack of space, to deal with local New York problems as fully as they might and to touch effectively the lives of the mass of workers. Hence they rank, like most large dailies, as class organs and the crowds go to the *Daily News*. Both the *Times* and the *Herald Tribune* are positively committed to the established order. Neither can claim to be an originator of causes, or a powerful creator of public opinion as was Horace Greeley. The *Herald Tribune* especially cannot be accused of imitating its founder in setting up idealistic aims at the risk of error and ridicule.

Unfortunately the latest figures show that the *Herald Tribune* is not holding its own in circulation, its daily sale having shrunk by 63,000 purchasers in the last three years, doubtless in considerable part owing to paper shortage and other war conditions. Its cleanness, its excellent typography, its special news dispatches, alone entitle it to increasing public patronage. It has long been known that Mr. and Mrs. Reid would like to purchase the *Times* to combine it with the *Herald Tribune*. That

CHAPTER X

The New York DAILY NEWS

THE QUESTION which confronts anyone who undertakes to judge the New York *Daily News* is a simple one: Has Joseph Medill Patterson solved well the problem of producing a decent, intelligent, honest newspaper for the masses? For generations journalists have wondered how it would be possible to create a daily which would interest large numbers of the people who cannot be reached by newspapers like the *Times.* Mr. Patterson seems to have found the answer. The tabloid form which he chose had been experimented with long before he entered the New York field, and so had the daily illustrated newspaper, years before technical and press conditions were ready for a mass-production undertaking. To Bernarr Macfadden, the journalistic apostle of physical culture, for example, the opportunity once seemed ripe and he put forth a sheet, the *Graphic,* which sought to live by sensations, by lurid pictures, by a frank appeal to the baser instincts, with a close approach to pornography, and by discarding the elemental rules of truth-telling. Never was there a more conscienceless crew of newspapermen brought together, as one of them, Emile Gauvreau, has since frankly confessed. It is enormously to the credit of the New York public that the *Graphic* met an early and thoroughly deserved death.

To Mr. Patterson, or to someone near him, also came the vision of a tabloid which should be tempered to the needs of the workers who have little time to read, are jammed in the subways in the rush hours with no space in which to fold and unfold an old-type newspaper, and have neither the taste, inclination, nor the education to absorb in their homes the news reports or editorials of the old-line dailies. That he found the medium and the technique he sought and others failed to devise is evidenced by his having achieved with the *Daily News* the greatest newspaper circulation in the history of American journalism, and probably in the world. Whether or not it is true that Mr. Patterson and his cousin, Colonel Robert R. McCormick, both then of the Chicago *Tribune,* founded the *Daily News* in the hope that it would be a losing venture and so aid them in meeting their heavy income taxes due to the success of the *Tribune,* there can be no question as to the astonishing financial results of their New York plunge. Far from decreasing the Patterson-McCormick bank accounts and taxes, the *Daily News* has largely increased them. Instead of being a lame-duck venture, its daily circulation is now 2,080,000 copies, while the Sunday circulation has risen to 3,880,000 copies, the latter having gained 100,000 in a year despite a price of ten cents beyond a certain distance from New York. In war and peace, in depression and prosperity, its circulation goes up. There is no stopping it; the bitter hatred of the Washington Administration and its great following and the warmongers affects it not at all. Whoever conceived the magic formula, the sesame is there and condemns the owners to larger and larger incomes and taxes despite the paper's holding to its two-cent price on week-days, now a rarity.

The remarkable fact about the growth of this paper is that it has gone on attracting readers by becoming soberer, less sensational, and less cheap, and pandering less to reader weaknesses. At the beginning it gave much space to matters of sex and went pretty far with some of its photographs — it still goes much farther than most dailies. But it has emphasized sex less and less, though, as Mr. Patterson frankly admits, it believes in printing sex stories and will continue to do so since it is a "major human interest." It still delights in a nice, big sex murder. The paper shortage has, however, helped it along the road to better taste and standards as appears from the following editorial announcement: "We have taken numerous steps to meet the previous [paper] cuts. From the editorial content of the paper, we have removed a number of once popular and valuable features: the news index, handwriting analysis, 'How He Proposed,' Embarrassing Moments, beauty and love answers, daily true-story illustrations, one comic strip, all comic-strip overlines, George Rector's recipes, book reviews, Poems You Ought to Know, and Aesop's Fables." So the *Daily News* is less vulgar than formerly and it is fortunate in not having to resort to some of the devices which keep many publications, notably in the magazine field, afloat. Its cheap paper and black headlines give it a worse and cheaper aspect than it really deserves. Its news pictures in the main are excellent; the news itself is well compressed and on the whole adequate. Its remaining features are of the popular kind, but some are of value and informative.

Thus there are a short story and an installment of a continued story. There is a "Garden Guide," and there is news of the radio and screen stars, the inevitable crossword puzzle, and much advice for the unhappy and those who are in spiritual difficulties. Doris Blake advises the lovelorn; Dr. Cutter gives medical advice; there are suggestions for parents, the latest recipes and patterns, with many household hints, including a recommended "daily dish," and so on. Its comic strips are the same as those which make so much for the success of the Chicago *Tribune,* and with the latter the *Daily News* shares the services of John O'Donnell, the Washington correspondent, who has earned the especial dislike of Mr. Roosevelt because of his searching criticisms of the President himself, his Administration, his policies and inconsistencies. The *News* also has its "inquiring reporter" to print daily samples of public opinion as picked up on the streets, and its letters to the editor headed "Voice of the People" contain many attacks upon the *News* and its political policies. Still the circulation grows, despite the foolish charges that the paper is disloyal, if not treasonable, and the increase in price.

In an endeavor to meet the increasing paper shortage the *News* makes no effort whatsoever to increase its circulation; its growth is therefore entirely spontaneous. How to check it without injury is one of the serious problems of the management, which, by the way, welcomes the boycott against it which has led to the canceling of some advertisements — again because of the lack of white paper. Indeed, it has restricted some of its advertisers and has deliberately added ten per cent to its advertising rates in the hope of holding down the advertising copy offered to it. Still the paper continues extremely prosperous; the flood of dollars into its treasury is unabated.

The chief criticisms now applied to the *Daily News* relate to its editorials and to its political point of view. All Communists and thick-and-thin, right-or-wrong followers of Franklin Roosevelt denounce it because it has not shared their views on the desirability of our going to war and entering into international alliances. I have seen it dubbed "Fascist" without the slightest foundation for the allegation. Its refusal to accept the modern cult that we must welcome everything that the Bolsheviks and their ruthless dictator, Stalin, say and do as beyond criticism because the Red armies have fought and defeated the Nazis so marvelously is one of its chief offenses with the Left-wingers. I have read many of its editorials. If I cannot agree with an able and learned friend who declares that they are always the best-written and most direct editorials in New York, I can see not the slightest ground for the demand by the bitterest and most intolerant of our patriots that the *Daily News* should be suppressed because of its "treason." Often its editorial page is so quiet, so unstudied, so guarded as to create no ripples whatever, although informative and expressing intelligent opinions. In my judgment it is not often exciting. Certainly no one can truthfully claim that it favors the Germans, and it certainly hates the Japanese. It seems just the work of an editor who has not lost his head or discarded his judgment in this crisis, who continues to pass upon issues with peace-time detachment and unbiased scrutiny of what is going on.

A cogent criticism of the editorial page might be that it is too limited — one double column — and therefore fails to touch on many vital subjects. But this is in keeping with the policy that it is written for hard-working people with little time to browse in the printed page, who are often without learning. The *Daily News* does not crusade or undertake deliberate propagandizing, and it has never imitated the Jewish *Forward* by playing down to its readers, seeking to change their social manners as well as their political thinking. In other words, it could be much more educative, but it cannot be charged with using its tremendous power for radical, anti-social, or illiberal policies. Here Mr. Patterson's personal influence is discernible. He was formerly a Socialist and was the more willing to leave the Chicago *Tribune* and move to New York because of his inability to see eye to eye with his reactionary relative, Colonel McCormick. If not so far to the Left now as he was, it cannot be truthfully said that he has gone over to the big-business camp. That is a familiar indictment of newspaper proprietors by Left-wingers — often with justice — but I have never heard that charge brought seriously against the *Daily News*. The criticism usually stops with the fact that, after all, Mr. Patterson is an enormously wealthy man, and that that places him as against labor and the New Deal.

Actually that is not the case. But it is hard to say just where Mr. Patterson stands at the present moment. There are those who look upon him as a completely disappointed man, unhappy in any political camp, and not too pleased with life despite the tremendous success he has achieved. At this writing in his sixty-fifth year, he was captain of a battery of field artillery with the 42nd Division in the last war, with long service at the front. It is years since he has published any books; the titles of those that marked his younger years, *Little Brother of the Rich, Dope, The Fourth Estate, By-Products,* and *Rebellion,* illustrate the current of his thinking at that time. The idealist of that period has vanished, but there is nothing in him of the irritating aggressiveness and stubbornness of his cousin. He is extremely modest and plainly seeks to avoid publicity by his refusal to put himself forward or to accept office, or generally to play the role so often assumed by proprietors of influential newspapers. One could almost say that when the fires of youthful passion burned out they left him dulled and almost hopeless. If he now has ideas as to the future world, they are not being put forth comprehensively and consecutively. But whatever his views as to the future of the United States, he is as much entitled to be respected for them as anybody else. Any attempt to portray him as a danger to the country, or disloyal, is false on its face.

As for the future of the *News,* Mr. Patterson has nothing to say. He admits frankly that he never had a clear-cut program or plan, and that the paper has just grown like Topsy without prevision, without even certainty that the road to success had been found. He insists that he is not thinking about the next five years or the next ten. He has no idea what will happen to American journalism after the war. He is not busying himself with the moot question whether the next step in journalism will be deeply affected by television and further developments of the radio or not — there are competent observers who think that the coming evolution of our dailies will mark an even more radical change than the arrival of the tabloid with its great popular appeal. The decrease in the number of dailies, the trend to monopoly, the loss of standards in the press as a whole leave Joseph Patterson cold. He is in an impregnable position, and he is content to let the journalistic world drift as it may.

Meanwhile Mr. Patterson's contribution to American jour-

nalism and to the welfare of New York City is a highly important one. It is easy to sneer at his paper, as is the custom in the
fashionable clubs where it is portrayed as a mere picture daily
intended only for servants, the illiterate, and the "unwashed."
That is as unjust as it is snobbish. One has only to consider what
the feeling would be if Mr. Patterson had imitated the example
of the *Graphic,* or were to carry on the conscienceless, self-seeking, insincere methods of Mr. Hearst, to realize how great the
debt owed to him for presenting the news to the masses as
cleanly, decently, and honestly as he does. Of course the *News*
was intended as a picture daily; it still calls itself "New York's
Picture Newspaper," and as such the run of its pictures is superior in some respects to those of *Life.* It no longer plays up the
nude female form, and does not give us the horrible portrayals
of crimes and battle scenes which have helped *Life* to build its
2,000,000 circulation in such an extraordinarily short time. It is
not a crusader, but it serves its community. It may even prove
in the years to come to be a great tower of strength for our
American institutions, just as it has never been afraid to face
government opposition and attack in its challenge of what it
considers the wrongful acts and policies of the New Deal and of
Franklin Roosevelt. In my judgment it could have gone much
further in this direction with truth and could have attacked even
more vigorously than it has. Perhaps, however, the quietness of
its editorials ensures their going further and therefore exercising
more influence.

Possibly the crusading spirit of his youthful days may in the
future again inflame Mr. Patterson and through him the *Daily
News.* Today my answer to the question at the beginning of this
chapter is that on the whole Mr. Patterson has solved pretty well
the problem of producing a decent, intelligent, and honest newspaper for the masses.

CHAPTER XI

The MONITOR, a Christian Daily

THE *Christian Science Monitor,* founded in 1908, "to injure no man but to bless all mankind," continues to be one of the outstanding newspapers of the United States, deserving the highest praise for its ability, the cleanliness of its columns, its remarkable foreign and domestic correspondence, and its freedom from practically all the evils of business-office control. It stands so high, indeed, in the regard of the profession that it has earned the coveted distinction of being a newspaperman's newspaper. Journalists feel that its own news service is entirely to be trusted. They know, too, that its foreign correspondents are of the best quality, some of them, like Joseph C. Harsch, being outstanding in that field.

It has, moreover, steadily improved during the last twenty years. While still the creation and property of the Christian Science Church, it is no longer so much of a house organ as it was, and it has outgrown its least worthy characteristics and inhibitions. These restrictions upon the news which it was allowed to print were not originally planned for it, but had come with time and through the control of the Christian Science Publishing Society, which owns it, the daily's directors being also those of the Mother Church in Boston. Mrs. Eddy's own policy for the *Monitor* was probably best stated in the issue of November 25, 1909, the first anniversary of its founding. It read thus:

It is not to be understood that the *Monitor* has stooped to censorship so narrow or opinionated as to render its news service inadequate, inefficient or incomplete. Far from it. Whatever is of public importance or affects the public welfare, even though it be news of what is ordinarily reckoned as crime or disaster, is printed in the *Monitor* in completeness sufficient for information but without unnecessary embellishment or sensational display. The emphasis, however, is reserved for the helpful, the constructive, the encouraging, not for their opposites.

Under the editorship, however, of Frederick Dixon, an English-born and bred journalist of distinction, who guided the newspa-

per from 1914 until 1922, the *Monitor* went beyond this platform
by refusing to print the names of those lost in such a calam-
ity as the sinking of the *Titanic,* and even ignored the deaths of
prominent persons, save only the President of the United States
and other outstanding personalities. Record the dying of poor
man or millionaire, wife or widow, it could not. In the *Monitor's*
code it was not fit to print. Indeed, after Mrs. Eddy's "passing,"
upon which there was a period of uncertainty as to the future
of her Church, the *Monitor* leaned over backwards in its extreme construction of what was then held to be the Christian
Science attitude toward public affairs.

This made it impossible for the *Monitor* to carry stories of
train wrecks or automobile accidents, the loss of ships, or such
a terrible labor disaster as the massacre in Herrin, Illinois, of
some mine workers. During the first World War the *Monitor*
only spoke of "terrific casualties" and "colossal human sacrifices," though occasionally it did admit that in war there are
killed and wounded — chiefly by acts of the wicked enemy.
Atrocities, curiously enough, one learned of — that is, the enemy's atrocities. The same standards were applied to the otherwise admirable advertising columns. Tea and coffee, liquor, tobacco, medical or hygienic articles, and insurance policies could
not be offered to its readers through its columns. If you lost your
pet police dog or found someone's gold watch, you could not
advertise either fact in the *Monitor,* not at any price. Rouge and
powder, henna and peroxide were forbidden, and so was any
offer to give a "permanent wave." Today the *Monitor* is far
wiser and more liberal, though it still refuses to take advertisements of drugs, medical articles, tobacco, wines and liquors, tea
and coffee. But the ban is now off cosmetic and beauty-parlor
announcements, lost-and-found notices, life-insurance solicita-
tions, lightning-rod recommendations, and want ads calling for
nurses.

It is greatly to its credit that its advertising columns are still
most carefully edited to protect its readers and to maintain the
highest standards in the United States. Many of its business announcements are still as limited to bare facts as were those of
the New York dailies of 1805. A large number of them are unsolicited goodwill advertisements, inserted by faithful followers
of the Christian Science Church, but they appear to produce

sufficient response to make them profitable to the advertiser. Before the war an astonishing percentage of these came from abroad. Similarly, in the news columns the domination of what might be called a narrow Puritanism has been about ended. It does print the news of disasters and is a pretty complete newspaper, and it is to its credit that it still avoids mentioning crimes, scandals, misery, and vice unless such mention is compelled by the relationship of the event to the public welfare.

While the chief editor has always had full liberty of expression, subject to the general Church conception of what the *Monitor* ought to be and the restrictions placed upon it by the Christian Science creed, the *Monitor* was in 1927 placed under an editorial board of four to five members which continued until December 1939 as the executive editorial head of the *Monitor*. Today there is no longer any such board. The present managing editor, Erwin D. Canham, is in direct charge, but responsible on business policy to the board of trustees of the Christian Science Publishing Society, and on editorial policies to the board of directors of the Mother Church. He is an able and experienced newspaperman who believes that the *Monitor* owes its strength not to any individual, but to the ideals behind it, and thinks that the daily should display much more vigor and freedom — the vigor and freedom which Mrs. Eddy intended should be the hallmarks of all her publications. He wishes to realize the promise made by the editorial board on September 4, 1934 that it is "the goal of the *Monitor* to give to its readers a newspaper which will be vital, realistic and comprehensive, which will give to the good news, to the encouraging news, and to the constructive news the prominence it rightly deserves." The board also promised at the same time that the *Monitor* would ignore nothing "essential to a penetrating understanding of those aggravated social conditions to which readers of the *Monitor,* particularly, can give healing attention."

It is undeniable that of late the *Monitor* has been more friendly to the farmer and the worker than is the ordinary large city newspaper. It is giving more and more attention to regional developments in the United States, sending reporters on cruises throughout this country to observe and report. It has naturally been responsive to the New Deal social aims and humanitarian purposes, but as an independent newspaper has freely made use of its right to criticize Roosevelt's methods, and the political abuses in connection with relief measures and appropriations; and it earnestly opposed Roosevelt's plan to pack (and thereby to destroy) the Supreme Court. It also stood strongly, like so many others, against the third term as increasing the danger of personal rule. It has always been eager to uphold civil liberties and minority rights. It is thus basically liberal and holds steadily to its belief that reform comes more effectively through a change of thinking in individuals than through legislative measures.

But if it throughout has relied more on light than heat, it was and is open to just criticism that it does not crusade or strike out vigorously enough against wickedness and injustice. It is far better than it was, but in confronting the eternal questions as to whether reforms are best achieved by being soft-spoken or by hitting straight from the shoulder, its religious affiliations and creed have distinctly handicapped it. Its occasional lapses into hot indignation are therefore to be welcomed as weakening the charge against it that its editorial policy was based on the familiar principle that a successful journal must not hurt people's feelings. To be soft-spoken is noble and generous and, to an extent, Christian, but it does not thrill nor interest, nor stir readers as does the editor who from time to time gives rein to the indignation that is within him — certainly Christ knew how to reach the heights of criticism and denunciation. I believe that the *Monitor* has suffered in the past because it did not take sides more ardently and did not cry out with emotion and passion against human injustice, wrongdoing, and wickedness. I do, however, of late seem to find in it, and especially in its support of the New Deal, a greater desire to be heard on the side of the masses rather than of the privileged.

The *Monitor's* attitude on the question of war I have never been able to understand in the light of its devotion to the teachings of Christ. It was unfortunate that during the early years of the first World War the *Monitor's* policy was in the hands of Mr. Dixon, for he could not overcome his pro-British proclivities nor hold the scales even. Nor did the *Monitor* otherwise live up either to the ideals which it set for itself, or to what seemed to be the principles of Mrs. Eddy's Church. More recently it has given a great deal of attention to the removal of the causes of war and the building of an international brotherhood as the basis for a lasting peace. It has done an excellent job in printing many articles on the "World We Want," and in insisting that spiritual and mental forces must and will determine the physical form of world organization and the character of the peace to come, and it has bravely championed liberal trade policies, such as the Hull reciprocal agreements, as essential to peace and progress.

None the less, in its active and positive urging of forcible resistance to aggression it has leaned to the side of war and American participation in it. Here it is the conventional daily, and here it has perhaps been greatly influenced by the burning sense of outrage which has imbued those of its correspondents who have viewed at close range the bloody horrors and the printable and unprintable barbarities of the Axis leaders; here it has been in decided contrast to its policy of seeking to emphasize healing rather than hatred. How a newspaper which speaks for the doctrines of Christian Science can take any other attitude than one of absolute opposition to all war I cannot understand. What is the use of seeking to teach people to conquer illness by mental and spiritual health and power, to rise above or ignore the existence of death, all on the ground that sickness is a state of mind and can be overcome by the individual, if you then give yourself to the wholesale support of wars in which millions upon millions are killed, and heaven knows how many more are tortured by suffering which no amount of will power, or ignoring of physical facts can overcome? Certainly the war-time editorials of 1917–18 in the *Monitor,* founded to injure no one and "bless all mankind," made one wonder how it was that the bottom did not drop out of the Christian Science Church when its authorities laid down the doctrine during the last war that opposition to it was "merely an academic objection to the use of the sword."

Think of it! The Church which objects to advertising tea and coffee, liquors, dyes and bleaches, sees only "academic objection" to the greatest evil on earth, to that combination of murder, rape, and pillage which kills and maims in a couple of days more human beings than Christian Science can aid or cure in decades! If it has become much more outspoken in regard to politics since 1922, and even more interested than previously in international affairs, it could well have been a leader in pointing out to all the

churches of the land the danger of their losing the remaining
hold they have upon the American people if they did not do their
uttermost to prevent the coming of the present war, from which
humanity will not recover in generations. I am sure that the
Monitor must have printed Lloyd George's warning some years
ago to the Welsh Church, that if the churches of America and
England permitted a second World War to come they might as
well lock the doors of their edifices, as there would be no use for
them after the struggle was over. This may have been exaggeration, but the danger thus portrayed of another war destroying
the faith of all peoples in religion has been so evident that it is
difficult to understand the relative complacency with which the
Monitor has seen and even approved and upheld the approach
of this second Armageddon.

It is only just to add, however, the *Monitor's* own statements
of its position. Here is one: "It is not simply that Britain must
win. Something very much bigger than Britain or America must
win the tremendous struggle now going on. There must be a
victory won in the interest of all the world, for the idea of freedom under law, of security from aggression, of adjustment by
peaceful means." It has freely admitted that it does not believe
that a victory for democracy obtained by force will settle the
question of war, but it thinks that "such a victory will permit the
continuance of the slow but steady progress toward war's final
destruction and the furtherance of the brotherhood of man,
which Christianity and democracy have been making down
through the centuries, often through the sacrifices of heroic
men and women. Whereas were the aggressive, anti-Christian
forces to be victorious, this progress would be set back number-
less years." Since it cannot see that war is the most dangerous
enemy both of democracy and of the Christian religion, it must
be admitted that its present position that "the greatest wrong
that could be done the peoples of the aggressor nations themselves is to permit them to continue on their self-ruinous course
of plunder, enslavement, and murder," and that "the only true
kindness is to check the evil as promptly and as efficiently as
possible," is as ably stated as possible.

It is greatly to the credit of the *Monitor,* its editor and proprietors, that it does not cast a Christian Science hue over all that
it prints, and indeed proselytizes extraordinarily little. It is not

necessary to be a Christian Scientist in order to be a member of the editorial staff or one of its foreign correspondents. There is no pressure exerted upon such a non-believer. Questions about the metaphysics upon which the faith is founded are answered with courtesy, frankness, and friendliness, but without effort to convert. The idea is that when a person is ready for Christian Science he will seek it, and he is never sought and is not held in disrepute for not being a Scientist. The *Monitor* continues to carry on an inside page ("The Home Forum Page") a metaphysical article which is Christian Science propaganda, the only direct expression of dogma in the paper. This is translated each day into some language — it may even be Arabic or Chinese. The reading of the *Monitor* has never been made obligatory by the Church and it has never been used as an official journal, however great the temptation may have been. Indeed, the editors are proud of the fact that at least ten per cent of their readers are not Scientists, and that clergymen of all denominations subscribe for it because of the extent of its news and the cleanliness of its columns.

There is not only no reason why the non-Scientist should not read it; it is a cause for genuine regret that it does not have a far larger general circulation, for its treatment of the news is of the very best. Its correspondents and reporters have no other instruction than to write the facts as they see them. Herbert Adams Gibbons, who was long one of its numerous non-Scientist correspondents abroad, once wrote that he was happy to represent "the one great newspaper in America that has a world vision, whose policy is to cover the entire world and to present the news of the world. I mention the *Monitor* because it is this conception of journalism that is the hope of the world." It is true that the correspondence from abroad has at times been unequal in quantity and marred by padding, and rewriting after the event. But the outstanding fact has been that the *Monitor* has sought to place its foreign correspondence on the level of that of the best English newspapers and to give an intelligent survey of what is happening in all parts of the world. For a long time it boasted that it printed more cable news than the New York *Times*. It never buys or sells syndicate matter, because of its widespread circulation. It feels that it would be a drawback to have a subscriber in Los Angeles read dispatches in its news service that had already appeared in a Los Angeles daily. Hence for years it was not a member of the Associated Press or of the United Press, but relied upon its own news-gathering forces. Now it has joined the former association. It really has to conceive of itself as almost more of a daily magazine than a newspaper; that is, its editors have to consider how their editions will read from six to eighteen days after publication.

This conflict between its magazine ideals and the daily news is one of the genuine difficulties which confront the *Monitor,* and it is not solved by the fact that it prints three editions, called the Atlantic, the Central, and the Pacific for those three sections of this country. Actually there are seven, for the Atlantic seaboard edition has five special variations, one for all New England except Boston, one for Boston, one for the New York and the lower Atlantic seaboard, one for Canada, and one for overseas, the last of which is greatly affected by the war. Each of these seven variations is made up differently and contains matter of special interest to the district to which it is sent, such as local news, advertising originating in the section, and so on. For example, the edition which circulates in New York and New Jersey has featured excellent articles attacking Boss Hague and supporting those seeking to overthrow his evil regime. The excellence of its general, its educational, and its literary articles must be stressed, for they are well and seriously done, often by experts, and give no one the feeling that they are written just to fill space.

An effort is thus made to offset the disadvantage of the *Monitor's* appearing, say, on the Pacific coast so long after its publication in Boston where it competes with its news-stand rivals in timeliness and news display. It is in California — state of isms — that the *Monitor* has found its largest group of readers — 19,146. In its and Mrs. Eddy's home state, Massachusetts, it has, surprisingly enough, only 15,781. There are two schools of thought as to the *Monitor's* problem — that which thinks that the emphasis should be more and more upon the magazine aspect, with perhaps a corresponding change of format, and another which believes that the *Monitor* should build more and more on its general national and international news, as has the New York *Times,* and rigidly adhere to the policy of getting out the highest-grade large-sized daily in the United States. It still refuses to print a Sunday edition. While it is copiously and admirably illustrated, it has not yielded to comic strips or to any cheap, catchpenny circulation devices. It keeps its news standards up and calls upon its readers to rise to them.

How financially successful has it been? This is not easy to ascertain, but its managers think that if it were free from certain obligations which it carries as the creature of the Christian Science Church, it would be well in the black and could be made to show a handsome profit. It is, of course, intertwined with the other activities of the Christian Science Publishing Society, in whose magnificent building it is housed, and to which, it is presumed, it does not pay rent. Its circulation has varied extraordinarily. Mr. Dixon's retirement on January 30, 1922 from the editorship came as a result of the quarrel between the directors of the Church and the trustees of the Publishing Society as to the control of the latter. While the *Monitor* took no position editorially on this as on many other issues, the conflict within the Church was almost a death blow to the paper, for its splendid circulation of 140,000 to which Mr. Dixon's great talents had raised it, fell away to less than 20,000. On February 1, 1922 there were only 17,500 readers. After that under the excellent editorship, from 1922 to February 1, 1927, of Willis J. Abbot, an old-time liberal and associate in former years of men of the type of Henry D. Lloyd of Chicago and Governor Altgeld of Illinois, the circulation again grew rapidly. It seems, however, to hover around 140,000 — it was 145,000 at the end of 1942. It has risen since the war began, but it has never attained the goal of 250,000 which it ought to achieve and which seemed quite possible in 1925. Occasionally when there are special issues it reaches that figure. But so admirable and so relatively free and independent a newspaper of such standards ought by rights to have in this country a circulation approaching the million mark, for it has enterprise, efficiency, vigor, and far more liberalism than all but a few of our dailies, and the highest ethical standards.

The warmest praise must be given to the *Monitor* for the excellence of its make-up and typography. Here is an outstanding exception to the general rule of indifference to type and appearance which has come to mark the press. This has been recognized a number of times by awards of one kind or another. Thus in April 1943 the F. Wayland Ayer Cup was awarded to it in the thirteenth annual exhibition of newspaper typography conducted by N. W. Ayer & Sons, Inc. The cup was given to the *Monitor* for "excellence in typography, make-up and press work" above all others. Its constant public service has also been frequently rewarded. Thus in December 1942 it received the Maria Moors Cabot award for distinguished service in the field of inter-American relations, and in May 1943 it was given the award of the University of Missouri for distinguished service in journalism. All associated with it have every reason to be proud of their product — and the whole profession likewise.

Because the *Monitor* is the organ of a society established upon an ethical basis; because it is entirely without the profit motive; because it has conceived its mission to be international, it has been from the start one of the most interesting and challenging of American journalistic experiments. It cannot be overlooked by anyone who seeks an answer to the riddle which reads: What is to be the newspaper of the future and how can it be kept free from that commercial control which has so degraded the press of today? Even with the disadvantages of its Church ownership, in the hidebound conservatism, sensationalism, utter editorial conventionality, and general cheapness, not to say sordidness, of Boston's press it shines as the one bright star, the sole remaining daily to recall the Hub's lost reputation for high intelligence and literary and intellectual taste.

CHAPTER XII

The St. Louis POST-DISPATCH

ANY HONOR ROLL of American journalism must place the St. Louis *Post-Dispatch* at the head of the distinguished, politically independent, and outstandingly honest American newspapers. Senator George W. Norris was correct in calling it the *Manchester Guardian* of the United States. Founded by Joseph Pulitzer, that it escaped the fate of his two New York *Worlds* was nothing less than a piece of extraordinary good fortune for the newspaper profession. Many things favored the *Post-Dispatch* which were absent in the New York situation. For one thing, the *Post-Dispatch* was inherited by the one son of Joseph Pulitzer who was endowed with something of his father's journalistic ability besides bearing his name. Curiously enough, the father, whose judgment of his sons was entirely mistaken, thought that Joseph Pulitzer, Jr., was the worst instead of the best of them from the journalistic point of view. He made things just as difficult as possible for all three of them to become good journalists, and he left the bulk of his property to the youngest one, who was only fifteen years old when his father died and had of course given no evidence as to his promise.

Overcoming the difficulties in the way, Joseph Pulitzer, Jr., soon made himself respected by his staff, with which he has labored quite in his father's spirit, and in the main along the lines of his father's policies. He and his newspaper have had the good fortune to be served by many great journalists, men of extraordinary loyalty to their newspaper and to the profession, and fired with the desire really to benefit the city, the state, and the country in which they lived. Again, St. Louis is a remarkable newspaper city, well located for the control not only of a considerable journalistic field in Missouri, but of a large slice of Illinois territory as well. Whatever the reason, taking its three journals as a whole, the *Post-Dispatch,* the *Star-Times,* and the *Globe-Democrat,* no other American city has maintained a finer group of dailies, or one with higher journalistic standards. They have clung remarkably to the older-fashioned, dignified newspaper forms and traditions. They are strong, editorially able, highly competent news-gatherers, and fight for their ideals with ability and power. As a whole they are amazingly independent and do not find it necessary to stoop to sensationalism or cheapness in order to obtain readers. The city has actually never had a tabloid, and by some divine blessing has never been cursed with a Hearst publication.

Its newspapers, moreover, have represented differing political viewpoints, so that the citizens of St. Louis have full choice of opinion, and they have profited by the fact that the state's political complexion is subject to change. If they have not succeeded in purifying a bad state government and in improving political methods sufficiently to make Missouri democracy a thing to be proud of, it is not because all three, but particularly the *Post-Dispatch,* have failed to reveal political corruption and to throw light upon the familiar alliance between certain forms of big business, notably public utilities, and the politicians. All three of them have been served by men of unusual journalistic capacity, but here again the *Post-Dispatch* has been outstanding. The loyalty and devotion of its employees constitute the greatest tribute that any journal can desire, and those qualities usually derive from the feeling of the workers that they have freedom of utterance and intellectual independence and are able to portray the truth as they find it. All these conditions and qualities have distinguished the *Post-Dispatch* ever since the days of Joseph Pulitzer the elder — in the main, that is — but there have been some lapses of late years. I cannot recall any other group of editors, correspondents, and reporters which has rendered more outstanding service than has for more than sixty years the staff of the *Post-Dispatch.*

It cannot be classified as a muckraking publication, for it is far less actuated by a desire for sensations than by the determination to expose corruption and malgovernment wherever they can be found in public life. To list some of its achievements, two members of the staff once published a thirty-one-page pamphlet without exhausting its important accomplishments. Only a few of them can be cited here. Its Washington bureau has been especially distinguished. To its brilliant correspondent, the late Paul Y. Anderson, goes much credit. It was he who took up the demand of the first Senator La Follette for an investigation of the leasing of the naval oil tracts at Elk Hills and Teapot Dome, and it was through him and his associates that so many facts were brought out that the far-reaching official Senate investigation was finally instituted. A few other newspapers and weeklies stood by, but the other leading dailies utterly ignored or, like the New York *Times,* deprecated and denounced the inquiry.

Fortunately there was in the home office of the *Post-Dispatch* Oliver K. Bovard, one of the greatest managing editors in the history of our journalism. He not only recognized the significance of the tremendous "story" which Anderson was unearthing, but backed him to the fullest possible extent and gave him and his Washington associates most helpful aid and suggestions. For weeks the *Post-Dispatch* was the only newspaper to maintain a special reporter at the hearings. Then, when the truth began to come out, which eventually revealed the trail of corruption that led straight into the Cabinet room of the Harding Administration, the rest of the newspapers of the country finally joined in the hue and cry. I know of few other instances in which one journal has so clearly demonstrated the tremendous power of the press when it is sincerely and unselfishly devoted to the revealing of public wrongdoing. Later, in 1927, the *P-D* again forced an inquiry into a phase of the bribery of Secretary Fall — the disposition of $3,000,000 worth of bonds which represented the profits of a curious concern known as the Continental Trading Company. The bonds used to purchase this shameless Cabinet official came out of the $3,000,000, the rest of it being divided among some of the foremost heads of the oil industry, or dispensed for political purposes — that is, corruption.

As a result of this inquiry both the major party platforms of 1928 came out for full publicity for political campaign contributions, a great step forward in the purifying of elections. It is not surprising that Senator Walsh of Montana, who distinguished himself in unearthing the whole story and in relentlessly probing to the very depths of every transaction, should particularly have complimented the *Post-Dispatch,* not only upon its enterprise, but also upon its "discriminating and helpful editorial comment in contrast to the hostile attitude of the press generally, until outraged public opinion forced a change."

But the exposures of the *Post-Dispatch* have never been limited to national affairs. State and city events have likewise always been within its scope. It was its superb reporting of the East St.

Louis race riots of 1917 that resulted in the appointment of a special Congressional committee to obtain the facts. This committee in large part drew its information from the work of a *Post-Dispatch* reporter, whom it described as "thorough and trustworthy," as one who reported the facts without fear of consequences to himself, who "defied the indignant officials whom he convicted of criminal neglect of duty; ran a daily risk of assassination, and rendered invaluable public service by his exposures." It is not surprising that the name of this brave reporter was Paul Y. Anderson.

Corrupt public utilities in the St. Louis district have constantly been in the *Post-Dispatch's* spotlight. It put an end to long-term franchises in St. Louis. It denounced the overvaluation for speculative purposes of the Laclede Gas Light Company, by which efforts for rate reductions were in large degree defeated. Single-handed it drove out of their positions the three chief executives of the Union Electric Company of Missouri, who had been guilty of legislative lobbying and the use of money to influence the election of public officials, and compelled their replacement by new officers appointed by the holding company, the North American Company. Examiners of the Federal Securities and Exchange Commission, in investigating the Union management, discovered that "slush funds amounting to more than $300,000 had been obtained in 'kick-backs' from padded expense accounts, bogus fees for professional services, and secret rebates from supply concerns, none of which funds appeared on the books of the company," but were disbursed by these crooked officials of the Union Electric Company through political and legislative channels. Again, the *P-D* has especially devoted itself to the improvement of the judiciary, with the result that the wheels of justice have been speeded up. In the case of a Federal judge, George W. English of East St. Louis, its revelations compelled his resignation in 1926, after the House of Representatives in Washington had voted 306 to 60 for his impeachment.

Sixteen years later its editorials protesting the appointment by Franklin D. Roosevelt of Boss Hague's minion, Thomas F. Meaney, to the Federal bench were reprinted throughout the state of New Jersey and became a factor in arousing the citizens to an effective revolt against the Meaney-Hague-Smathers deal at the polls in November 1942. In 1936 the *P-D* received the

Pulitzer Prize for proving wholesale padding of the St. Louis list of registered voters and forcing a recanvass, which showed that 40,000 names carried were those of persons who did not exist. The complete success of this campaign was achieved when the Governor of Missouri removed his own unfaithful or worse board of election commissioners. In every case the courage of the *P-D* has been beyond praise. Sometimes its experiences have been distinctly unpleasant. Thus in 1940, after denouncing intolerable conditions in the local courts due to politics and personal favoritism, it was bitterly attacked by one of the judges criticized. He issued a citation charging the *Post-Dispatch* and certain of its staff with contempt of court. Mistakenly believing that Ralph Coghlan, the present editor of the editorial page, had written the editorials to which he objected, instead of Irving Dilliard, another vigorous and able member of the staff, the judge sentenced Coghlan to twenty days in jail and fined him $200. Daniel R. Fitzpatrick, the distinguished *P-D* cartoonist, received ten days and a $100 fine, and one of $2,000 was assessed against the Pulitzer Publishing Company. The case was taken to the Missouri Supreme Court and there the freedom of the press was upheld in an opinion which scrapped much of the old restrictions on editorial freedom of speech imposed by a contempt-of-court case of a generation ago that had theretofore acted as a precedent.

The *P-D's* editors and reporters have constantly done their duty at the risk of imprisonment and bodily attacks, and have found great rewards for taking such risks in the thrill which comes to every honest journalist when he succeeds in exposing some rascality or driving some faithless public official into private life. Even these brief accounts of some of the *P-D's* activities are completest proof that its staff and its owner have in the news-gathering field lived up to the highest ideals a patriotic daily can set for itself. It has remained a brilliant newspaper in the technical sense, which fact has contributed no end to its successful public exposures. As I have written, for years it rejoiced in the services of O. K. Bovard, who could be trusted not only to pick remarkable subordinates, but knew enough to encourage initiative in them and to back them to the limit. But the list of outstanding *P-D* men contains many other names. One of the greatest of them was George Sibley Johns, for forty-eight years an active newspaperman who became editor emeritus in 1930. Twice dismissed from the *P-D,* he was reinstated on both occasions. For years he was Mr. Pulitzer's mouthpiece in the paper, with practically unlimited powers, for the owner publicly stated that he was interested in the *P-D* only to the extent of the size of the checks which he received. Long after the death of the senior Pulitzer, Mr. Johns dominated the editorial page, if not the whole office. He was so deeply versed in the Constitution and the story of its creation, and so reverenced our fundamental law, that it was called his religion. It was he who picked Mr. Bovard for a reporter's position and started him on his career.

Clark McAdam went from a typesetter's case to the *Post-Dispatch* as a result of an imaginative snake yarn he sent in from Alton, Illinois, which so pleased Mr. Bovard that he at once gave him a job on the staff, which eventually led McAdam to the headship of the editorial page. He, too, was a really great journalist of the finest American liberal strain and a columnist of distinction. He fought unceasingly, with rare humor and the passionate crusader's sincerity, for freedom for the common man. His style was vigorous, clear, and compelling. It was his epigrammatic skill and wit that made him during the Hoover regime characterize the battle between the reactionaries and progressives of American life in these words: "The issue is between the country and the country club." Into the promising phases of the New Deal which marked its inception Mr. McAdam threw himself wholeheartedly, believing that by it the United States could and would be made over. It was rightly said of Clark McAdam that his "rich reward was the universal respect of the entire newspaper fraternity for his high editorial courage." His convictions were deep and profound, his faith unshakable, and his spirit ever youthful in its enthusiasms.

Unfortunately Mr. Pulitzer dropped Mr. McAdam from his position in 1934 because the latter's zeal for the New Deal far exceeded that of his employer. This was one of the younger Pulitzer's worst blunders; it dealt a severe blow to the prestige if not to the solidarity of the staff. Some years later Mr. Bovard left the office of his own accord, because of irreconcilable differences between him and the proprietor. While it is not apparent that Mr. Pulitzer's views have been directly molded by his wealth and fortunate situation in life, he does seem at times to lean to

the conservative side, while unswerving in his devotion to his
father's newspaper ideals, to the freedom of the press and of the
individual, and to the liberal tradition as a whole. He supervises
the paper and its editorial expression somewhat as did his father
those of the two *Worlds* — but not always fortunately. Often he
edits editorials, and occasionally an editorial appears over his
signature. It must be added that he does not seem to have been
personally responsible for some of the political positions taken
of late years by the *Post-Dispatch* which have injured its editorial influence.

Thus, despite its enthusiasm, in the main, for the fundamental
principles of the New Deal, this newspaper supported Alfred
Landon in the Presidential contest of 1936 because of mistrust
of Mr. Roosevelt's leadership. As the next Presidential election
came on, the *Post-Dispatch* violently opposed the President's
international policy because of its correct judgment that he would
lead the United States into war. When, without consulting Congress, the President sold fifty over-age destroyers to England
and leased for one hundred years British possessions in this
hemisphere for naval bases, the *Post-Dispatch* wrote that "Mr.
Roosevelt today committed an act of war. He also became America's first dictator. . . ." When the 1940 election approached,
however, the *Post-Dispatch,* whose able and unanswerable editorials had heartened the anti-war forces all over the country,
suddenly turned around and urged Mr. Roosevelt's election.
Never was there a more sudden or more violent *volte-face* in
American editorial writing. Naturally the St. Louis *Star-Times,*
always for Roosevelt and all his works, seized the opportunity
to deal the hardest blows ever given to its rival by reprinting
some of the anti-Roosevelt statements of the *P-D*. The *Star-Times*
appears rather ridiculous now when one recalls that it defended
the destroyer and naval base deal with the words: "It was not
an act of war, but an act to keep war away from America, now
and forever!" It is assumed, since there were no resignations
from the staff of the *P-D,* that it approved this sudden determination to support the very man against whom it had made the
most serious charge that could possibly be leveled against an
American President — that he was seeking to become a dictator
and leading the country to war.

As one looks back, this incident is the more remarkable because the *Post-Dispatch* very soon returned to the attack upon the third-termer, and at this writing it seems inconceivable that it could possibly advocate a fourth term for Franklin Roosevelt. It has sincerely and loyally supported the war since it came, and has done more than its share in revealing the tragic maladministration of the home front. It has been unceasing in pounding the White House bottleneck, in attacking the President for his failure to maintain discipline in his official family and for his constant playing of politics even in war-time. Probably the *Post-Dispatch* thought in 1940 that it could not in any circumstances support the candidacy of Wendell Willkie when it had always specialized in criticizing corporation managers of his type. If this is a correct theory, the proper answer would have been to refuse to support either party. This is a most difficult position for any daily to take, but has been cheerfully assumed in the past by other journalistic exemplars of the very political independence which distinguishes the *Post-Dispatch*. Other liberal journals, like the New York *Evening Post,* the Springfield *Republican,* and the old Boston *Herald,* have at times deliberately refused to take sides, to choose the lesser evil.

None the less, the *Post-Dispatch's* standards and editorial courage remain of the highest. Often newspapers as old as this one go through periods of standing still or of positive intellectual decline. I cannot seem to find any time when this has been the case with the *Post-Dispatch*. Its vitality is remarkable. Not the least of its achievements is that it has remained a politically-minded and outspoken journal in the day when few of our newspapers give any evidence of a knowledge of American political history, or of a desire to judge contemporary events in the light of previous political happenings. In this respect the average newspaper reflects not merely the decay of the editorial page, but the prevailing failure of our schools and colleges to teach American history adequately and also the bases for our political faiths, and to liven the problems of the day by parallels drawn from our national experience. There is no other daily which has so clearly inherited the political tradition and insight, not only of Joseph Pulitzer the elder, but of Edwin L. Godkin, Samuel Bowles, Henry J. Raymond, Henry Watterson, and other apostles of American journalistic liberalism as has the *P-D.*

It has today several men upon its staff, including Mr. Dilliard,* who are political specialists, who value the favorable position of the *Post-Dispatch* in the great Mississippi Valley to check and counter-check every Midwestern political development and activity, and in consequence to report, often before any other newspaper, new trends and new events. Mr. Dilliard's political prescience is remarkable. He "scooped" the entire press by his correct forecast of what would happen in the Congressional election of 1942, and he also foresaw what the Republican gains would do in stiffening Congress to resist, and at times to defeat, the President. He is one of the few really deep students of our political drifts. In no other department does the paper prove more clearly that it is living up to a great, continuing tradition. In this field it is also tremendously reinforced by its extraordinarily able, outstanding Washington staff, composed of Charles G. Ross, Raymand P. Brandt, Richard L. Stokes, and Marquis W. Childs. There are numerous larger staffs in Washington, but none that surpass in intelligence, understanding, and vigilance these *P-D* men.

In other words, the *P-D* as a whole closely lives up to the ideals set for his papers by Joseph Pulitzer when he retired from active journalism and called upon them never to forget to "fight demagogues of all parties," never to "lack sympathy with the poor, and always remain devoted to the public welfare." It was a noble platform and has nobly been lived up to by the *Post-Dispatch* because the paper has had freedom, courage, and the complete independence given to it not only by its owner, but by its continuing financial success, which has enabled it to pay unusually high salaries. But no financial reward could account for that loyalty and devotion of the staff, already cited, which means so much, not merely to the paper and to the profession, but also to the Republic.

* Mr. Dilliard is now in the army.

CHAPTER XIII

Colonel McCormick and the Chicago
TRIBUNE

By AN EXTRAORDINARY turn of events, as a result of our involvement in the second World War, Robert R. McCormick, the most unpopular newspaper publisher in the United States with the exception of William R. Hearst, has been placed in the position of defending the rights and liberties of the American press. This will not be conceded by the many who are demanding, in the name of the Four Freedoms, that the Chicago *Tribune* be forthwith suppressed, together with its affiliated newspapers, the Washington *Times-Herald* and the New York *Daily News.* None the less it is a fact, whatever one thinks about the Chicago *Tribune* and Colonel McCormick. It is of course not the first time that a man who has typified narrow reaction and ultraconservatism has suddenly been able to render a great public service.

Since I long ago described the *Tribune,* which so impudently, brazenly, and falsely calls itself "the world's greatest newspaper," as one of the world's worst, I will hardly be accused of being a partisan of this daily. But whether one abominates the *Tribune's* international policies or its opposition to the Roosevelt regime, or approves of them, in its dissent from the President's pro-war program prior to Pearl Harbor and its vigorous criticism of the Administration's conduct of our part in the war since then it is keeping alive the historic American right of press dissent even in war-time. Multitudes deplore the *Tribune's* methods and modes of expression and dislike the personality of its editor, but share its viewpoint and are ready to champion its refusal to approve of the President, while supporting the war against Japan and Germany. They did not believe that the *Tribune* was guilty of a disloyal or improper action when it reported that the American admirals who fought the brilliant and victorious action against the Japanese at Midway had been informed in advance of the Japanese plan of campaign, and they rejoiced when the United States government's effort to bring about the punishment of the Chicago *Tribune* for revealing war secrets was promptly thrown out of court.

This was again not due to any love of the *Tribune,* but to a belief that the *Tribune* would never have been prosecuted by the Department of Justice had it been on the side of Mr. Roosevelt. It is largely because of this governmental antagonism toward the McCormick-Patterson group of newspapers that the Colonel has appeared to some of the public as a champion of free speech and freedom of the press, even though he uses that freedom illiberally and has none too great a regard for the truth. To the best of my belief, the Chicago *Tribune* has not been guilty of any unpatriotic dissent; certainly, had it been, the government would not have lost an hour in moving against it for other offenses than its enterprise in revealing the secret that through one means or another our American Naval Intelligence Service was so clever as to have ascertained the program of its Japanese adversaries. At any rate, it is a fact that more than 967,000 Americans daily purchase Colonel McCormick's *Tribune* and nearly 1,300,000 on Sundays, which hardly could be the case if it were the unpatriotic and treasonable sheet so many of its critics allege it to be; nor would its total advertising linage have increased as considerably as it did in the year following Pearl Harbor, especially as there is now in the Chicago *Sun* a competitor to which dissenters and critics can turn.

The truth is that, whatever else may be said about Colonel McCormick, he has in his stubborn way steadfastly fought for the right of the press to live up in fullest degree to that one of the Four Freedoms which pertains to it. That freedom can never be delimited by good manners or good morals or restricted to "wise" political views, and should not be enchained even in wartime. In every war in every democratic country there will always be the fight as to what constitutes just military censorship, for every governmental censorship inevitably reaches out not merely to suppress military information which might directly or indirectly benefit the enemy, but to control the opinions of the press. This is the case in the present war, when American censors are refusing to allow American editorial and news opinions to go to England, and the English censors are preventing British points of view from coming to the United States. Anyone, whether liberal or reactionary, who throws himself into the breach and challenges this drift toward governmental control of public opinion renders inestimable public service, however mistaken he may be in his political viewpoint, or in his opposition to or championing of certain governmental policies. This Colonel McCormick has done.

Actually he illustrated his devotion to the freedom of the press long before the coming of Pearl Harbor. Thus, in the celebrated case of the so-called Minnesota gag law, enacted in 1925, he took the lead to have it declared unconstitutional, in his capacity as chairman of the Committee on Press Freedom of the American Newspaper Publishers Association. Under this statute the Minneapolis *Saturday Press* (a far from admirable or worthy newspaper) was enjoined from publication after it had exposed numerous instances of local political corruption. Colonel McCormick contended that the suppression of this newspaper violated the First and Fourteenth Amendments to the Constitution. He proposed to the membership of the A.N.P.A. to carry the case to the Supreme Court of the United States and obtained an almost universal endorsement of the members for this plan. It resulted in a complete victory, the law being declared unconstitutional in 1931. He also led the A.N.P.A. fight against the tax on newspapers imposed in Louisiana under the Huey Long regime, and this law, too, was declared unconstitutional by the United States Supreme Court. In addition he has championed several local newspapers held in contempt by various state courts, and he is still chairman of the A.N.P.A. Committee on Press Freedom. No one can deny, therefore, that he has proved that in this vitally important field he has been not only a consistent, but a most meritorious defender of the freedom of the press.

That the Chicago *Tribune* during this World War took the position that it did in opposing American entrance into the struggle was hardly to be expected if one recalls the attitude of the *Tribune* in being one of the outstanding warmongers in the first World War. Then it was for war to the hilt, and there was no bitterer antagonist of the Germans in the whole country, nor one more intolerant of the very sort of dissent which it has itself practiced during the present struggle. Colonel McCormick's defense of this may well be that he learned the lesson of the last war (in which he served as an officer of artillery), that he has never forgotten that we achieved nothing permanent in that war and bettered the world and America not at all by our sacrifices, which merely helped to pave the way for the coming of the present catastrophe. There was nothing unpatriotic or un-American in the Chicago *Tribune's* desire to keep the country out of the second World War, certainly nothing more unpatriotic than were Abraham Lincoln's bitter attacks on President Polk's conduct of the Mexican War, which led to Lincoln's being defeated for re-election to Congress; nor John Jay's and all New England's sharp opposition to the War of 1812, which even led to threats of secession at that time. No one can accuse Colonel McCormick of any ulterior motive in seeking to keep his country at peace — it would have been to his financial advantage, perhaps, had he gone the other way. The point is, again, that he maintained a historic American right when he fought to the last to keep the country out of war.

It is an amusing irony of fate, however, that the *Tribune* should be so roundly abused because of its beliefs, since this colossus among dailies was long savage in its attacks upon all liberals and everyone with whom it disagreed. If its advocacy of its peace policy has been subject to widespread doubt of its integrity, it is because for decades it has typified illiberality, plus very great inconsistency, and constant hostility to those who have fought for ideals for their own sake. Yet its career has not always been marked by ultra-conservatism. Thus, while ordinarily upholding the *status quo* and the great business influences which have done so much to bar true prosperity and genuine progress in the United States, it did champion the Republican Progressives from 1909 to 1916, and with skill and courage. For years it opposed the traction barons, and especially Yerkes, the bribe-giver and franchise-grabber. It has stood for a moderate tariff and for progressive and high taxes on inheritances. Although itself the creator of great wealth and the instrument of very rich men, it has advocated the breaking up of great fortunes, which it considers a menace to the Republic. It *is* independent in its viewpoint, eccentrically, inconsistently, and self-contradictorily so. And at any time it is capable of rendering a distinct public service at the risk of financial loss.

Indeed, it may be said that inconsistency is its watchword. It has been outspokenly against Southern political ideas, and then it turns around and serves the cause of race hatred with equal facility and venom. One can never be sure where it is going to stand, and whether it will be reactionary and vicious or, accidentally, will be found on the side of progress and enlightenment. It poses as a great defender of law and order, but it endorsed the Ku Klux Klan. It opposed Prohibition as an attack upon personal liberty, but favored the law to prohibit the use of revolvers. Years ago it bitterly opposed the seating of Senator Lorimer because of corrupt practices, but it favored the seating of Senator Newberry of Michigan because his opponent, Henry Ford, was a dangerous internationalist! In its attacks upon wrongdoers it is often so abusive, so vituperative, and so savage as to arouse a feeling of sympathy for the object of its bitter venom. That was the case in its great fight against former Mayor Thompson of Chicago. It abandoned every rule of dignified editorial practice to vent its feelings against Thompson, precisely as it abused pacifists and radicals — it has never observed any Marquis of Queensberry rules as to when and where to hit. Yet despite its bitter hostility Mayor Thompson or his candidates were re-elected again and again.

On international questions the *Tribune* has generally been cynical, reactionary, militaristic, and jingo, which added to the surprise that it should have taken the anti-war course that it did prior to Pearl Harbor. It has been enthusiastically for universal military service, and for a huge navy, just as it carries on its masthead Decatur's mischievous motto: "My country, right or wrong." To sneer at morality in foreign relations is the *Tribune's* stock in trade; it was a staunch defender of President Theodore Roosevelt when, contrary to morals and international law, he "took" — to use his own word — Panama by fraud and violence from Colombia. Its nationalism has always been narrow and immoral as well as militaristic. Of course it opposed our entry into the League of Nations, less because of the League's obvious and fatal weaknesses than because the *Tribune* was opposed to all international organizations. It has wanted to clean up Mexico and impose our superior morality upon the Mexicans, whom it would have annexed without hesitation. Naturally it favored our conquest of the Filipinos and felt that it was our "manifest destiny" to rule over them. Its training of its guns upon Japan after Pearl Harbor was not merely a move of expediency; for years the *Tribune* had done everything that it possibly could to attack Japan and to convince the Japanese that the United States was bound sooner or later to go to war with them. To have been consistent it should have been pleased and proud that the Japanese did us the favor of attacking us.

As for Russia, of course the *Tribune* has been the voice of privilege and power against the Bolsheviks from the beginning. Like the New York *Times* during the 1920s, it lost no time or opportunity to discredit the Soviets. On its record it should find itself in completest sympathy with Hitler's assertions that the Soviet government is the world's greatest menace to humanity and that it should be eradicated by force. Second to the Communists, in its bad opinion, could only be the New Dealers in Washington. Everything that they have attempted in the way of progress this once ardent champion of the Theodore Roosevelt Progressives, who were in some degree the forerunners and sires of the New Dealers, has opposed. No other newspaper has circulated so widely its belief that the real underlying purpose of the New Deal is to destroy the fundamentals of American life and government. Its attacks upon Franklin Roosevelt have known few bounds; they have hurt that gentleman frequently, it must be admitted, because its editors have told unpleasant truths and brought out his failures and blunders, his administrative inefficiency and incapacity, and his all too frequent insincerity, this with unsparing ferocity and unending iteration and complete failure to credit him with his good deeds and aims. Where other newspaper-owners have yielded to the President's power and prestige, the *Tribune's* have defied him with contempt and disdain, even in war-time, so that the President has felt impelled to strike back whenever he could.

Latterly Colonel McCormick has brought out his scheme for the reorganization of the world, which has been ignored as unworthy of discussion by most of the American press, but has received undue publicity in England because its author is the head of so powerful a journal. He has announced that after this war, if the democratic white members of the United Nations wish to do so, they should be graciously permitted to enter the American Union. His permission awaits them. Of course England must give up her King and her aristocracy to do so, but otherwise he sees few obstacles. Even France and Latin Americans might be permitted to enter our Union, which would then doubtless make a League of Nations unnecessary and take over the task of patrolling the world. He would naturally be ready to take in Canada, Australia, and New Zealand, and by this plan he has achieved the distinction of being the first American ever to propose that the American Union should extend beyond both the Pacific and the Atlantic. At least, it is no such unblushing demand that the United States alone dominate the future world as has marked the utterances of Henry Luce with his demand for an "American Century." Both proposals, however, are distinguished by the same repelling condescension, national arrogance, and overweening American self-esteem.

As for the Colonel himself, one of his employees once amusingly described him as "a cross between a Russian Grand Duke and Dogberry, with a liberal dose of plutocracy," but this is surely too severe if the Colonel is to be credited with the good things that the *Tribune* does, and especially with his fight for the independence of the press. It is undeniable that he is an able, if crabbed, journalist. He assumes full authority over his daily's development. Within his office he has been the unchallenged monarch of all he surveys since his cousin, Joseph Medill Patterson, went to New York to become the head of that phenomenal tabloid the New York *Daily News.* Up to that time the cousins had shared the direction of the *Tribune* and had frequent differences of opinion, which were successfully reconciled, however, though the editorial writers and executives could never be sure in advance which of the cousinly opinions would dominate at a given moment. Today the Colonel's mind is reflected by the *Tribune,* for he himself is inconsistent, constantly shifts his ground, is arrogant, and nationalistic to the full of the sinister meaning of the modern Know-Nothingism so rudely broken in on by this war. The Colonel plays an increasingly large role in the Associated Press and is conspicuous in other press gatherings. But he cannot lay claim to being popular with the fraternity, however much he may be looked up to because of his achievements, his great means, his power, and his obstinate fearlessness and courage.

Under the Colonel's management the *Tribune* has risen to great financial success and maintained it despite depressions, wars, and periods of great unpopularity. It stands as a product of the fierce newspaper warfare which was for generations carried on in the city of Chicago and gradually resulted in the destruction of one morning newspaper after another, until the *Tribune* almost alone survived in the morning field. In that warfare the *Tribune* played frequently an unworthy, yes, a despicable role. More than any other paper it helped to make impossible the success of the Chicago *Record-Herald* when James Keeley, long the distinguished managing editor of the *Tribune,* took over the *Record-Herald* for some rich men who wished to establish a worthy rival of the McCormick daily. With the aid of the corrupt city government and its subservient police, the other newspapers of Chicago made success impossible for the *Record-Herald*. Dealers were terrorized, stands smashed, copies of the *Record-Herald* destroyed, men beaten, slugged, gravely injured, until its sale was made impossible. This in the second largest American city! When Mr. Field's *Sun* appeared, the *Tribune* again threatened newsdealers with the loss of the privilege of selling the *Tribune* unless they declined to handle the *Sun*. In this case, however, violent measures were not resorted to, and after a year the *Tribune* abandoned its vicious tactics, so that the *Sun* has no difficulty now in getting on the newsstands.

The *Tribune* has for long been in a position to snap its fingers at any advertiser if it so wishes. It is a "commercialized newspaper." To use its own words: "The Chicago *Tribune* is not a philanthropic institution nor is it a religious or a political institution. It is a *commercial* institution." Exalting its virtue, it adds: "The *Tribune* is so prosperous that no bribe is of even passing interest. It is the weak newspaper with regular deficits that the 'interests' pick up cheap to serve as a tool" — as to the truth of which one may have one's doubts. Its able business management has always studied its field with the greatest care and adjusted the paper to it; wherever possible it has harmonized editorial policy with its business progress. It has spent money freely to obtain special service from correspondents all over the world and to purchase sensations; but its sensations usually — there are exceptions — never interfere with the popularizing of its news columns. Among its foreign correspondents have often been men of outstanding ability and of international renown; yet of late years other newspapers, notably the New York *Times,* have out-stripped it.

Like many another big daily, it throws away most of the news it receives and often cuts the Associated Press reports to snippets because of lack of space. Since it is a newspaper obviously made, above all else, to sell and not to educate or to convey information, it constantly slights national, state, and municipal matters of great importance. In its local news it is as biased and inaccurate as many of our metropolitan dailies, and it has never hesitated to reveal malice in its reports of the doings and utterances of those whom it does not like; there are plenty to accuse it justly of falsification; its news reports are not beyond question. The *New Republic* in its supplement of March 17, 1937 spoke of its conduct in the election of 1936 as "one of the most slanderous campaigns in the entire history of American journalism." It has always catered not only to the city of Chicago, but to the surrounding territory in the states near by. For years it has claimed that it dominated the votes of the electorate in this great territory — by no means always a truthful assertion. It would be idle, however, to deny the great influence that the paper has exercised in this rural field, and even in neighboring cities. If the Ku Klux Klan had a brief life in Illinois, it undoubtedly prospered while it lived because of the *Tribune's* aid. That the paper could not have pursued its isolationist policy as it did if it had not had large community support has been pointed out. It is true, however, that it lost 63,000 readers for the morning edition in the twelve months following March 31, 1942.

Beyond question Colonel McCormick has made his journal "live" and the center of much controversy and public interest. There are often straightforwardness, directness, and forcefulness in the statement of the newspaper's opinions, and sometimes most useful realism. When it comes to belles-lettres, it has often failed. The *Tribune* is not always authoritative in arts and letters. In the past its musical criticisms were often condemned by resolutions of the Chicago musical societies. Its book-reviewing is far superior. Its editorial page, as said, hits hard and effectively, but a large percentage of the readers of its news columns have shunned its editorial page as if it were pestilent. It has for generations been disliked and despised by those who have made the profoundest contributions to the social, civic, educational, and moral progress of the city. If the good opinion of the men and women of brains and character in a given community is the truest test of a newspaper's greatness, then the *Tribune,* despite its fine qualities, has stood very low in the scale.

CHAPTER XIV

Frank Knox and His DAILY NEWS

PAGE FRANK KNOX! Vice President Wallace has declared there should always be a Horatio Alger in America. He meant that we should always have with us the American success story of the boy who started from the bottom with nothing and wound up at the top by hard labor, by astuteness, and by achieving millions. Well, Frank Knox, as he sits across the Cabinet table from Henry Wallace, must give the Vice President no end of cheer and comfort, for he is the perfect type of the hero of a Horatio Alger romance. Now the Lord High Admiral of the American war fleet and a member of the Cabinet, to say nothing of the ownership of one of the greatest and most remunerative American newspapers, Frank Knox, originally William Franklin Knox, began work as a newsboy at a salary of $2.25 a week. If ever there was a home-town boy who made good, Knox is he. On the face of his record this would seem to indicate a man of outstanding ability, an executive of tremendous driving force, of broad vision, of statesmanlike quality. Mr. Knox possesses hardly one of these traits.

The truth is that, as in the case of so many other Horatio Algers, luck has played a considerable part in his rise, and that if his career is analyzed, he appears possessed of only ordinary ability aside from his unusual gifts as a newspaper manager. He has a parochial viewpoint and so limited an understanding of the great problems of this shattered world as to make it obvious that he can contribute nothing in that direction to the war effort. It cannot even be claimed for him that he is a well and thoroughly educated man, or master of his own language. His very rise to the Cabinet was not due to any popular demand or to any sudden discovery that he had just the qualities needed in the head of the navy during the rearming days of 1940. It was due solely to the fortuitous circumstances that one morning it popped into Mr. Roosevelt's head that he might induce the American people to believe that by inviting into his Cabinet two prominent Republicans he was creating a union government of Republicans and Democrats to confront the Fascist dictators

[138]

in the name of a united people. It was easy for him to choose Henry L. Stimson for the War Department, because he had been in that job once before and had long been a warm supporter of the President's foreign policy. Mr. Knox, however, had been calling F. D. R. all kinds of uncomfortable names, had been insisting that we must get rid of the President if the Republic was to survive, and also that this country must stay out of active war.

If the President hesitated over this, it was not for long. After all, Frank Knox had been the Republican candidate for Vice President two years before and therefore was a perfectly good symbol. Fitness for the Navy Department? None whatever; that was never even considered. It was just a political move and the navy had to accept what it got. Frank Knox honestly said on taking office that he knew nothing about the navy, and his career as Secretary has proved that he told the truth. As he himself put it: "Any layman would be a damned fool to get himself mixed up in the professional business of trying to fight a naval war. . . . My job is to find out what the top admirals want to put across, talk it over with them, and then do my damnedest to see that the job gets done as economically and as efficiently as possible." If there were those who remarked then that nothing could illustrate more clearly than these words Frank Knox's lack of knowledge of the true function and duty of the civilian head of army or navy to direct and control the top admirals and generals, or his complete ignorance of the history of the army and navy in war-time, why, these critics were just miserable carpers, who, as Mrs. Roosevelt would say, were obviously actuated merely by hatred of the President. So Frank talks gaily to the press, to the public, and to Congressional committees as if he really were an authority and knew all about things.

It is rumored, however, that once he did blush when, after telling a Congressional committee that Dakar was only 800 miles "below" Gibraltar, he was sharply told that it was actually distant some 2,000 miles. And he must have been a trifle annoyed that his announcement that "the navy is ready" appeared just when the Japanese had struck and so badly damaged our unready fleet at Pearl Harbor. His engaging frankness was demonstrated by his admitting publicly that the numerous magazine articles which had appeared over his name since he entered the Navy Department were ghost-written for him. He saw nothing wrong in that and made haste to point out that he had hand-somely rewarded the writers who helped him to put over this swindle by giving them a considerable percentage of the checks sent him by the magazines for the use of his name. That in giving it he deceived the public never occurred to him. A go-getter of this type really must not be expected to waste time in delicately considering people's feelings or to have a fine sense of the fitness of things. Indeed, if he had been afflicted with any sense of ethical considerations, he would not have been able to enter the President's Cabinet, and then where would the country have been? No doubt the Japanese would have burned Seattle.

So Frank Knox has never been troubled by his entering the Cabinet so soon after he had fired broadside after broadside at his new boss from all the intellectual mortars, anti-aircraft weapons, and 16-inch turreted guns he possessed. As long as the President understood that calling him names was, as Wendell Willkie explained a similar turn-about a year later, all just a bit of friendly campaign badinage, why, what difference did it make? Who would let a little thing like describing the President of the United States as a man seeking to ruin our institutions keep the denouncer from jumping into the ruiner's Cabinet to help save us from the dangers ahead? Not Frank Knox. True, he had liked so well the volleys he had fired at F. D. R. during the 1938 campaign that he brought those high indictments together — doubtless with some ghostly aid — in a pamphlet the year after the campaign. Therein this good-natured raillery that Frank Knox passed out to his nice, gullible Republican audiences is embalmed for all time. He called it: *We Planned It That Way,* using a phrase that the President had made famous and it contained some "hot ones," one of the best being his charge that the President was "raping democracy" and grafting "political coercion onto the American system."

Another was Frank Knox's assertion that "any discussion of the New Deal concerns the misuse of public funds. No one likes to think, let alone say, we have in public office men who are guilty of wrongdoing. The facts are as they are." His next point was that we had in Washington "a federal Administration that issues false and misleading statements to undermine public confidence in private enterprise. The facts are as they are." Again he wrote: "No one likes to think, let alone say, we have in Mr.

Roosevelt a Chief Executive who has to be continually watched lest he slip over legislation depriving the people of more of their rights. The facts are as they are." As for the New Deal propaganda machine, Colonel Knox wrote in this pamphlet that it "is the equal, if not the superior, of the machines set up to praise Stalin, Hitler and Mussolini; it is a machine which functions along lines quite similar to the organizations of Stalin, Hitler and Mussolini; it is a machine which has been set up in open contempt of laws prohibiting using public funds this way." He denounced the President for spending huge sums upon press agents employed "to exploit the Administration," and he demanded that Congress "force the Administration to obey the law." His motive, he asserted, was only "the maintenance of our traditional American form of democratic government." How those two jolly souls, the two Franks, must rock with laughter when they recall that pamphlet and the 1938 campaign!

But all Frank Knox's gems are not in that pamphlet. According to the Baltimore *Sun,* in a speech at Waterbury, Connecticut, he got off this remarkable literary nugget:

The Federal Government, attempting to substitute its arbitrary judgment for the combined wisdom and energy of these millions, is a preposterous King Canute attempting to sweep back the sea with a broom. Nature has twice punished us for this monstrosity with a ruinous drought.

As far back as 1935 Frank Knox sounded a warning tocsin that if Mr. Roosevelt were not retired in 1936 *"perdition is just around the corner."* In Toledo he asserted that "it is my sober and solemn judgment that four more years of such a government may destroy our system of free enterprise and our system of constitutional government." He told the North Carolina Republicans that the President's "political" use of relief funds was "a national scandal." Under F. D. R., he said, "no life insurance policy is safe; no savings account secure." But the future Secretary of the Navy was too busy to reply to General Hugh Johnson, who during the 1938 campaign listed nine statements made by Knox and declared them to be "false, known by him to be false, and made with intent to deceive."

So there Frank sits in the Cabinet, a model of patriotic abnegation and of the subordination of his own views to the nation's needs. Cheerfully he is now part and parcel of that propaganda machine that is "the equal, if not the superior, of the machines set up to praise Stalin, Hitler and Mussolini." He is part of the group of radicals who, he asserted, were compelling Congress to embark "upon a course far away from the American form of government and toward a dictatorial form of government," with "perdition just around the corner." There, with complete self-sacrifice, he silently watches the President undermining public confidence in private enterprise. He, too, is a confederate of those who are making no life insurance safe, and no savings account secure.

From one point of view the President made no mistake in choosing Secretary Knox for his Cabinet, for, like the President and Wendell Willkie, he was more than ready to change his announced position of opposition to our entering the war. Thus, when testifying on July 2, 1940 before the Senate Naval Affairs Committee, Colonel Knox stated in the most flat-footed way that he would not favor sending any of our boys to Europe under any circumstances. Senator Holt asked him: "Even if the vital interests of the United States can best be served by sending our boys over there?" To this Colonel Knox replied: "Let me say this again, so there will be no doubt about it. My position has consistently been from the first that we ought to aid them in a moral and economic way, never in manpower." Senator Holt next asked him "if the moral and economic way would not be sufficient for them to win, would you feel that we should go the rest of the way?" Again Secretary Knox replied: "No." More of the colloquy follows:

SENATOR HIRAM W. JOHNSON (R. Cal.): What do you mean by "short of war"?

KNOX: I mean everything short of sending military assistance, either navy or army assistance.

JOHNSON: Now you would not go to war under any circumstances in this particular misadventure that is occurring in Europe, would you?

KNOX: That is right.

JOHNSON: You never, on any occasion, would attempt to send our boys, as we term it, abroad in an European controversy?

KNOX: That is right.

CHAIRMAN WALSH: Colonel Knox, several members of the committee have asked me to ask you this question: Does the committee understand that you favor moral economic aid to the Allies through the sale by the United States of goods, products, and munitions by the businesses and citizens of the United States, but you do not favor direct economic aid to the Allies by the United States government itself, or any steps by the United States government which will involve this country in war?

KNOX: That is my conviction.

Exactly one year later, on June 30, 1941, Secretary Knox told the Governors' Conference at Boston that "the time to use our navy to clear the Atlantic of the German menace is at hand. . . . Now is the time to put in motion the huge machine we have been building since the war began. We can insure, beyond the shadow of a doubt, the defeat of the pagan force, and insure victory for Christian civilization" — this, be it noted, was six months before Pearl Harbor and constituted so deliberate a threat to Hitler as alone to justify him in declaring war upon the United States. Indeed, as time went on, Mr. Roosevelt used Secretary Knox to make speeches which were obviously intended as trial balloons to find out what the public reaction would be. Thus, on October 1, 1941, Colonel Knox made an address before the American Bar Association which the White House later certified through Mr. Early, the President's secretary, had been approved by the White House. In it Colonel Knox declared — two months before we entered the war — that the foreordained outcome of this struggle would be domination of the oceans by the United States and England. These are his exact words: "It is the hope of the world that sea-power for the next hundred years at least will reside in the hands of the two great nations which now possess that power, the United States and Great Britain." This was certainly a much more modest declaration than Hitler's boast that the Third Reich would dominate the world for a thousand years.

Just how did Frank Knox rise to his high position in newspaperdom? Well, by the development of real management ability and intense application, together with an undoubted sense of civic responsibility, plus complete conformity. He is a born Rotarian of the peculiarly American species of back-slappers, glib talkers, kind-hearted, cheery, convivial companions certain never to hurt anybody's feelings. Wherever he has worked he has been a pillar of the Church, a good and useful citizen who never disturbed anybody's night's rest by suggesting something new and unusual. He began his career as a newspaper-owner when but twenty-seven years old, after having served for a couple of years as reporter, city editor, and circulation manager of the Grand Rapids, Michigan, *Herald*. It was in 1901 that he purchased the Sault Ste. Marie, Michigan, *News* with $500 cash, a good part of which he had borrowed. When he sold it, in 1912, it was for $50,000. Those eleven years were by no means quiet and peaceful ones. He found a corrupt government and a rather bad town and he set to work to clean it up, and did. Once a bullet crashed through his office window, and at least once he wasn't afraid to use his fists upon a threatening, aggressive opponent. Undoubtedly the town profited by his residence in it, but in 1912 he moved on to Manchester, New Hampshire, with which state he was identified until he moved to Chicago after purchasing the Chicago *Daily News*. With some of the money earned in Sault Ste. Marie he purchased the Manchester *Leader,* within one year allying with it the Manchester *Union* and suppressing another rival, and he still owns the press monopoly he thus created.

In Manchester, too, he is remembered as a good citizen, and he resided there for fourteen years until he was lured away by William R. Hearst to become the publisher of Hearst's Boston *American,* Boston *Daily Advertiser,* and Boston *Sunday Advertiser*. Here he did so well that Mr. Hearst promoted him to be general manager of all the Hearst newspapers, which position he held until January 1, 1931, when he left for Chicago. Meanwhile this career of successful publication was interrupted by his military service during the first World War. As a boy he had left Alma College in Michigan to join Roosevelt's Rough Riders, serving with them from April to September 1898, and thereby he became an adorer of Roosevelt the First. That this devotion was sincere and complete is evident from the fact that he left the Republican Party when Theodore Roosevelt accepted the Bull Moose nomination. It would probably hurt his feelings to remind him that the Bull Moose platform contained some of the New Deal proposals which, until he entered the Cabinet, seemed to him the quintessence of Socialism. But he would have gone with Theodore even if the Rough Rider had come out for Communism. The friendship did not last indefinitely, however; there came a day when Mr. Knox discovered that after all his idol was not beyond a bit of double-dealing. Then the Colonel, like almost all the Bull Moosers, went back into the Republican fold until another Roosevelt lured him out of it.

In the World War he made a good if not a distinguished record. Commissioned a captain of field artillery on August 14, 1917, he was promoted to the rank of major on December 1 of that year, and served with the 153rd Artillery Brigade overseas from May 26, 1918 until February 10, 1919. For a time he kept up his interest in military affairs and was made colonel of the 206th Reserve Field Artillery Regiment. It is a testimony to the sincerity and the selflessness of his service in the World War that he began it by enlisting as a private soldier, although then forty-three years of age, a fact that he did not mention in compiling his biography for *Who's Who*. Neither did he list there the number of times he ran for office only to be defeated. But these were local and state offices which he sought until a year came when both the Republican nominations for President and Vice President were going begging. He announced his candidacy for the Presidency with his usual frankness, worked hard for it, and then gladly accepted the Vice-Presidency when Mr. Landon walked off with the top prize.

The great business opportunity of his life came to him when, after the death of Walter Strong, the trustees of the Strong estate decided to sell the estate's controlling stock interest in the *Daily News*. They consulted a number of people, including such a magnate of the press world as Adolph S. Ochs. All those interviewed said: "If you can get Frank Knox, you are made." The Colonel, in partnership with Theodore T. Ellis, bought the Strong stock and later acquired the Ellis holdings. The *Daily News* was a great institution when he and Mr. Ellis bought it. It was a genuine part of Chicago, and had always been owned and edited by men who had grown up in that city and were devoted to its interests. Moreover, during the ownership and direction of Victor Lawson, who was its founder and creator, the *Daily News* had built up one of the three or four outstanding special news services in the United States, notably strong in the foreign field, where it was represented by as distinguished a corps of correspondents as has ever been assembled by an American daily.

Mr. Knox was wise enough not to interfere with this service or to change the fundamental character of the paper. He has always published clean and decent papers, except for the period of his association with Hearst. None the less, it cannot be said that the *Daily News* stands as high now as it did under Lawson and Strong. The reason for this is probably that the Colonel has not a real Chicago background, and that he has gone actively into Republican politics. Will Irwin once said that the *Daily News* under Lawson was "an honest newspaper, first, last and all the time. . . ." I doubt, however, if Will Irwin could today say of it as he also did that "it goes far beyond any contemporary in allegiance to the truth." It always injures the independence and the standing of a daily when the owner runs for office; whether justly or unjustly, the public then regards with suspicion the utterances of the editorial page. It was impossible for Frank Knox to become one of the standard-bearers of the Republican Party and not support all the party's candidates at an election. Today there is criticism that independent civic organizations receive much less publicity and much less support in their campaigns since Frank Knox took the *Daily News* over.

Today it ranks rather as a conservative Republican organ with occasional lapses into independence — Mr. Knox, for example, to his credit, has demanded a break with the protective-tariff policies of his old party when this war is over. Indubitably he showed courage and independence when he advocated the Roosevelt war-headed international policies, for Chicago was strongly anti-war. Actually it affected neither his circulation nor his advertising. Indeed, he added 25,000 readers in 1940 to those that he had in 1939, and the circulation in 1942 was 443,057. As for his attitude toward labor, he was willing in 1936 that his reporters and editors should join the American Newspaper Guild, and he denied the charge that they had been intimidated in the matter of joining. When Heywood Broun asked him to post upon the bulletin board of the editorial department a notice that his employees were free to join the Guild without danger from the "payroll axe," the Colonel declared "the employees of the News have always been given to understand that the management of this newspaper has no concern with their political, economic, social or religious beliefs and affiliations. From the first talk about the Guild it has been understood in this office that any man who wished to join it was free to do so. That was our position, is our position, and will continue to be our position."

It would be wrong, however, to portray Secretary Knox as being as friendly to labor as are his other associates in the New Deal Administration. True, he has upheld the forty-hour week, but only on the ground that its abolition "would result in confusion and delay in the war program." On the other hand he has advocated our freezing of open and closed union shops for the duration of the war. His attacks upon the Wagner Labor Act continued until he entered the Cabinet of the Administration which had drawn that act and of the President who signed it; in 1938 Colonel Knox asserted that it had "fomented more strikes, more labor disturbances, and fostered more class feeling than any piece of legislation ever written into the statute books of the United States." He was then also calling for the indefinite suspension of the Social Security contributions for both employers and employees "on the express condition that the money thus saved be earmarked for men and women put to work in the ranks of the unemployed." Even since Pearl Harbor the Colonel is said to have declared that to call in labor as such to help speed up production through labor-management committees would be "bolshevism."

When he was asked if he officially approved of Rear Admiral W. H. P. Blanding's public statement at Macon, Georgia, in November 1941 inciting to criminal lawlessness and violence, the Secretary replied: "I am in thorough accord with the sentiments thus expressed." The Admiral, referring to the cessation of labor in war plants elsewhere by order of "misguided local leaders," had said: "I am confident that no such stoppage of work can happen here, but if it should come about that any of these disloyal citizens shall [*sic*] approach you with any such suggestion, I hope you will ride them out of town on a rail as if they were wearing swastikas on their sleeves." This is but one more example of the fact that under Mr. Roosevelt Cabinet members ride their horses in various directions.

His labor critics don't allow you to forget long that Colonel

Knox once made a radio address in Chicago under the auspices of the Crusaders, an anti-labor, semi-Fascist organization set up by big business which is said to have been watched pretty carefully by the Federal authorities since this war began. Mr. Knox's natural conservatism, and the company he keeps, are best illustrated by some of those who are the directors of the *Daily News*. These are J. E. Otis, of the Central Trust Company of Illinois and a director of various public utilities, of other banks, and of the Dawes Pure Oil Company; Max Epstein, of the General American Transportation Company; John Stewart, President of Quaker Oats and a director of the International Harvester Company; George E. Scott, president of American Steel Foundries; and Sewell Lee Avery, who is affiliated with the United States Gypsum and Montgomery Ward. Several of these have contributed to reactionary, Red-baiting organizations. As George Seldes sarcastically remarks: "These men are proof that the *Daily News* is not controlled by big business interests; it is merely directed by men of big business."

His employees on the *Daily News* like Frank Knox very much, both as a man and as employer. They give glowing accounts of him as a publisher and, according to Raymond Gram Swing, have never seen him come to what they considered a fundamentally wrong decision on a major business issue. They say that they have again and again seen him do the right thing when it cost him a good deal to do so. Mr. Swing insists that Frank Knox has refused to subordinate the *Daily News* to his political life and that it is not his political organ. One of his best reporters nearly lost his job by asking Colonel Knox how he wanted him to write a certain story. When the Colonel was trying for the Presidential nomination, Howard Vincent O'Brien, a columnist, criticized the Colonel on the *Daily News's* editorial page by saying: "I am convinced that Frank Knox would be a good President, efficient, worthy of all trust; but I am equally convinced that as President he would do things that are utterly abhorrent to him now, and perforce leave undone practically all the things he now advocates" — the correctness of which statement Mr. O'Brien's boss proved when he entered the Cabinet of the man he said he despised and detested. On the other hand, the *Daily News* has several times omitted Westbrook Pegler's articles, as when he attacked Governor Landon, and indirectly Colonel Knox. There is also at least one case when a Washington correspondent of the *Daily News,* who was criticizing an action of the Hoover Administration, was promptly warned by the home office to change his attitude.

Every evening when the Secretary of the Navy has finished his day's chore of listening to the top admirals and then doing his best to help them to get what they want speedily and economically, and has given out whatever good news he can to his newspaper conference — wisely suspended for many months after the Pearl Harbor disaster — he goes aboard the yacht *Sylph* in the Potomac River, on which craft he lives, calls up the *Daily News* and talks shop. Admirals and such are all very well in their way, but his heart is true to Poll and to the *Daily News.* The long-distance telephone comes into service and he gets his daily report of what has happened in *the* office. Doubtless the circulation and advertising figures are read to him; perhaps he gets reports of the reaction of the Chicago public to the events of the war and the big boss's speeches, and to the trial balloons which the Lord High Admiral sends up whenever the White House desires it. Then the Japs may do their worst, and the U-boats, too, but Frank is back on the job to which his heart belongs.

CHAPTER XV

The Marshall Field Newspapers

Fortune has written that Marshall Field, the third of his name, will be the last very rich man to found daily newspapers in this country. That seems a venturesome statement if one considers the great fortunes that still remain, despite taxes and death duties. One thing is clear, however: no other rich man can possibly be found to make greater mistakes in putting huge sums into journalism, or to produce on the whole less for his investment than has Mr. Field. He has declared — and then withdrawn the statement — that he was perfectly willing to lose all his means in backing newspapers and that that was his affair. Like the other rich men in journalism who entered it entirely ignorant of the business, he has needlessly wasted much of his money, has achieved little that has altered the profession and nothing that has uplifted it. It is true that his New York tabloid, *PM,* has distinct features and does without advertisements, but as the Chicago *Sun* stands at this writing, it is "just another" daily, interesting only by reason of its contrast to the Chicago *Tribune.*

The *Sun* is a profound disappointment to all the liberal forces in Chicago which had for years hoped that the *Tribune's* practical monopoly of the morning field would be challenged by a powerful journal capable of genuine social and political leadership. It is true that the *Sun* has grown rapidly; at the end of its first full year it had attained a circulation of 275,000 copies and printed no less than 11,000,000 lines of advertising. This is no inconsiderable achievement, especially in view of the fact that in the first few months of the *Sun's* existence the *Tribune* waged a nasty and severely injurious campaign against its new rival in the circulation field by threatening newsdealers with withdrawal of the *Tribune* from their stands if they also handled the *Sun*. Yet I have found no one to assert that the *Sun* has lived up to its intellectual and professional opportunities. There is much complaint not only that it has the faults of the conventional big-city daily, but that it is the Chicago *Sun* printed in Chicago for residents of Chicago largely by non-Chicagoans who do not know the territory which they are trying to serve. Just as Thomas W. Lamont turned the New York *Evening Post* over to men wholly inexperienced in journalism, so Mr. Field entrusted the birth of his Chicago daily to editors imported from distant spheres. Many liberals feel that it has not yet established its political independence, nor won esteem for authoritative editorial utterances.

Beyond question its faults were in large measure due to the conditions in which it was created. The year 1941 was an extremely bad one for the development of a journalistic enterprise. Mr. Field, on coming to his decision, turned to the liberal Nashville *Tennessean* for his manager and publisher in the person of Silliman Evans, a Texan of ability and experience. Mr. Evans did everything in his power to bring the new daily to life with the utmost speed. Arriving in Chicago in the middle of September, he published his first issue on December 4, 1941, three days before Pearl Harbor. Actually Mr. Evans labored under semi-war conditions; for example, the voluntary censorship was already on and newspapermen in droves were seeking government positions or overseas assignments. In Mr. Evans's defense it is stated that with every desire to obtain a Chicago-trained staff, he found himself largely unable to do so. It was almost impossible to wean employees from the newspaper that so falsely calls itself the "World's Greatest." Whatever else may be said about the Chicago *Tribune,* it does have the loyalty of its staff.

The fact that Chicago had only four dailies all told gave Mr. Evans a limited range in which to look for recruits, and many men would not leave their jobs for the uncertainty of the Field venture. Forced to look elsewhere, he induced Turner Catledge to leave the Washington bureau of the New York *Times,* lured Irving Brant of the St. Louis *Star-Times,* took H. R. Knickerbocker from Hearst to head the *Sun's* foreign staff, called Bascom Timmons, an experienced correspondent, to lead the *Sun's* staff in Washington, put in Rex Smith as editor and George DeWitt as managing editor. It was a group that could not last and it did not. Catledge, Brant, DeWitt, Smith and others have already resigned. Mr. Field has now become his own editor, participates in the daily editorial conferences, and, it is reported, has actually written several editorials himself. If he sticks to this, he will surely learn quickly a good many things about journalism he needs to know. The chief editorial writers are two younger men who, Mr. Evans believes, will in due course make names for themselves and the *Sun.* They were for some time aided by editorials from Irving Brant. But whether he did not see the need or could not fulfill it, Mr. Evans did not call to the editorial chair any outstanding editorial personality to win immediate attention and to clothe the editorial page with genuine authority.

Another difficulty was that the *Sun* was committed to the support of Franklin Roosevelt and our entering the war, and was printed in one of the territories most hostile to our joining in the international holocaust. The advantages Mr. Evans hoped to gain by opposing the isolationist policies of the *Tribune* instantly came to naught because of Pearl Harbor, after which the *Tribune* clamored for all-out war against Japan. Because of the threat of imminent war Mr. Evans could not even take the time to buy presses. Indeed, he was lucky to be able to share those of the *Daily News,* for obtaining new presses is no longer possible. It was an amazing achievement that Mr. Evans produced a daily in such a short time, even if he had the advantage of unlimited sums of money to work with — Mr. Field's fortune is a mere $164,000,000. Millions can buy a great deal in this world besides being able to hire dash and enterprise in the overcoming of obstacles, but they cannot buy a soul or ideals for a newspaper. Mr. Field has plainly no real idealism to offer despite his upholding of the New Deal, and he has given no personal leadership. His first objective — to humble the *Tribune* — was born of a defensible hatred. His second, to support Mr. Roosevelt and his policies, was apparently not based upon any deep economic and political philosophy. At least I have not found in the *Sun* any burning advocacy of radical social changes, nor any clear understanding of the fundamentals of the world revolution in which we are involved, in which this war is surely only one phase, however great.

Doubtless this was too much to expect from one who until a few years ago was largely a playboy and then suddenly decided that he would devote himself and his vast wealth to reforms and to public causes. Perhaps under the circumstances he had to concentrate attention upon his hates and war desires and to leave

the working out of a well-rounded policy for America to another time. The upshot is a journalistic product which leaves
most readers cold; they purchase an ugly newspaper, badly put
together, without marked individuality, and they see no reason
why they should be the ones upon whose reactions the editorial
writers are to rise to future greatness. It is possible, of course,
that the *Sun* may survive its birth pangs and achieve high standards. But those who refused to join its staff because of uncertainty as to the paper's future were not without reason. They
were justified in asking: what if Mr. Field should die suddenly
before the paper is earning money? It is certainly not a compelling necessity in Chicago, nor an established Chicago institution. Yet its remarkable possibilities were made clear when no
less than 220,000 prospective readers took the trouble to write
letters urging names for the new journal after Mr. Field and
Mr. Evans offered $10,000 in prizes for the best name for the
daily — the *Sun* is the outcome of that contest.

Mr. Field's journal offers much pabulum to its readers. It
has been said of it: "The *Sun's* personality is split one hundred
different ways; even more than the *Tribune* it offers all things
to all men." Thus it prints about 170 columns of editorial content daily by contrast with the 130 in the *News,* and it has done
its utmost to obtain all the amusement features and "comics"
that it can. But here the *Tribune* holds a monopoly of the very
best comic strips and the *Sun* cannot shake it. Perhaps if the
government had been successful in obtaining the Associated
Press service for the *Sun,* it might also have induced the courts
to declare the *Tribune's* present unquestioned monopoly of
Andy Gump, Little Orphan Annie, and other popular favorites another combination in restraint of trade. That would help
the *Sun* enormously, far more than the Associated Press news,
for, with humiliation must it be admitted, Chicago is a comic-
strip city in which adults by the tens of thousands turn to the
unending adventures of their favorite strip heroes before reading
the sports pages and then — perhaps — the war news. The sober-
est journalists admit with shame that a daily without strips
could not succeed in the Windy — and superficial — City. If
this is an indictment of our democracy and our public educational system, it cannot be gainsaid.

Nevertheless it would seem that if Mr. Field, instead of producing the present unattractive *Sun,* had deliberately undertaken to produce a New York *Times* in Chicago, he would have made a vastly more substantial contribution both to journalism and to the city which has produced his wealth. At least it would have shown whether the power of pure news, and plenty of it from all over the world, to draw masses of readers exists in Chicago or not. The *Sun* has a large group of special correspondents and prints the columns of a number of well-known commentators, despite its being handicapped by war-time paper stringency. But it is in its failure to develop the local field more carefully and voluminously that it has disappointed many who desire to be its ardent admirers and supporters. A heaven-sent opportunity for a Sir Galahad in journalism faced Mr. Field in that his city, or the city of his origin, is in the grip of one of the worst and most corrupt political rings to be found in the United States — one of the few remaining of the type that forty years ago made practically all our municipalities the public shame of America. Whether it was impossible for a new daily, dependent upon the city government for its opportunity to go on sale, to strike out at the ring; whether the prosperity of the Marshall Field store and Mr. Field's accumulated wealth made a frontal attack upon the machine impossible, or whether the cynical political friendship between Mr. Field's reforming hero, Franklin Roosevelt, and Boss Kelly prevented, the *Sun* has not as yet poured out vials of wrath upon the Kelly gang.

It is, of course, wholeheartedly for the war and most of the Roosevelt policies — it deals with the President's administrative weaknesses quite gingerly. It rightly champions the President's efforts for social security and greater opportunities for the workers, although it has not found it easy to get on with all the local union leaders. It is true that it serves a useful purpose in offering the alternative it does to the newspaper reader, who prior to the *Sun's* appearance had no choice save that of McCormick's *Tribune* or of Hearst's Chicago daily. That is why it has done as well as it has in gaining readers. But when one considers how tremendous the opportunity was which offered itself to Mr. Field and then views what he has done, it is pitiful that so much money has been paid out with such a relatively inadequate result. There are no substitutes in journalism for high character, high aims, effective and brilliant technique, and a fighting spirit.

To turn to Mr. Field's New York venture, it was started not by him alone, but by a group of owners brought together by the skillful persuasiveness of Ralph Ingersoll and lured also by the prospect of a crusading daily wholly without advertising and supporting the New Deal. It is characteristic of the way very rich men venture into journalism that when, well prior to the first issue of *PM,* I asked one of its backers what *PM* was to be, this sponsor confessed that he had no idea what it would advocate, or whether it would urge our going into the war, or what its specific objectives would be. His knowledge of the enterprise, to which he gave thousands of dollars, was limited to the fact that it was to be free from all temptation to knuckle under to advertisers, and that Ralph Ingersoll was to be its editor. *PM* started with a bang, but, as is so often the case, when it was no longer a novelty its circulation fell rapidly, and before long it came into the hands of the largest contributor to its funds, Mr. Field, who paid something to the other sponsors and now cheerfully meets all its large deficits. After three years of life *PM* reported a circulation of only 134,455, on April 1, 1943, but at this writing is claiming 200,000 readers. It is asserted that if *PM* can attract 250,000 a day it will be able to make both ends meet.

From the outset it did achieve a personality of its own. Its typographical originality is commendable, its make-up and readability are excellent, and it remains a refreshing contrast to the general run of tabloids. Mr. Ingersoll plainly had some new and worth-while ideas. Yet when this is said, there is not much to add, though it is today improving. At first, however, it was a dreadful mess, with an outstanding lack of character and news integrity. Its over-large staff was loaded down with Communists and "fellow travellers," which made it extremely fitting that there were in due course vigorous, if not bloody, office purges. Whether all the Stalinites are out is not clear. Like most Communistic enterprises its beginning was marked by a complete indifference to truth and by inaccuracy, whether deliberate or accidental or both, in its reporting. The viciousness of its attacks upon those, like Colonel Lindbergh, with whom it was at odds, was all its own. It set out to be a reckless, highly sensational, muckraking organ and it succeeded. It is much quieter and far more reliable now that Mr. Ingersoll is no longer its active editor, but it still does not appeal as a first-rate, trustworthy newspaper and its staff should be purged again. It does do a certain amount of useful spade work; it does often present phases of the Washington scene that deserve to be brought out and for this and for other reasons it is widely read by newspapermen in order to obtain tips and to watch its special articles. These men tell you, however, that they do not read it without many reservations. They appreciate scavenging, but not always this scavenger, whom they do not regard as an ornament of the profession.

Here again there was a fine opportunity which Mr. Field has so far muffed. There was a chance for a daily bent on doing in its field what the liberal weeklies have at times done in the past — printing facts the conventional newspapers will not handle, or which they overlook, and speaking up continuously for the underprivileged, the victims of hate and prejudice. It could have told the truth and shamed the journalistic and political devils. The prerequisite, however, was the establishment of a solid reputation for sincerity and integrity and ability in its news and its editorials. Curiously enough, I have found that *PM's* brethren on the Chicago *Sun* seem to respect *PM* least of all. Indeed, I have reason to believe that *PM* is one subject which Silliman Evans does not discuss with Mr. Field because of the extreme divergence of their views of that organ. But in its opposition to reaction and its undiscriminating adulation of Franklin Roosevelt and approval of everything that he does, *PM* remains steadfast. I suppose that all of its readers are convinced that when anything goes wrong in Washington it is due first to the machinations of big business, or second to the failure of many of Mr. Roosevelt's choices for important offices to live up to the ideals of the man who appointed them. Mr. Roosevelt personally appears impeccable, and a fourth and doubtless a fifth term absolutely essential to the welfare of the Republic — even if Mr. Ingersoll was drafted into the army contrary to his and to Mr. Field's wishes and the latter's public appeals to the selective service, which rightly decided that neither Mr. Ingersoll's contributions to *PM* nor the newspaper itself were so worth while as to make it necessary to excuse him from joining the army.

How great a service, if any, *PM* will furnish to a new organization of society when the war is over is difficult to estimate. Again the trouble is that there is no outstanding personality connected with this newspaper. I know well that men of the old-fashioned, four-square type of editor can be found only with difficulty, yet there are columnists in plenty, men and women, who make names for themselves and carry some weight, and it would not be impossible for Mr. Field to find a journalist whose personality itself would give immediate promise that *PM* meant to play fair with those whom it interviews, and would assure the public of its integrity and determination to lead toward liberal reforms. It now has no editorials worthy of the name, for an old-fashioned editorial page was never visualized. It was apparently held to be as superfluous as advertising. As in the case of the Chicago *Sun,* one can only hope that it will yet evolve and become a publication worthy of its possibilities before Mr. Field loses his interest in journalism.

CHAPTER XVI

Frank E. Gannett and His Chain

FRANK E. GANNETT is the *bête noire* of most liberals. In their eyes his offenses are many. He owns twenty-one newspapers. He is opposed to the extravagances and wastes of the New Deal. He is "a complete reactionary," hiding behind his National Committee to Uphold Constitutional Government, with which organization he did more than anyone else to defeat President Roosevelt's effort — quite needless as events soon proved — to enlarge and make over the Supreme Court. He has always been strenuously opposed to this country's going to war — especially into World War II. He has not favored our mixing into political affairs all over the world. He has charged that the Roosevelt Administration was responsible for the great depression, and has declared the Wagner Act "a potent factor in promoting strikes" and in discouraging production. Liberals admit that he occasionally has humanitarian ideas, but that does not save him, nor does the fact that he once offered his newspapers to both sides during the fight for the Tugwell Pure Food and Drug Bill for the expression of their opinions. Finally, he is decried as "a self-seeker"; he has openly sought the nominations for Governor of New York and President of the United States, and has cheerfully faced ridicule and criticism for doing so without the backing of important politicians. In addition, he served as vice-chairman of the Republican National Committee during the Congressional campaign and election of 1942.

To most of these indictments Mr. Gannett would undoubtedly plead guilty, though not to still one more, charging him with hostility to labor, and particularly his own labor. In January 1928 the Tri-City Newspaper Guild charged his company with using stool pigeons and strike-breakers during a printers' strike and discharging twenty-seven members of the union out of the twenty-nine he dropped when he amalgamated the Albany *Knickerbocker Press* and *News,* but I have found no real evidence to indicate hostility to the workers. As a matter of fact, Mr. Gannett has not only been deeply interested in plans for profit-sharing between capital and labor; he has decided not to leave his newspaper properties to his family and has provided for a foundation which will hold the common stock in his newspapers, or as much of it as belongs to him, in trust for the employees of his journals. The preferred stock is to be held largely by executives and employees and, after dividends have been paid to them, the remaining profits are to be used for "public, charitable, educational, and general philanthropic causes and purposes." There is to be a self-perpetuating board of directors of eleven, of whom eight must be working newspapermen, and each director must hold at least one hundred shares of stock. His farm paper, the *Agriculturist,* is to be directed by a manager chosen by the readers, with its profits turned into a fellowship fund for agricultural research. But even this remarkably broad-minded and unselfish plan to turn over his newspaper properties to the workers on them does not save him from the charge that he is essentially "anti-social," which is the epithet applied by some to all who do not favor the New Deal one hundred per cent.

As for Mr. Gannett's political ambitions, it is true that they represent a break with his earlier belief that a newspaperman and an owner of dailies should not take an active part in politics. It is certain that he became an active candidate for office not because of any selfish political ambitions, but because he honestly and sincerely felt that we had reached such a crisis in our national affairs that it was the duty of every citizen to do what he could to oppose the tendencies which, in his opinion, are rapidly undermining our American institutions. Few men would have the courage to do this, or possibly the lack of imagination necessary to a full understanding of what he risked. Most men would hesitate lest they run a quite insignificant race for such great prizes. I respect Mr. Gannett for having done so, believing that if there were more of this open and aboveboard seeking for the opportunity to hold public office, without standing in first with the political bosses, our public life would be better off. At the same time, I cannot recede from my position that it is best for the profession and the country to have newspaper-owners and editors take a self-denying oath so far as politics are concerned. There are few cases on record in which editors have really been successful in public life, or made noteworthy contributions in public office, and it is a sad fact that one of our worst Presidents was the editor who reached the White House.

Curiously enough, a remarkable aspect of Mr. Gannett's ownership of newspapers seems highly praiseworthy to many critics
and quite censurable to others. It is that when he purchases a
newspaper he permits it to continue the editorial policy which
it followed when he obtained control. Thus, when he acquired
the Hartford, Connecticut, *Times,* he purchased the most influential Democratic newspaper in New England outside of Boston. Most new Republican owners would promptly have made
the editorial page over and supported the other party. Mr. Gannett preferred to allow it to retain its individuality and the political beliefs that it had so long held. Those critical of his policy
say that he did it with his eyes solely on the profits of the counting-room, which they think would rapidly have diminished had
Mr. Gannett alienated its Democratic following. Had he done
the opposite, however, he would certainly have been attacked
as a selfish capitalist who jeopardized the welfare of the staff and
the future of the newspaper in order to impose his political ideas
upon the public. Not having done this, he is charged with
double-dealing — with supporting political theories with which
he does not agree, for purely financial reasons! In this case it is
certainly impossible to please or to satisfy everybody.

After most careful consideration, it seems to me that Mr. Gannett's policy is entirely defensible, especially if there are other
newspapers of a different political faith in the particular city involved. In Hartford, for example, there is the *Courant,* one of
the cleanest, ablest, and best edited of American newspapers. It
is strongly Republican. It would certainly have been a pity if the
Times had become another exponent of the doctrines of the
Republican Party. In other words, there is at stake the principle,
elsewhere touched upon, of having both sides, or all sides, of
political questions represented — at least in our largest communities — as vital to our democracy. Many years ago a conscientious stockholder in the Springfield *Republican* asked my judgment as to whether she could continue ethically to hold her
stock if that corporation carried out its purpose of purchasing
the competing newspapers in that city and continuing their
political policies, with which she was not in agreement. My
response was that while any press monopoly in any city is hateful to me, it seemed to me to be less objectionable if it pro-

vided the three different political viewpoints which in this case the company intended to express and has since expressed.

I do not think that Mr. Gannett can be charged with influencing his newspapers to boost him or his political ambitions. Indeed, when he sought the Presidential nomination he instructed his editors to treat his candidacy just as they would that of any other prominent citizen of Rochester. I am certain that if he had achieved either of the nominations which he sought, he would not have objected to his Democratic newspapers assailing his candidacy and showing up his weaknesses. He is a remarkable owner in the freedom he gives to the executives of his various properties. I have known cases in which he has expressed his desire to the various heads to have certain features appear, and they have not appeared. In other words, he upholds the principle of local autonomy within each shop, which is only just and proper in view of the fact that he holds the executives responsible for the financial success of the properties — a responsibility enhanced by the fact that a considerable amount of the stock of the Gannett newspapers is in the hands of the public. When it comes to advertising, it is true that in one respect Mr. Gannett has enforced his personal views — he has barred all liquor advertising.

For a time Mr. Gannett changed his policy. After the failure of Prohibition and the return of beer he felt that "no matter what my personal views may be, I have come to appreciate that it may be dangerous to exclude advertising not in conflict with the law. . . ." He thought then that exclusion might threaten free speech and a free press, but later on he returned to his earlier policy and again excluded this advertising. He was always an ardent Prohibitionist and still feels that liquor is one of the greatest enemies of human society. His antipathy to it dates back to his boyhood, when in the course of his hard struggle to maintain himself and to get ahead he was for a time, as a high-school student in Bolivar, New York, a bar-tender's helper in a local hotel. In his own words: "After watching booze ruin men I made up my mind that if I ever got a chance I would fight it," and fought it he has, consistently and courageously ever since.

No one can deny that Mr. Gannett publishes clean and decent

newspapers, both in their news and in their advertising columns, a fact that his critics do not begin to stress or praise adequately. His platform is that "the Gannett newspapers are dedicated to the welfare of all the people. Theirs is the pledge to publish each day clean, wholesome, educational, and entertaining newspapers. Knowing no selfish interest, no entangling obligation, each newspaper within this group can be, and is, fair, just and tolerant, ever sympathetic with the unfortunate and eager to present all sides of any question. Each of these newspapers has ever before it the idea of Lincoln, to be for and *of the People.*" The slogan of his newspapers is: "The integrity of a Gannett newspaper must never be questioned." Opinions will differ as to how rigidly this program has been lived up to. But certainly no suspicion of any corrupting influence has ever attached to the Gannett dailies. They are not afraid to present unpopular opinions, and they are conspicuous by their readiness to print criticisms of themselves and of their leading contributors in their letters-to-the-editor department. If editorially they are as a whole not among the most distinguished American newspapers, though some stand out, it must also be said of them that their appeal is chiefly to the middle class. There is no originality in their handling of the news, and they have most of the faults in presenting it that mark the majority of our dailies.

But Mr. Gannett has had the wisdom not to make them all look alike in make-up and typography as is the case with the Hearst and other chains; he has preserved their individuality, and he has not overloaded them with star contributors and special correspondents. Moreover, although they are directed in some degree from the central office, Mr. Gannett has avoided the mistakes of other chain managers and, like the Scripps-Howard owners, has not deprived them of their identification with their localities and has urged their devoting themselves to the upbuilding of their communities. He is eager that their editors and workers should be outstanding men in their towns. Indeed, as Frank Tripp, the general manager of the Gannett papers and Mr. Gannett's closest associate, has put it: "Frank's newspapers are as local as the town pump." Mr. Gannett has also been clever enough to avoid the tendency of chains to become top-heavy and over-costly at the top.

It remains to be pointed out that he has never founded a newspaper. His creative instinct has run exclusively in the direction of purchasing and amalgamating, of taking over the work of other men and improving upon it. His shrewdness lies in usually picking the right ones to acquire, and when he buys a daily his assuming control is usually marked by a dinner or reception in his honor given by the local Chamber of Commerce or merchants' association. Mr. Gannett invariably takes this opportunity to explain why he does not interfere with the old management, and why he holds to the belief that each of his papers should be part and parcel of the community from which it draws its subsistence. If any of his listeners feared, or hoped to find, a new first page on their breakfast tables, they were completely disappointed.

There is one criticism of Mr. Gannett that would seem to have much justification. It is that he is apt to take the color of those with whom he is. He is warm-hearted, sympathetic, sincere, and generous, and those qualities make him inclined to sympathize with the group he may be in contact with. He reads and appreciates liberal publications, even when they criticize him. None the less, it is his conservative viewpoint that undoubtedly controls when there is a conflict between the two schools of thought. But it should never be alleged that his opposition to the New Deal is due to any lack of appreciation of the pressing need for bettering the welfare of the masses. He is profoundly interested in the progress of all the people. If he seems not always to work for this along lines that are open to him, it must again be charged to his temperament, perhaps to his associations with the men of whom he sees the most, rather than to any deliberate espousal of non-progressive doctrines or policies. Even so severe a critic as George Seldes declares him to be "sincere, humanitarian, a man of good intentions." Mr. Seldes's chief criticism of Mr. Gannett is that the latter is "one of the most confused persons in public life today."

That there is some justice in this charge is doubtless true, but Mr. Gannett has conscientiously endeavored to keep himself abreast of what has been going on in the world, and, on the occasion of one lengthy trip to Europe, wrote a series of articles for his papers which showed an excellent appreciation of the real situation abroad and of the threat of the second World War. When it became apparent that under Mr. Roosevelt's leadership we were deviously heading into that second World War, Mr. Gannett redoubled his efforts to keep the country at peace, and while not seeking to influence the individual policies of his newspapers, placed himself squarely on record as being opposed to our entering the war and did everything in his power to defeat Mr. Roosevelt's candidacy for the third term. In this he was, of course, but exercising the American citizen's inalienable right of dissent from those in office. He is a truly patriotic man.

The worst indictment of Mr. Gannett's judgment is to be found in his having borrowed in 1928 the sum of $2,781,158.30 from the International Paper and Power Company. In May 1929 the Federal Trade Commission brought out, through a cross-examination of Archibald R. Graustein, the president of the company, the fact that it owned some $10,000,000 of the securities of twelve newspapers, in addition to having just previously purchased a half interest in the Boston *Herald* and its evening edition, the *Traveler*. Mr. Gannett explained that, when attempting some rather extensive financing in the fall of 1928, he found the money market so unfavorable for the issuance of securities direct to the public, he fell back upon an advantageous offer from the power company, instead of going to his bank for aid. The four newspapers affected were Mr. Gannett's Brooklyn *Eagle,* the Albany *Knickerbocker-Press,* and Albany *Evening News,* and the Ithaca *Journal-News.* As soon as the revelations appeared, Mr. Gannett wrote a letter to Mr. Graustein in which he said:

We entered into the arrangement in good faith; it was a straightforward, entirely legitimate business transaction, mutually advantageous and desirable, which should not be questioned; but there has been criticism of the policy of your company holding even a minority interest in a newspaper. Without discussing this contention, I feel it is better to remove all possibility of a misinterpretation of the motive which actuated our relationship.

With this letter he sent a check for the total amount of the indebtedness of his newspapers to the paper trust.

It was never alleged that Mr. Gannett's newspapers had been influenced by this business arrangement. Indeed, they had consistently favored the retention of power resources by the public. But Mr. Gannett should have realized that as soon as there was public knowledge of this arrangement it was bound to cast suspicion upon the independence of his entire chain. As it was, the revelation did affect the progress of the Brooklyn *Eagle*. It was in 1928 and 1929 that Mr. Gannett expanded his chain most; he then purchased the Hartford *Times,* the Rochester *Democrat and Chronicle,* the Albany *Knickerbocker-Press,* the Albany *Evening News,* and the Ogdensburg *Republican-Journal*. The prices he paid for them in that get-rich-quick era were incredibly high. His technique was to acquire them by the aid of borrowed sums and to sell preferred stock or bonds or both to the public, while retaining the common stock for himself. As rapidly as possible he then paid off his loans.

Mr. Gannett's judgment also erred when he sought to stop the sale of a book called *Under Cover* which unfairly and even libelously attacked him and the Committee for Constitutional Government of which he is the head. It is a typical muckraking book, containing insinuations and misstatements, and Mr. Gannett had full reason to be aggrieved. His putting book-sellers and news companies on notice that they were liable to suits for libel if they handled the book laid him open to the charge that he was trying to suppress the truth. It actually greatly stimulated the sale of the offending volume, as is usually the case under such circumstances. He should have sued at once, or taken action in other ways — or borne this injustice with the resignation of persons who are similarly ill treated by the press or by book publishers and usually cannot, for one reason or another, obtain the redress to which they are entitled. In England the law is so strict that book publishers there are often afraid to publish statements already in print in the United States relating to men no longer living. Mr. Gannett would certainly have had justice done him there, and should have received it here.

It is certainly not true that his political ambitions have played any great part in Mr. Gannett's expanding his chain. Once asked if he had any definite purpose in extending his group, such as the endeavor to influence public opinion in increasing measure, he replied no, that he merely enjoyed enlarging his personal field of activity. In other words, he had no more conscious motive than that which leads a man to buy six more drug stores if he has made a success of one or two. He might readily have gone on and added many more dailies to his chain, but the coming of the collapse of 1929, and especially his inability to carry on with the Brooklyn *Eagle,* checked any further developments until the 1940s. It was understood at the time that in reselling the *Eagle* he lost two million dollars. He was undoubtedly wise in taking that loss, for that historic old paper, which once exercised such a commanding influence in Brooklyn, has steadily gone downhill. In making his purchases Mr. Gannett has concentrated upon New York State with three exceptions, his Hartford, Connecticut, Danville, Illinois, and Plainfield, New Jersey, papers. He has always been devoted to the state in which he was born. His latest purchase was announced on June 18, 1943. It was the thirty-nine-year-old Binghamton, New York, *Press,* which made the total number of his newspapers twenty-one.

Mr. Gannett's newspapers are successful because of careful management, clever buying, constant, careful supervision, conventional make-up, and his reduction of the evils of chain ownership to a minimum. It is to their credit that they make no pretense of being anything else than what they are. If Mr. Gannett himself is not one of the most brilliant of our newspaper managers, he is beyond doubt one of our ablest publishers. He has had the satisfaction of demonstrating on a considerable scale his ability to succeed in the newspaper field. He is not a splurger and he has proved that he has no desire to increase his personal wealth, and no unwise ambitions for his children, by his provision for the foundation already cited and for the passing of his dailies to those who create them.

CHAPTER XVII

Scripps-Howard and the United Press

WHEN ONE RECALLS the place held by the Scripps-Howard news-papers twenty-five years ago in the regard of the liberals and progressives of that day, they now strongly suggest champagne without the cork. They still believe themselves to be liberal or-gans of public opinion, and they are in their progressiveness su-perior to the great run of newspapers. They still have brilliant men writing for them and evince a greater interest in labor than most dailies. They have a better interpretation of many overseas events than most. But the old spirit of championing the under-dog, of battling for the liberal way of life in America, is no longer there. I do not sympathize with those intolerant New Dealers who charge everyone with treason if he does not go along one hundred per cent with every phase of Mr. Roosevelt's winding course and who now say that the Scripps-Howard newspapers have gone completely over to the enemy's camp and lay the whole blame upon Roy W. Howard, the head of the chain. The Scripps-Howard dailies have not done so. But it is evident that there is far less reforming spirit, far less eagerness to fight for the people's rights and to champion new and even unpopular causes at any cost than there was two decades ago.

The responsibility for this does lie at Mr. Howard's door. There is no doubt that he has journalistic ability and made his mark with Scripps in the United Press when he was still an ex-tremely young man. The great rise of the United Press was in considerable part due to his energy and enterprise, as well as to those of the remarkable group of men who were, and are, its heads. But Mr. Howard is obviously not as deeply devoted to reform and to the liberal cause as was Edward W. Scripps, who, with his brother, founded the chain of newspapers and the United Press. A suppliant for aid for a good cause was rarely turned away by Scripps; Mr. Howard is not as easily moved. But his refusal to approve many of the acts of the New Deal must not in itself be taken as a sign that he has gone over to the reac-tionaries and become merely another newspaper tool of big business. He has grown much more conservative, but in his opposition to the New Deal in such matters as the packing of the Supreme Court he has been one with great groups of liberals, some of whom supported Mr. Roosevelt ardently for re-election and later for a third term. Indeed, more than two thirds of the newspapers which supported the President for re-election were antagonistic to him on his Supreme Court issue.

The truth is that Roy Howard was never meant to be a great leader, or a great champion of the people's cause. He has not the stature nor the vision nor a sufficient understanding of moral values. He cannot outline large policies and fight for them effectively day by day. His rise was too rapid, his egotism is too great, and the necessary background for distinguished leadership is lacking. Hence one misses in the Scripps-Howard papers today that open determination to make America the property of the common people and not of the privileged classes which used to distinguish it. One does not get the feeling of a continuity of editorial effort, of continuous campaigning for a clear-cut program. Particularly is this true of the *World-Telegram* in New York, which is directed by Mr. Howard personally. There is sound sense in its foreign editorials, but there is no distinction in anything else outside of its columnists. Even when one reads its criticism of the Roosevelt Administration one gets less and less the feeling that it is due to Mr. Roosevelt's break with the true principles of the New Deal. It sounds so much like the familiar big-business complaints as to explain why many people feel that the Scripps-Howard papers differ little in their editorials from the New York *Times* or *Herald Tribune*.

It cannot be said that the Scripps-Howard dailies are today outstanding technically. More than a decade ago I wrote that it was a pity that "their reporting is sometimes poor, their make-up and typography wretched. They sorely lack high standards in these respects, but the answer is the old one — 'we must stoop to get circulations in order to put our ideas over.' " The *World-Telegram* is especially unattractive in its make-up. Its front page is a mess, with huge war headlines whether they are warranted or not. Indeed, its war news is by no means as well handled as that of its chief rival, the *Sun*. Mr. Howard has not forgotten that James E. Scripps, the brother and partner of Edward W. Scripps, built up this newspaper chain upon the psychological principle that the plain man reads newspaper items in the inverse ratio to their length. He therefore leans to filling his papers with a large number of short bits of news. So the tendency with the Scripps-Howard papers is not only to hand out much news in small nuggets, but to run a few lines on the first page and break the rest of the "story" onto inside ones, which puts many headlines on the first page, but also makes against the appearance of a well-rounded and attractive newspaper.

Beyond their columnists these papers lack distinction and differentiation from the general run. Mr. Howard like many others is quite aware of the usefulness of featuring the female form, and specializes in that in his Saturday edition, which is the most difficult to circulate and to make pay. His paper is also too much routinized. The features, even when quite different, give, by reason of their make-up and position, the feeling that the reader is getting the same old thing. The strength of the chain lies in its columnists. Ludwell Denny, Westbrook Pegler, Peter Edson, William Philip Simms, Lyle C. Wilson, Thomas L. Stokes, Ernie Pyle, Major Al Williams, Fred W. Perkins, and others appear regularly, or irregularly. And Mrs. Roosevelt, too, but not because of any admiration for what she has to say or how she says it. I think Mr. Howard would freely admit that his taking Mrs. Roosevelt's nauseating "My Day" into his columns is due solely to the fact that it is a great circulation creator. In other words it is purely a matter of dollars and cents.

Often one wonders whether the Howard columnists and political reporters are not just a trifle too numerous. Certainly the "by-line" has been carried to the utmost limit in the Scripps-Howard papers. The reader is tempted to believe that he is being offered not a well-rounded, solid newspaper entity, but a galaxy of stars who sometimes overlap and repeat themselves, and sometimes find it difficult to write freshly and ably six times a week. There are missing the strong, informative, long-length dispatches, obviously written with inside knowledge, which distinguish the *Times,* though there are exceptions here, especially from the pen of Mr. Stokes. Sometimes it seems as if the Washington news was too clearly filtered through the eyes of the reporter. A long, unsigned column of detached paragraphs and subjects which appears in the *World-Telegram* from Washington on Saturdays is by all odds the best contribution it prints from the nation's capital. Here one gets the note of inside knowledge, of prevision and outspokenness. Of course Mr. Howard faces keen competition in the New York field. Still he sells nearly 380,000 copies a day, as contrasted with the 600,000 of Hearst's *Journal-American,* while the *Sun,* the business man's favorite, runs 100,000 copies behind the *World-Telegram,* with the *Post,* a tabloid, selling 220,000. Undoubtedly the *World-Telegram's* reputation for liberalism, even if somewhat diluted, is responsible for its surpassing the *Sun* in circulation.

As for the whole chain, it now comprises nineteen newspapers well scattered over the United States. Since 1930 there has been a loss of eight newspapers, sold or discontinued, while three others have been added. In eliminating weak members of the group Mr. Howard showed the same excellent judgment which led Mr. Hearst's creditors to make him jettison the money-losers in his chain. It is quite easy to carry a combination of weak and strong dailies when economic conditions are favorable; it may become dangerous when times are bad. Another danger to any chain is that the editorial policies are dictated by the central office. The Scripps-Howard members, however, are free to deal individually with local issues and thus to avoid the appearance of being wholly absentee-owned. Their local editors are aided in buying stock in their papers, and are expected to spend their lives in the Scripps-Howard service. They are constantly urged to "know your town" and "feel its pulse," which admonitions are offset, however, by the occasional transfers of editors from one city to another. Even with the above rules it is not easy to make a chain daily seem quite the same as one owned by a native known to all his fellow citizens and nurtured in local traditions and objectives. On the other hand there is a certain advantage in the freedom of the chain editor from occasionally embarrassing local entanglements, social, business, and financial.

While Scripps wanted his editors to be stockholders in his dailies, he ruled that they should never invest in any enterprises which would interfere with their complete freedom of opinion and action. He rightly wished them to be newspapermen and nothing else. As to the business side of the chain, there is a general manager in New York in complete control of the business affairs, but it is a pleasure to add that no business department exercises any control whatsoever over editorial policies. Thanks to Scripps, there is still another unusual feature of the Scripps-

Howard control. At election times the leading editors have been brought together to discuss the situation and to decide on the policy to be followed. One of the first cases of what seemed a departure from liberalism by them was their decision to support Herbert Hoover for the Presidency, something that they later surely repented in sackcloth and ashes. However much democracy and local independence there still is in the Scripps-Howard management, the chain, being a chain, cannot escape considerable standardization of features, illustrations, and so on.

When the chain has the remarkable luck to develop an Ernie Pyle, whose dispatches from the front in Africa and Sicily were by all odds' the best which came from the scene of war because of their pictures of the life of the individual soldier and the reactions of the men under fire, the whole group profits. But there is an ever present danger that what is very valuable and completely understandable to the reading public in New York City, or San Francisco, or Cleveland, is not as suitable for the audience in Evansville, or Covington, Kentucky, or Knoxville, or Memphis. Nothing can take the place of a strong, vital individuality, fighting through the columns of the paper with which it is wholly identified. The *Gazette* of William Allen White will always mean far more in its community than a reflection of the views of Roy Howard and his editor-in-chief, George B. Parker, however wise they may be, when published in California.

But it must not be assumed from this that there are not editorial latitude and divergence among the various members of the Scripps-Howard chain. The Pittsburgh *Press,* for example, differs from the *World-Telegram.* The chain as a whole was not eager to have the United States enter the war — Mr. Howard thought after a trip to Japan that it was very essential we should immediately increase our fleets, although he has since been accused of being pro-Japanese! Since Pearl Harbor his papers have stood up very straight in supporting the war effort. But they have rendered their greatest service by speaking out with complete veracity and vigor about the breakdown of the Roosevelt leadership, or rather lack of leadership, on the home front. It has not been an undiscriminating criticism, but often genuinely constructive, particularly in dealing with developments in the economic field. Still one feels the lack of deep leadership and of a strong continuity of effort in the delivery of sledgehammer blows. I am not at all sure whether the *World-Telegram* has a real conception of what it would like the post-war world to be, and what it and its allied newspapers will do to bring about a better state of international society. That may, of course, be a failure on my part to understand what is given to the Scripps-Howard readers. But it is my feeling that the Scripps-Howard papers today lack the clear aims they seemed to have in the bitter days after the first World War, when reaction took over the United States.

Closely allied with the Scripps-Howard chain is, of course, the co-ordinated United Press, also founded by the late E. W. Scripps. He was opposed to a monopoly in news, favored a liberal interpretation of it, and, being particularly interested in evening newspapers, established the United Press with the special purpose of serving evening dailies. Not until 1920 did it include morning newspapers. In many respects it is the exact antithesis of the Associated Press, being wholly without any co-operative features. Scripps and most of the managers from the beginning did not pretend that theirs was a public enterprise, but just another commercial profit-seeking institution. They declared themselves to be not journalists, but business men, but were careful to stress the fact that the United Press has no policies of any kind and no desires save "to present to its clients throughout the world a world-wide service of news objective and impartial, without prejudice of any kind, national, sectional, economic, social or religious." Against great obstacles it has steadily progressed, thanks in large measure to the skill and ability of Scripps, Karl Bickel, Roy Howard, James H. Furay, Hugh Baillie, Robert J. Bender, and James I. Miller, and the other executives, all of them part owners, who carried the company on.

One reason for their success is that they were untrammeled by conventions. They could go ahead, moreover, without first having to consult the heads of their member dailies. If any subscriber to the service did not like what they were doing, he could go elsewhere. The United Press was the first to develop the use of the telephone for the transmission of a "pony" (i.e. small) news report; this made it possible to provide a larger service than by telegraph and for less money. It was the first to use extensively the printer-telegraph machine and to welcome the radio, in which it saw not a competitor, but a valuable ally. And it asserts that its use of a national hook-up during the general election of 1924 compelled its rivals to abandon their opposition to the radio and to see in it a necessary adjunct of any news service. Karl Bickel once attributed the remarkable expansion of its world service to the fact that it has always been free from nationalistic bias and was not tied up with those foreign news agencies, official and semi-official, from which Kent Cooper finally freed the Associated Press. The United Press has also felt that its system of not relying upon member newspapers for its news, but upon paid correspondents responsible solely to it, has aided it in that its paid correspondents were not usually serving two masters — their immediate employers and the press association.

The year 1929 was a record one for the United Press; at that time the New York *Herald Tribune* and the Chicago *Daily News,* both pillars of the Associated Press, subscribed for the United Press service. That marked a tremendous step forward, for Victor F. Lawson, the founder of the *Daily News,* had been the strongest director in the Associated Press, and it seemed like treason that two such newspapers should take the service of the rival news organization. It was some years before the New York *Times* followed suit. The simple truth is that the United Press has established itself all over the world, notably in South America, as a first-rate and trustworthy news-gathering agency, with a much more liberal slant and a greater interest in social and economic developments than its rival. It will probably never get over the fact that through a misunderstanding by others Roy Howard himself transmitted to the world the greatest news blunder of modern times, the mistaken announcement of the fake armistice on November 7, 1918. This is far in the background now and I have heard of no recent criticisms of the reliability of the United Press, and much praise for certain features of its service.

It is an interesting development of the present war that the Associated Press, the United Press, and other news agencies, American and foreign, have clubbed together and sent joint representatives to the front to accompany the troops or the fleets in different spheres of action. In this way competition has been ended. Since news-gathering in war-time is not free, but subject to the limitations imposed by the military and naval authorities, this does not mean that there will necessarily be a continuation of this when the war is over. But the inevitable argument that there is an economic waste in having duplicating news services, two correspondents to transmit the same story that one could handle just as well, will inevitably make itself felt. The rising costs of producing newspapers will undoubtedly make many a newspaper manager feel that here, too, is a possibility of making large savings to offset the ever increasing expense bills.

Mr. Gannett's chain of twenty-one newspapers now surpasses in numbers the Scripps-Howard group, so that the latter stands second in size of the major chains.* Its influence on American thought is still much greater than that of the Gannett newspapers, not being restricted as the latter are largely to the smaller cities of one state, and of the Hearst newspapers with their notorious loss of editorial influence. Backed as the Scripps-Howard dailies are by the United Press, they have it in their power in the dangerous and difficult years ahead to render very great service to their country — provided that they hold fast to the ideals which actuated Edward W. Scripps and his brother when they founded the chain for the purpose of helping to make the America of the future something different from the self-satisfied and socially reactionary country in which they worked and rose, by their industry, enterprise, and liberalism, to influence and affluence.

* The Hearst chain also comprises nineteen papers, but two of them appear only on Sunday.

CHAPTER XVIII

Boston, a Journalistic Poor-Farm

IF, as it has been so wittily said, Boston is the abandoned farm of American literature, journalistically it is the country's poor-farm. Nothing in Boston astonishes foreigners more than its press; nothing more clearly illustrates the passing of what was once the Athens of America. To understand in full the low standards of its dailies one must know not only the city's history, but also the extraordinary transformation which has come over the stronghold of the Puritans; one must realize that the Boston of today has comparatively little in common with that city when New England flowered. A thin blue line of descendants of the colonials, who learn nothing and forget nothing, is intrenched in the suburbs, on the Back Bay, and in State Street and does its best to confront and hold back the multitudes of Irish, Jews, and Italians who today comprise the bulk of the city's population. The Puritan is yielding to the Catholic; the Catholic in turn may yield to someone else.

Now, the decay of the press has naturally not been due merely to the city's changed character; it has followed the whole trend of the press throughout the country. The surprising thing is that the ultra-conservatism of Boston did not retard the change, but, I am inclined to think, rather accelerated it. Perhaps the explanation is this: One of the worst faults of the Boston press is its parochial character. No other large American city has such localized newspapers. That trait comes from the Back Bay. Even when literary Boston was in fullest flower, its attention was riveted chiefly upon itself. It knew nothing of the rest of the country and did not wish to know anything about it. Some years ago a charming young bride from Albany, descendant of the most patrician of Dutch settlers, was taken to visit on Back Bay two of her husband's maiden aunts, then nearing their seventies. They looked upon her with mingled trepidation and wonder. "So you come from the West," said they. "Well, from Albany," faltered the guilty bride. "Well, *we've* never been further west than Worcester!" The bride felt properly crushed. In peace-times one reads the Boston papers and is convinced that some of the editors have never been further west than Worcester.

Fifty years ago the Hub rejoiced in some excellent and most intelligent journals. There was the old *Post,* a fine Mugwumpian morning paper of the type of the New York *Evening Post* of Godkin and the Springfield *Republican*. Under John Holmes the *Herald* was independent, honest, and aboveboard. The *Advertiser* personified Republican dignity, respectability, and conservatism, with the *Record* not far behind. The *Traveler,* too, once had its day. But the *Post* failed, was bought up, and became, under E. A. Grozier, a particularly low but successful scarlet woman of journalism. The *Herald* fell upon hard times and bartered its virtue like any drab, actually taking the dollar-a-line bogus reports of the famous insurance inquiry in New York. The *Record* and *Advertiser* had their ups and downs; the *Record* has gone to Hearst and the *Advertiser* in its old age has sunk dreadfully to being a Hearst Sunday tabloid. Of all of them it must be said that they are narrow and provincial and that they glory in it and are convinced that concentration upon local news and local crime, and the use of large black headlines, constitute more than ever the road to business success in 1943. To all of this, however, the *Christian Science Monitor* is the brilliant exception.

Despite the tremendous changes in the world's aspect and the global war, the last twenty-five years have seen only an intensification of these discouraging Boston press changes. The headlines are blacker and larger, the typographical make-ups more eccentric and more repellent, the devotion to sensation greater. With the disappearance of the Boston *Transcript* there vanished the last survivor of the old-type journalism which deemed itself a dignified profession intended to educate and illuminate, to uphold intellectual standards and to treat news as news on its merits and not merely as possible material for a sensation. The Boston poor-farm is poorer than ever, and is without a single daily to compare favorably with those in St. Louis or Washington, to say nothing of New York, whose journals naturally make a larger appeal to what is left of the thoughtful reading public in the Hub. There remain in Boston today only the Hearst group, the *American, Record,* and Sunday *Advertiser;* the *Monitor;* the *Post,* still owned by the Grozier family; the morning and evening *Globe,* the property of the Taylors; and the *Herald,* with its evening edition, the *Traveler.* Not one except the *Monitor* would be outstanding in any national survey of the American press, but they dominate all of New England, notably the *Post,* with its shockingly low standards, for it pervades, degrading as it goes, destroying ideals, lowering the public taste, and familiarizing many homes in five states with crime, scandals, and the basest aspects of life. The only encouraging fact about it is that it once sold 540,000 copies of its Sunday edition and now sells only 270,000, while its daily edition has stood still at 377,000.

It is beyond dispute that E. A. Grozier, who built up the *Post,* achieved a great material success. Those who think only of financial results have praised him and his successors for pluck and dogged persistence in the face of tremendous obstacles. To achieve that success, however, they subordinated news accuracy and reliability as well as all vestiges of good taste and dignity. The *Post* did, however, start out with the democratic idea of being a daily for the man in the street. As for the Hearst newspapers in Boston, they differ not a whit from the others owned by Hearst. Undoubtedly in the past they have occasionally championed in Boston as elsewhere some excellent policies, notably in the matter of the street railways. For many years their managers believed that their strength lay in editorial liberalism or radicalism. The amazing thing about them is that they have been less bizarre, scandalous, and sensational than the *Post.* The *Record* has the largest morning circulation in Boston — 289,000 — with the exception of the *Post.* The tabloid *Advertiser* dominates the Sunday field in Boston with 600,000, while the Evening *American* sells 164,000.

It was General Charles H. Taylor of the Boston *Globe* who first understood how best to exploit the new-type residents of Boston. He achieved a great journalistic success by several simple policies. Sensational headlines and the playing up of crime contributed, but what is a far more important explanation lies in his issuing orders that, if possible, every reader of the *Globe* must find his name in the paper at least once a year. Main Street must have its day in the journalistic court. So it then printed long lists of "among those present" and gave pages and pages to clubs, societies, and society news, to meetings of fraternal orders — anything which made possible the printing of names, names, and names. In a city as self-centered as any parish, the *Globe* was as parochial as it knew how to be. A true story of General Taylor further illumines his policy. Being informed one day by an excited employee of the alarming news that the Boston *Herald* had engaged another London correspondent, the General exclaimed: "Then, by God, we'll have to get another in South Boston!" To this must be added General Taylor's second recipe for sure success: Never say anything unfavorable of anybody in your daily if it can in any way be avoided; never give offense. It was his desire, too, that no "story" should appear in the *Globe* whose writer could not shake hands the next day with the man about whom he had written.

That rule has long governed the *Globe*. General Taylor adopted it not merely because it was good business, but because he was himself a simple, sweet-natured person, undiscriminating, conventional, ignorant that there were such things as deep economic currents and terrible economic injustices. A kindly employer, whose gentle spirit of goodwill permeated his whole printing plant and made him very popular in the Associated Press and wherever newspaper publishers or writers met, General Taylor none the less became distinctly cynical in public and professional affairs and more and more materialistic. He was typical of many an idealist who, under the spell of this extraordinary cold-blooded, and business-mad period in our history, more and more yielded to its influence. He was without a vestige of a social policy. With a really creative mind, he should have been a man of action instead of a publisher who owned fifty per cent of his paper (Eben Jordan, of the Jordan & Marsh drygoods store, owned the other fifty per cent) and made money much too easily.

This paper is the inheritance that was left to General Taylor's sons, of whom the younger, William O. Taylor, is now the head of the *Globe*. Generous and worthy, he inherited his father's kindly heart and has been politically and socially content to move on in the same old highly successful groove. As the years pass, the *Globe* changes little. Its morning edition is purchased by 130,000 people and its evening by 180,000, while its Sunday edition touches 353,000. The latter is quite standardized in its features, but always clean and timely. The war years have brought it increased prosperity. Why should its owners care if it is entirely conventional and typographically cheap and ugly, seeking in the evening edition to outdo its rivals in splash and sensation? Why should it do anything to make Boston journalistically little better than a Sahara?

Curiously enough, it does do something worth while; it usually contributes the best editorials printed in any Boston newspaper. One appears daily over the signature "Uncle Dudley," which has hidden the personalities of a group of able and meritorious writers. "Uncle Dudley" has often found pleasure in dwelling upon fundamentals, in dealing with the basic ideals of spiritual and moral liberties, usually in generalities, but none the less valuable. In its news columns the *Globe* has often done yeoman service by giving the only accurate, unbiased reporting of labor troubles or of important trials. The accounts of the famous Lawrence strike handed in by a veteran reporter, Frank Sibley, were the best reporting done in New England in years and became a part of the subsequent court record. Similarly, in that terrible miscarriage of justice, the Sacco-Vanzetti case, Mr. Sibley distinguished himself and his newspaper. An attendant at all the court sessions, he was personally entirely convinced of the unfairness of the judge and the innocence of Sacco and Vanzetti. It was again Mr. Sibley who during the first World War gave to the *Globe* the most interesting and valuable accounts of the fighting of the New England Yankee Division.

Since the Taylors have done so much along these lines, it has always seemed a great cause for regret that their ambitions could not have carried them further. The present head knows that he has continued to hold for the *Globe* the respect of a large section of the public which believes in the essential integrity of the paper. Like his father and his now deceased elder brother, William O. Taylor has been a model employer and has the merited confidence of his employees to a rare degree, as he has the confidence of his readers. Yet the *Globe* has been sadly subservient to the great advertisers. Editorial puffs of them and their doings appear in its columns and never unfavorable comment. When Eben Jordan of the drygoods firm of Jordan & Marsh backed a season of opera in Boston, the *Globe's* musical critic invariably went into raptures over every performance. I fear that there are many "keep-outs" and "must-nots" in the *Globe* office in addition to the fundamental policy of being as kindly to everyone as possible.

When one turns to the Boston *Herald* one comes upon the greatest disappointment in Boston journalism. It had, as I have said, an excellent name at the turn of the century, and it should have been developed into the great, broad-minded newspaper of Boston, with a metropolitan touch. It had the opportunity to be to Boston what the Baltimore *Sun* has been to that city, but it had reached the lowest possible ebb financially, and it fell into the hands of men who did not have the means or the desire to make it great, and a great news-organ. Next it became the property of very rich men and certain large corporations, and therefore became the mouthpiece of State Street and of the big-business world. Among these owners were Senator W. Murray Crane of Massachusetts, the New York, New Haven & Hartford Railroad, some of those connected with the United Shoe Machinery Company, and Morton F. Plant, who made an enormous fortune in Florida. Even with this sort of backing the paper could not be made to pay — which is entirely to the credit of the public. In their effort to save the paper the owners called to the editorship and position of general manager Robert Lincoln O'Brien, a Harvard graduate, private stenographer to President Cleveland during his second term of office, and then for years Washington correspondent of the Boston *Transcript* and for a time its editor. Mr. O'Brien had a wonderful opportunity before him and the experience and ability to put the paper on its feet.

He succeeded financially, but by methods that lowered rather than lifted its standards. Through him the paper became rich and powerful, without, however, maintaining ethical standards. He sold himself to the god Success, received a large salary, and now, in retirement, is one of the largest stockholders in the corporation and the recipient of a large annual income from his holdings. It is true that he put an end to some of the worst delinquencies of the paper as he found it, for it was then deliberately venal, as proved by Charles E. Hughes when he brought out the fact cited above that during the insurance scandal in New York the *Herald* was being paid a dollar a line by the insurance companies to print bogus news of the Hughes inquiry. It is still a creature of the big corporations; it has always been subservient to the big advertisers. Nor has it always been square in its advertising. Years ago it joined in the general abuse of Joseph Pelletier, the then District Attorney of Boston, for not punishing or interfering with the perpetrators of the Emerson Motors swindle. But while properly berating Pelletier, it failed to state how many thousands of dollars had gone into its treasury for the extensive Emerson Motors advertising in its columns, through which many dupes lost their savings.

Once Mr. O'Brien, as editor, personally equipped with letters of introduction a gang of rascally advertising solicitors who sold to prominent people rotogravure pictures of themselves in the *Herald* at $400 a half page until these solicitors tried it upon Mr. Plant, then a chief owner, after which the gang moved elsewhere. Its book reviews and its criticisms have been suited to its advertisers — at one time it even ruled automobile accidents off the front page on Mondays to oblige the motor-car advertisers. Once it actually printed the headline "[Governor] McCall and Moxie at Barnstable Fair" — the Moxie Company was a big advertiser. Whereas General Taylor's policy of offending nobody was in part due to his own kindly philosophy, with the *Herald* it was business pure and simple. Of course it had plenty of people to berate. It always lambasted the radicals, hammered the Communist leaders, Trotsky and Lenin, while they lived, and all Bolsheviks, the pro-Germans, the German people, all American labor leaders, and of late years the New Dealers. Upon all unpopular persons, especially those who threaten the present economic order, its blows have fallen thick and fast. It is one of the institutions which State Street swears by, but when the bad times came and the respectables lost a great deal of money through the failure of Lee, Higginson, which had also played a considerable role in the affairs of the *Herald,* the Back Bay centered some of its rage upon that newspaper. When the great First National Bank became highly unpopular, many people vented their grudges upon the *Herald* because it was supposed to be very closely affiliated with that bank.

Curiously enough, it was even blamed directly and indirectly for the tragic ending of the *Transcript,* presumably on the ground that its competition in the evening field with the *Traveler* helped to bring about the downfall, and perhaps because it failed to help the *Transcript* when its owners appealed for aid.

The public felt that even its book reviews and criticisms of the arts were colored to gloss over the truth in the interest of advertising. There have been periods in its recent history when it has had to do a tremendous amount of promotion and use the local radio stations freely in order to hold its circulation, because of competition, notably in 1941, when it raised its price from two cents to three and the *Globe* refused then to go along. Of late, however, neither the *Globe* nor the *Herald* has cared to add much circulation, especially in view of the stringency in paper due to the war. Their chief concern ever since 1941 has been to hold what they have. The *Herald* sells 131,000 in the morning and 204,000 on Sundays, while the *Traveler,* the evening edition, disposes of 220,000.

One thing must be added about the *Herald's* attitude toward the New Deal and President Roosevelt. As might have been expected, it has supported the President's international policies through thick and thin. It has been the mouthpiece of the large Anglophile group in Boston, something that has required considerable courage for a newspaper as attuned to the box office as this one. For, after all, a great section of Boston is Irish Catholic, innately hostile to England, and the Catholic Church has not been too ardently pro-war. But the large segment of Boston's population which was opposed to all aid to England and our taking part in the struggle was not restricted by any means to the Irish. Some men high in banking and political life, yes, some real bluebloods, were on the other side from the *Herald,* which is now getting what satisfaction it can out of the Rooseveltian mismanagement of the home front. It remains only to add that the *Herald* thinks, of course, that the charge of its being pro-English is unjust; it believes that it has been fighting the battle for freedom in America — though I am not at all sure that it did not come to this belief long after it first demanded aid for England and the delivery of American materials of war to it. In this policy the *Herald* has had the warm support of Mr. O'Brien.

All in all, the *Herald* typifies in nearly every way the faults and the weaknesses which the critical American, especially if he is of liberal tendencies and believes that American life should not be directed by State Street and Wall Street, thinks are responsible for the decay of the American press and its loss of public confidence. Its officers and directors speak for big business, wealth, and privilege. They will rarely be accused of taking any idealistic position or being truly progressive. They are for the *status quo*. If occasionally, especially under Mr. O'Brien, it has lapsed into the liberalism of President Cleveland, it can usually be counted on to be safe and sane, to go with the well-to-do crowd in times of stress. And above all else, it seeks not to offend those people from whom it expects to draw its income, and it sticks to its friends, especially if those friends are outstanding champions of conservative policies. It knew perfectly well what a sham Calvin Coolidge was — that he did not deserve the credit given him for his denunciation of the police strike after it was safely over and he had returned from his place of hiding. One of its editors once said to me at the time of Coolidge's nomination for the Presidency: "Never in years of political experience have I met a man in public life so despicable, so picayune, so false to his friends as 'Cal' and so unworthy of that office." But the *Herald* boomed him for the Presidency as if he were a statesman and an honor to Massachusetts.

When it comes to loyalty to one's friends, Mr. O'Brien was outstanding as an editor. With him it was loyalty, loyalty, and again loyalty to anyone with power and influence through whose friendship the *Herald* might advance. Once this led to a most amusing incident which belongs to the sagas of journalism. There was a certain Mr. X who in Mr. O'Brien's sanctum one day explained, with some embarrassment, that a publication would be made about him in the next few days and he did *so* hope that the *Herald* would deal kindly and gently with him. Mr. O'Brien assured him that it would; he could safely leave the matter in O'Brien's hands. The visitor departed, plainly much relieved. Mr. O'Brien, about to go off for a few days of vacation, left orders that not one single word should appear in the *Herald* in his absence about his friend, Mr. X. Three days later the news of Mr. X's honorable appointment to a high Federal office in Boston duly appeared in all the Boston newspapers except the *Herald*! Not until Mr. O'Brien returned could the lips of the loyal staff of the *Herald* be unlocked.

As for the late lamented *Transcript*, in an earlier volume I described it as "staid, dignified, the personification of reaction and conservatism, catering to the business men whose minds are closed and to the Back Bay conservatives, male and female, whose horizons are as limited as their prejudices are unnumbered." Yet its death was lamented because it was in many respects an excellent news purveyor, while its criticisms of books, plays, art, and music were free, honest, and often very able, rated by some higher than those of any other American daily. It did endeavor to keep up Boston's interest in things intellectual, but with the waning of its once fairly popular Saturday edition, it could no longer make money — all the Saturday editions of this type of evening newspaper were the chief source of revenue, and when the advertisers, largely because of the long week-ends in the country, switched to the Sunday morning newspapers, the doom of the *Transcript* and those in its class was sealed.

But the *Transcript* would probably not have survived in any event. Had it had the right kind of spiritual, intellectual, and political leadership it might have ranked very high, particularly if its owners had had the wisdom to follow the example of the Chicago *Daily News* and build it up as a great news daily with exclusive foreign dispatches. There the provincialism of the entire Boston press doubtless prevented, in addition to the bitter and aggressive conservatism of its owners, which was such that the *Transcript* long ranked with liberals as "the most hateful, viperish, and reactionary paper in the United States."

This, then, is the daily newspaper menu of Boston, chief city of New England, foremost inheritor of the Puritan tradition, and, in the eyes of many, predestined conservator of the ideals of the Revolutionary Fathers, with no more important duty to the nation than the prevention of any further revolution. This is the journalistic poor-farm which is Boston, whereas it should be the abode of editors eager to winnow the choicest fruits of the rich, scarcely touched soil of our American democracy and lead us in the evolution of the country toward a better, a more just, and a freer State.

CHAPTER XIX

Washington and Its Journals

TWENTY-FIVE YEARS AGO the newspaper situation in Washington was a grave reflection upon the nation's capital. Not only was it without a "Thunderer"; it had not a single daily which wielded a genuine editorial influence among the public men in Congress and in the government. No legislator or statesman ever turned to one of the Washington newspapers, unless to the *News,* with an eager desire to see what were the editorial opinions of the previous day's events. The *Star* was considered the mouthpiece of the District of Columbia and was especially devoted to the ever increasing army of government clerks. The Washington *Post* was known in the country as a whole chiefly because of the military march composed and named after it by John Philip Sousa. Its news pages and headlines undoubtedly exerted some influence on the breakfast tables it reached, and it did play an important role during the fight against the Treaty of Versailles and our entering the League of Nations. For the moment it demonstrated, through the tremendous propaganda carried on in its news columns, that a cause ably served by a Washington daily could make an impression upon the political public.

The *Post* was then in the hands of Edward B. McLean, the very rich playboy son of John R. McLean, long owner of the Cincinnati *Enquirer.* The son achieved unpleasant prominence especially as an intimate friend and host to President Harding. From the McLean ownership the *Post* gained not at all. It did not have the respect of the corps of correspondents or of the local newspapermen. They despised, disliked, and distrusted it and thought it not only a poison sheet, but a contemptible one, and they questioned its moral integrity. It was watched narrowly by some who thought during President Harding's lifetime that they could find in its columns some indication of the President's policies, as for example when it attacked the French occupation of the Ruhr, which helped so much to open the way for the rise of Hitlerism. But nothing that it did could put an end to the deficits that recurred as regularly as the seasons. It was always far inferior to the near-by Baltimore *Sun,* and of course to the New York dailies, which have always exerted a great political influence in Washington. It was therefore a relief when, after McLean's death, the paper found a new owner and a valuable one, who not only has given to the paper new life, but has made it a genuine and growing influence in the city which has now become the most important news and political center in the world. Indeed, no other newspaper in the whole country has made greater progress than the *Post.*

It is Eugene Meyer, a rich New York City Republican, who has worked this change. His appearance at the auction sale of the *Post,* ordered by a Federal court to satisfy a creditor's claims before it entirely collapsed, was entirely a surprise. He had not been mentioned as a possible purchaser. Indeed he had only a few weeks previously resigned as Governor of the Federal Reserve Board, on which he had served for three years by appointment of Herbert Hoover — the latter had then a high regard for Meyer's ability, his very useful services during World War I, and his loyalty to the Republican Party. Mr. Meyer had considered his active business career over and wished to spend his remaining years in quiet retirement upon his splendid estate in Westchester County, New York. But he could not resist the temptation to continue in the Washington limelight and purchased the *Post* for $825,000. Perhaps he had heard of Lord Northcliffe's saying that of all the American newspapers he would prefer to own the Washington *Post* because it reached the breakfast tables of the members of Congress. At any rate, Mr. Meyer took over, to the eventual satisfaction of Mrs. Meyer, who was and is an unusually able writer.

Most people groaned when they heard that a rich New York banker, a hidebound Republican, had bought the unfortunate *Post.* They counted upon his turning out a purely big-business daily. Possibly, some thought, this was a Wall Street move to build up a great organ in order to influence Congress on behalf of the Street. Others were certain that Mr. Meyer would make all of the mistakes which seem inevitable for the rich man who enters journalism without actual knowledge of the profession and thinks that all he has to do to create an important daily medium is to pour in sufficient money and hire the names of well-known writers. Mr. Meyer did make a number of mistakes;

he did hire a number of "trained seals" and high-priced executives. It took him several years really to orient himself, to learn to know his field and his business, and adequately to staff his paper, but within two years a Pulitzer Prize was awarded to its editor. Today no one would assert that the Washington *Post* is an organ of big business. It is conservative in many of its aspects, but it has profound liberal convictions as well, and instead of being a hidebound Republican organ it has strongly championed the Roosevelt Administration in many of its policies, especially its war program and its conduct of international affairs, so that it has often been called "the President's strongest supporter."

The outcome today is that Washington has a newspaper in which it takes genuine pride, whose influence is growing so steadily that it has to be watched day by day by the White House as well as by the members of Congress and the higher officeholders. The President himself has publicly commended and equally criticized some of its editorial positions. It has earned the hearty respect of the newspapermen. It has rendered signal service to that abominably ill-managed and ill-governed community in which it is published, and made notable contributions to the national welfare. Nearly ninety per cent of the leading officials in Washington read it and are more or less influenced by it. That does not mean that the *Post* has driven the Baltimore *Sun* and the two great New York dailies from the Washington field. They are still read and are still most influential. It does mean that Mr. Meyer has created a daily which presents its news well and soberly, yet carries on vigorous crusades for special causes, whose editorial writers are to a large extent encouraged to express themselves as they see fit. Occasionally Mr. Meyer makes suggestions of his own and seeks to give directions, but those directions may bring no response. His newspaper therefore rejoices in a strong editorial page, written with conviction and quite often with courage and independence — this whether one agrees with its policies or not. Sometimes Mr. Meyer contributes editorials.

Today Mr. Meyer is his own editor. He *is* the Washington *Post,* and he has won the respect and regard of his employees as well as the goodwill of the Washington public. From the beginning of his ownership the *Post* became his first job in life, and he is at his desk in his office in the familiar old building every day. From December 1933 until August 1940 Felix Morley, now president of Haverford College, was the editor. When he resigned, in part because he could not go along with Mr. Meyer's out-and-out interventionist policy, Mr. Meyer took over the title of editor as well as publisher. Both Mr. Meyer and Mr. Morley parted good friends, and the latter's nominee, Herbert Elliston, long a foreign correspondent and an editor and columnist on the *Christian Science Monitor,* is now associate editor in charge of the editorial page. Barnet Nover, whom Mr. Morley also brought to the *Post* as a specialist in foreign affairs, writes an able and well-informed column — some people think it outstanding. The editorial page to a considerable degree preserves the excellent quality upon which Mr. Morley always insisted.

It is Mr. Meyer himself, however, who today gives to the paper its courage and the independence that it has. He is afraid of nobody, nor of lawsuits or feuds or battles with political magnates. He is a good fighter, sometimes perhaps too bitter, but no one can accuse him of timidity or of that fear of authority which has made the *Star* the colorless and spineless daily that it is. He has shown that he can be a most intense propagandist, as when he attacked the isolationists in Congress who did not share his views and held that we should not go into the war. The justice and fairness of these attacks are, however, well open to question. In addition he printed a series of important exposures of foreign and domestic supporters of Axis policies and of agents for the dictators.

That his newspaper can make itself greatly resented by officials is shown by the physical attack made by Jesse Jones, the Secretary of Commerce, upon Mr. Meyer at a dinner of the Alfalfa Club. Meyer's offense was a particularly strong editorial assailing Jones for that procrastination in developing the stockpiles of precious material prior to Pearl Harbor, and in handling the rubber, aluminum, and magnesium problems, which led to the most sensational attack upon him by Vice President Wallace in July 1943. It is needless to say that the Washington *Post* editorial writers have kept right on attacking Jesse Jones. Indeed, one of the most valuable editorials which have appeared in any newspaper in aid of the war effort was that called "Conversion of Government" which appeared in the *Post* of February 12, 1942, demanding an end to unnecessary bureaus and overlapping divisions of the government. Few editorials have been more widely quoted; its importance was everywhere recognized. While it did produce some results in the way of governmental reorganization, unfortunately nothing could really change the administrative inefficiency of the President. A characteristic and notably valuable editorial attack upon Secretary Knox, in relation to the navy's failure to appoint a chief of staff for air warfare, appeared on August 4, 1943. As a matter of fact, its editorial page is today probably more often quoted in Congress than any other. Thus, on May 17, 1943 the *Post* was cited thirteen times in the *Congressional Record,* five of its articles being reprinted, one of them twice.

A criticism of the *Post* is the familiar one that all the Washington dailies are too much influenced by their proximity to the government. If that seems a contradiction and unjustifiable in view of the constant variety of the *Post's* attacks upon the Administration, there is still foundation for it. I doubt very much whether Mr. Meyer would go to bat with the government if the risk were serious damage to his paper, or its being attacked directly by the government. In my judgment, he has yielded too much to his patriotic desire to serve the government's war program, to prove his and his paper's loyalty beyond any question. His acceptance of the voluntary censorship instituted by Secretary Knox prior to the war is a case in point. With every desire to do justice to him I cannot conceive of his taking as daring and risky a stand against a national policy as marked the editorial policies of the New York *Evening Post,* the Springfield *Republican,* the Boston *Herald,* and the various other newspapers who fought against our taking over the Philippines, and our bloody conquest of those islands, whose people had never done us the slightest injury. There is also foundation for the charge that Mr. Meyer lacks the convictions of high principle, and regards ownership of the *Post* as an end rather than a means.

This explains why, in my opinion, Mr. Meyer has not accomplished more and does not seem likely to accomplish any more. He has always wanted to publish a good newspaper to maintain his reputation as an able and sound business man and, I suspect, because he would otherwise not have obtained the prestige which is now his. But many people doubt if he ever desired to publish a great newspaper and to face the risks involved — not financial

risks, but those unpleasant social consequences which follow
when one directs a hard-hitting independent newspaper and
does not count the cost of hewing to the line. There are no signs
that he is deeply concerned with what happens to the paper after
his death. He has the consciousness of having bought the *Post*
at a bargain price and enormously increased its value and its
standing in the community.

Washington newspapers, like those of New York, are too little aware of the rest of this vast country, its needs and its desires,
its views on public policies, its reactions to White House leadership. The *Post,* for all its independence, is still the conventional
American daily, not digging too deeply under the surface, not
liberal enough for those to whom liberalism is a creed and a way
of life. It does mean to champion the underdog, and its friendliness to the Negro is one of its best services, as is evidenced by
its active efforts to prevent the occurrence in the American capital of any race riots like those in Detroit. It is a sad fact, however, that with all the power of the Washington press it cannot
bring democracy to the District of Columbia and win suffrage for its citizens. In the war year 1943 Washington is one of
the worst cities in America for overcrowding, for venereal disease, for sickness of other kinds and threats of epidemics, together with every other form of misgovernment. It has not even
a decent police force or decent sanitation. Mr. Roosevelt has
never felt that any New Deal was needed for the District. He
has been too interested in purging Europe of the Axis dictators
and in keeping his political fences in repair to be able to clean
the very dirty house in which he lives. And so the efforts of the
Post, and the rest of the daily press, have gone almost for nought.
At least they have not been able to induce Congress adequately
to govern and sanitate the District in which it functions. The
Post undertakes varied crusades, sometimes with success, as in
revealing abuses in the food supply, the deficient traffic rules,
and so forth. But the sad fact remains that the District continues
to be a disgrace to the United States.

To Mrs. Meyer all this must be especially trying, for she has
a deep civic interest and a pen which never hesitates to lay bare
social evils. She has developed into a star correspondent. From
England she wrote in 1942 a series of noteworthy reports dealing
with the effect of the war upon the lives of the people, but even

more striking was a long series of articles she penned in 1943 describing a trip around this country, a journey anything but easy under war conditions. She dealt unsparingly with the frightful conditions of vice and disease, overcrowding, ill health, and bad sanitation in the many cities, towns, and camps she visited. Some of her articles, like that dealing with her visit to the mining camps in Pennsylvania, produced immediate results in that the government agencies affected acted immediately to remedy the bad conditions she described. But in the main it is the old story: we have billions to manufacture weapons to clean up Europe, but not enough to take care of our own people and to grant to all Americans the freedom to live decently and adequately, with proper food and housing. Mrs. Meyer's picture of the conditions in the bituminous coal region of southwestern Pennsylvania showed that the miners did have sound reasons for demanding higher wages. The burden of their complaint was: "Tell these folks in Washington to give us enough to eat at the right prices and we will go along. But if they can't make good, we have got to have more money. And we are not going to wait long for the answer." Mrs. Meyer added that the cost of living had risen 22 per cent since the miner got his dollar raise in 1941, and that he was worse off than he was then, since food is 40 per cent of the miner's total budget.

So far as the business of the Washington *Post* is concerned, it has prospered under its present owner. Its total advertising has increased from 4,592,006 lines in 1932 to 12,582,685 lines in 1942. In 1932 it stood forty-seventh among the morning newspapers of the United States in total week-day advertising; in 1943 it stood ninth. In 1932 it was fifty-seventh among morning papers in what is known as national advertising, and in 1943 it stood fourth. Its classified advertising has also shown a very large growth. As for the circulation, it, too, has trebled. On June 1, 1933 its daily circulation was 50,300; for the six months ending March 1, 1943 the total of the daily issue was 161,910. In the same period the Sunday paper rose from 62,447 copies to 159,780. When one considers how enormous has been the increase of the war population of Washington, this gain seems nothing like as great as it should be, but the growth has been steady and should continue. Actually there were only about 650,000 newspapers, morning and evening, sold in the District at the end of 1942.

Washington has never been a great newspaper city, but of course to the figure cited must be added the large number of out-of-town papers sold every day.

The Washington *Post's* only local morning competitor is the *Times-Herald,* which is one of the few papers that really publishes "around the clock," one edition following another, morning, afternoon, and evening, with a total sale of approximately 225,000 for all editions. It is well printed; some observers praise its make-up and type excessively. It is a most useful alternative to the *Post,* in that it presents an opposing editorial point of view, notably on international affairs. Despite the efforts made to bring the so-called isolationists into disrepute, here, as in Chicago and elsewhere, the dissenting newspapers have not only kept alive the historic American policy of presenting antagonistic opinions, but actually represented the bulk of the people in their opposition to American entry into the war. There were and are a great many persons in Washington in complete opposition to those policies of the President so ardently and passionately championed by Mr. Meyer and the Washington *Post,* and it is a fortunate thing that they have found in another newspaper the expression of at least part of their views, an outlet for their emotions.

To the *Times-Herald* its readers turn to read its anti-Europe editorials and its criticisms of the Roosevelt Administration. Many seek the column of John O'Donnell, Mr. Roosevelt's pet hate among the correspondents, which, whether one likes it or not, is a desirable astringent to those of the Roosevelt "fellow travelers." The *Times-Herald* does not cover the news field, local, national, and international, so thoroughly as do its rivals; it is "selectively" edited after the manner of the Chicago *Tribune.* It has made an especial appeal to women, for a time through Helen Essary's clever column, which is frequently witty, often courageous, and altogether useful. Originally meant merely to attract feminine readers, it has steadily broadened with the growth and experience of the writer. It is said that the paper has many Negro readers; if this is true it is not easy to explain. To most journalists the *Times-Herald* ranks neither as a very good newspaper nor as a bad one, and it cannot be said that it exercises anything like the influence of the Washington *Post,* and probably not that of the *Star.*

This is the more remarkable because there stands behind it a most interesting individuality, that of the owner, Mrs. Cissie Patterson. She comes rightly by her newspaper heritage since she is the granddaughter of Joseph Medill and the sister of Joseph Patterson, the creator of the New York *Daily News*. Her cousin is Colonel Robert McCormick of the Chicago *Tribune,* the three relatives sharing expenses and constituting what is known as the Chicago *Tribune* group. That Mrs. Patterson has ability goes without saying; stability is not so evident, nor deep fundamental principles and political beliefs. For all her brilliance, the *Times-Herald* does not reflect a vital personality through its pages. One feels also that it lacks drive and force, which is a source of regret to many who follow it because it stands for some of the old-fashioned American traditions that ought not to be abandoned.

Next to be considered is the Washington *Star,* which continues to be a rich source of income for the Noyes and Newbold families, and an unassailable house-organ of the District. Its proprietors early recognized that their field of endeavor necessitates the paper's being absolutely identified with local interests. The great army of government clerks, the cogs in the governmental machine, feel that they cannot be without the *Star* because of the departmental news it contains, the obituaries of local worthies, the notices of entertainments and lectures. It used to be said that there were many streets in which the *Star* was subscribed for by practically every house. To be such a local mouthpiece is a legitimate and useful journalistic function, but that is, of course, almost incompatible with the exercise of more than a local influence especially in view of the fact that from the beginning the editors and owners decided not to have either an interesting, or an informative, or an able editorial page. That has not prevented generations of readers from believing in it thoroughly, in its honesty of purpose and its devotion to their interests and those of their peculiar community.

Long dominated by Theodore W. Noyes, an agreeable character, and by Frank B. Noyes, so long the head of the Associated Press, the policy of the paper has always been to injure no one's feelings, to be kindly and fair, and, above all, to avoid criticism of influential persons, and especially of the government. It has been unquenchably conservative, has played safe, originated nothing, and made no contributions whatever to the intellectual life of the nation, to its method of government, or to the solution of any of its problems. If it did take a political position it invariably went along with the conservative business and social groups. It used to be said that the coming of war was a godsend to the *Star,* for then it could really cut loose and do some first-class "cussing" — of the enemy — without endangering its advertising or its circulation. It could then discard its careful balancing of both sides, the familiar "on-the-one-hand" and "on-the-other-hand" type of editorial in which the *Star* specialized, impressing the thoughtless, advancing no cause an inch, but not even adding to the gaiety of nations.

Formerly some of its editorials could not even be defended on the ground that the management was deliberately writing down to the lowest level of the intelligence of its readership. But as Washington has become the world's capital in point of interest and importance, the *Star* has been compelled to become more and more a part of this unhappy and bloody world. Only twenty-one years ago it was not impossible to pick up its editorial page and find that the editorials bore such headings as these: "Another Judge Needed"; "The Silver Spring Tornado"; "Flowers Blooming"; "Facilitating Traffic"; "Sugar Profiteers"; "Art Lights"; and "The Tight-Wad." One had to go far into the rural regions to some country weekly to find editorial writing of a more kindergarten nature. In other words, the *Star* was the incarnation of the poorest American mass mentality, the completest expression of Mencken's booboisie. But it is in other ways an admirable institution, and its care of its employees is beyond praise. For decades it was accepted by the newspaper fraternity that a job on the *Star* was equivalent to a government pension since nobody was ever discharged from this newspaper. It has been a home for old workers and for the relatives of the chief owners. Indeed, it is in danger today from the nepotism by which it has been distinguished, a nepotism that has produced at this hour no young, outstanding, vigorous personality. No other American newspaper of which I know has had so much direct proprietary control, or so much hereditary management.

Its annual profits have been enormous and it has long been included among the ten best money-making papers of the United

States. Its great wealth has enabled it to be independent of its advertisers and free in its news policies, save for the very considerable limitations of the ownership, and in its conception of the functions of a newspaper. Its managers have lacked intellectual courage and have been handicapped by their social surroundings and their personal popularity. They could never undertake a news policy which would make them unpopular or unwelcome. In advertising and news the *Star* is one of the cleanest of American newspapers, and it is willing to spend much money for news and features and for special correspondence. But it could never throw itself wholeheartedly and with passion or real leadership into any cause — even to redeem the District of Columbia. There were years when newspapermen had to be careful to turn to its last page as well as to its first, for the most important political news story of the day was then quite likely to be buried in the back of the paper, with its worth unrecognized. It still keeps up a high typographical standard, and it is without question an indispensable record of the life of its community. One finds newspapermen, however, wondering whether it can continue indefinitely as it is without before long paying too great a price for its managerial inbreeding.

Finally, the local newspaper field includes the Scripps-Howard tabloid *News*. It has the characteristics of its group, and like the others its liberalism has become somewhat diluted. It has faced the difficult problem of favoring the New Deal with very considerable reservations as to the individual leadership of Franklin Roosevelt. At many points up to the coming of war it was hostile to some of his war policies; when Roy Howard, the present head of the group, returned from a visit to China convinced that we must have a much larger navy and greater strength in the Pacific, the editorials swung in that direction. The *News*, like the others of this group, has made a strong appeal to labor and is sympathetic with its aspirations. In twenty years its readership has risen from about 40,000 to nearly 100,000. It continues to be usually on the side of the underdog, and to understand what liberalism means and in years gone by it exercised a valuable influence upon the whole Washington newspaper field by printing news of a kind not usually given by the other papers. It was for years the only paper in Washington with a sincere and consistent understanding of what the whole fight in America is about. If it is no longer so strikingly liberal and influential as it used to be, the change must be due in part to the metamorphosis of the Washington *Post* and to the weakening of the whole Scripps-Howard chain under its present leadership.

Twenty years ago William Randolph Hearst owned the Washington *Herald* and the *Times*. Next to the building of the Washington *Post* into a front-rank journal, the best thing that has happened to the newspaper situation in Washington has been the disappearance of Hearst. His two Washington dailies were typical Hearst newspapers, weaker than most, but peas out of the same pod, typographically ugly and messy, with all the usual Hearst standardized features. It is a striking measure of the weakness of Mr. Hearst's leadership, both in journalism and in our political life, that he possessed for a while this great opportunity powerfully to influence American national development at the seat of the Federal government and made no use of it. He had the means to create there the finest daily in the world, to confer honor and distinction upon the city and the country, but he was utterly lacking in any vision, even in any realization of what this opportunity could do for him personally, and Washington has gained by his disappearance. If a great newspaper publisher has not yet appeared in the capital, at least the opportunity is larger and the possibility far more attractive than ever before, for there is every prospect that for generations to come Washington will be the center of world interest.

CHAPTER XX

William Randolph Hearst

INDEED, William Randolph Hearst has lived too long. It is said of him that he is so much in fear of death that no one may speak to him about it or mention the possibility of his eventually leaving this mundane sphere. But at eighty years of age he has lived so long that he has seen a considerable change in his great newspaper enterprises and their once great influence, in addition to a marked decrease in his fortune and the almost total disappearance of his political power. Few politicians outside of a handful of cities care now what his political preferences are, and still fewer kowtow to him. No longer is he a champion of the dear people, a dangerous radical in fear of whom Wall Street and big business had many sleepless nights.

With the lapse of years he has come to see almost eye to eye with the "plunderbund" he once lampooned and denounced so vigorously. No longer does he portray a Republican President or his party manager in clothing covered with dollar signs as he used to caricature McKinley and Hanna. No longer does he startle the newspaper world by unprecedented features and sensations and unconventional departures. No longer do the political correspondents reckon with him in speculating what will happen at party conventions, in the primaries, and at the elections. I cannot recall that his name was even mentioned during the campaign of 1940. He is a lonely and disappointed old man who no longer lives in splendor at his vast estate, San Simeon, in California, which is almost as large as our smallest state, nor is he still surrounded by great groups of sycophants and toadies. He cannot even take great pride in the progress of his progeny. No one cares today whether he will be for or against a fourth term for President Roosevelt.

In 1923 Mr. Hearst was the sole owner of nine morning, fifteen evening, and fourteen Sunday newspapers. In addition he owned sufficient stock to give him practical control of the San Francisco *Call-Post* and the Los Angeles *Evening Herald,* and he practically owned several other newspapers which were, however, attributed to other proprietors at his wish. Today he has left seven morning newspapers, ten evening newspapers, of which eleven have Sunday editions, while two appear only on Sunday. The following is the list (the S indicating those that appear on Sundays):

MORNING	New York *Mirror* (S)
	Albany *Times-Union* (S)
	Boston *Record*
	Milwaukee *Sentinel* (S)
	San Francisco *Examiner* (S)
	Los Angeles *Examiner* (S)
	Seattle *Post-Intelligencer* (S)
EVENING	New York *Journal-American* (S)
	Boston *American*
	Baltimore *News-Post*
	Pittsburgh *Sun-Telegraph* (S)
	Chicago *Herald-American* (S)
	Detroit *Times* (S)
	San Francisco *Call-Bulletin*
	Oakland *Post-Inquirer*
	Los Angeles *Herald-Express*
	San Antonio *Light* (S)
SUNDAY	Boston *Advertiser*
	Baltimore *American*

His largest circulations are those of the New York *Sunday Journal-American* and *Sunday Mirror,* which have respectively 1,028,599 and 1,629,813. His largest daily circulation is that of the New York *Mirror* with 804,684, with the Los Angeles *Examiner* selling 235,530 copies. The *American Weekly* and the *Comic-Weekly Puck,* which are part of the Hearst Sunday newspapers and are also sold to other, non-competitive newspapers, have a weekly circulation in excess of 7,000,000, and 5,700,000 copies, respectively.

There is no question that Hearst's jettisoning of his other dailies and Sunday newspapers was a sound business move. It was forced in part by the great depression, but also by the fact that, despite his tremendous successes, Mr. Hearst was always a poor manager. If that sounds like a paradox, it is none the less true. At all times he had some great money-makers whose earnings offset the losses of the weak members of the group and gave him his profits. Ranking in the eyes of the profession as one of the great journalist-owners of America, he was never able to make a success of his pet daily, the New York *American,* which once sold 225,081 copies on week-days and 1,083,911 on Sundays. But he cheerfully faced its deficits for years until he was compelled to amalgamate it with his once famous *Evening Journal,* but as the *Journal-American* it is now just another New York evening newspaper, and today sells for five cents, a daring increase in price. For years the Atlanta *Georgian* lost more than $100,000 a year. The whole Hearst liquidation program, largely planned by Mr. G. J. White, the Hearst general manager in New York, has been successful and his group is now making money. Mr. Hearst himself is no longer able to draw out as much money as he pleases, but is on a salary which seems to have fluctuated between $100,000 and $500,000. As long as the properties were wholly his own he milked them as he saw fit, withdrawing enormous sums whenever fancy dictated or he yielded to his insatiable lust for buying objects of art, collections of all sorts and kinds, and more and more land for his "ranch" in California, which he now cannot give away.

A chief reason for his non-successes has been his inability to create happy and efficient organizations. At all times they were split into cabals and were hotbeds of intrigue and dissension, of jealousies and rivalries. When, despite their enormous earnings, his newspapers as a whole were compelled to turn to the public for capital, this laxity and extravagance of management could not, of course, continue. None the less, in applying to the Securities Exchange Commission for permission to float additional securities, he had the unconscionable impudence to certify that this capital which he asked of the public not only was to supply working funds for his properties, but was also actually to cover the cost of maintaining his famous Castle of St. Donats in Wales, and to provide for his personal expenses during his stays there on the ground that this was proper advertising and propaganda expense! Naturally he did not obtain what he asked; before the Securities Exchange Commission could decide against him, so much publicity was given to this piece of effrontery that the application was withdrawn.

There were many years when the bankers were practically in

full charge of the Hearst chain and of his surviving magazines. But by 1943, profiting by the war conditions and more efficient management, the Hearst chain paid off all its obligations to bankers and public and is therefore once more free and clear in the hands of its founder — an admittedly remarkable financial achievement. There were always times when he really tried to improve his business methods, as, for example, when in 1931 he asked the present Secretary of the Navy, Frank Knox, to become the general manager of all his newspapers, which position Mr. Knox retained with considerable success until he purchased the Chicago *Daily News*. Even then, however, the Hearst newspapers were notorious throughout the profession because of the continuing unhappiness of the working force. Some men, of course, like that distinguished prostitute of the profession Arthur Brisbane, received enormous salaries and profited greatly by the favors shown them by Hearst. But for all his campaigns against the plutocrats and the wicked capitalists, it could never be said of him that the workers he employed were distinguished above all others because of their pay, their working hours, or the pleasantness of their surroundings.

As the years passed, Mr. Hearst readily forgot all about those much vaunted crusades on behalf of the oppressed and the downtrodden, the workers and the underprivileged upon which he based his vain appeals for public office. One of his employees, Bradford Merrill, once thus defined Hearst's policies: "Are they not simply this: That the public affairs of every city, every State, and the nation as a whole shall be controlled by the inhabitants thereof, for their own welfare, and not controlled by privilege and plutocracy for the benefit of a few already privileged individuals?" But apologists for Hearst, such as he, forgot to mention the utterly despicable methods by which Hearst carried on his war upon privilege — the lying, chicanery, dishonesty, yes, at times the venality of it (as in his relations to the Southern Pacific Railroad in his early California days), and his measureless degradation of the public taste. Brisbane, of course, earned his chief's great favors by praising him to the skies, but if Mr. Hearst had been someone else to whom Brisbane owed nothing, his pen, which moralized so easily, would have found in the moral failure of his employer a wealth of material for "sermonettes" to present to the millions of his readers. As it was,

Brisbane asserted once that "for twenty years I have seen things appearing in the New York *Journal;* then I have seen them in [Theodore] Roosevelt's speeches; in the New York *American,* and then in Wilson's speeches. The public, of course, will in time know it — they won't know it while Hearst is alive because people never do, but they will eventually."

What Hearst did in the early days of his career to debase and degrade the newspaper business it would be impossible to exaggerate. The whole tone of American journalism was lowered by the example and the competition of one whose newspapers were not only unprincipled, but frequently dishonest. Few other dailies dared to attack him, as the New York *Tribune* often did, to its credit, before its amalgamation with the *Herald,* and notably during the first World War. Most of the fraternity kept silent because of a certain professional fellowship, or because of simple cowardice. Not only were they guilty of servile imitation and bowing down before his millions of readers; they did not even bring out the fact that at one time, if you were a theatrical producer and paid $1,000 for an advertisement, you could draw in return an Arthur Brisbane editorial praising your play with all the sophistry of which this chief of editorial trumpeters was a past master. Let any student of the American press turn back to the files of the metropolitan dailies as they were in the years just before Hearst came into the field and then compare them with editions of today, and he will see for himself how lasting has been the injury done by Hearst in the lowering of journalistic taste and standards. Yet our journalists wonder why it is that the standing of the daily press with the American people suffered so tremendously during the years of Hearst's period of influencing our journalism, and that the people ask why the profession, with few exceptions, never made an adequate protest against the sliminess of the Hearst career or dared to denounce it.

The worst case of journalistic failure to move against Hearst because of proved misconduct is credited to the Associated Press, whose refusal to expel Hearst from its membership was proof positive how dull some editors are to offenses which in any other profession would lead to the expulsion of the guilty man, to say the least. The Associated Press found that the Hearst International News Service was systematically stealing its news;

that in violation of its by-laws the Hearst publications which were members of the Associated Press were allowing its news to filter out to the non-member Hearst newspapers. The Hearst service bribed employees of the Cleveland *News,* an Associated Press newspaper, to furnish it with Associated Press news as soon as it came over the wire. This was then wired back to New York and was sent out as an International News item. International News systematically copied dispatches from early editions and bulletin boards of Associated Press newspapers, particularly after the British, Canadian, French, Portuguese, and Japanese governments had barred the Hearst service from their countries and prohibited the use of their cables for any Hearst messages.

The difficulty of running down dishonesty of this kind was obviously not slight, especially since the ownership of news had not been judicially or legally defined in the United States. To this task Melville E. Stone devoted himself, inspired by the desire to wind up a long journalistic career by obtaining a judicial ruling on the rascalities of Hearst and establishing a needed principle of enormous value to all who originate news. He was completely successful. Hearst's agents were convicted on every count of cheating and stealing from the Associated Press, which Hearst as a member was in duty bound to protect. When the case was won the Associated Press was duly jubilant, but its then board of directors, comprising such men as Adolph S. Ochs of the *Times,* Victor Lawson of the Chicago *Daily News,* Charles A. Rook of the Pittsburgh *Dispatch,* Clark Howell of the Atlanta *Constitution,* Elbert H. Baker of the Cleveland *Plain Dealer,* Frank B. Noyes of the Washington *Star,* and others, did nothing to relieve the Associated Press of the odium of Hearst's presence in the association which he had not only betrayed but deliberately sought to wreck, or, if expulsion was not possible, to make clear their moral condemnation of his acts by a resolution of censure and reprobation.*

So far as the public is aware, the question of Hearst's disciplining was never brought up before the board of directors or in

---

* I was a director of the Associated Press at the time of the suit and have been criticized on the ground that I did not move against Hearst. This was in response to suggestions from within the Associated Press that it would be best to await a final decision in the case before acting. The decision of the Supreme Court was rendered December 23, 1918; my resignation as a director had been sent in on August 8, 1918.

the annual meetings of the members. What more striking illustration could there be of the depths to which the leaders of the profession have lowered it? These men were not willing to purge themselves of Hearst's presence in what is avowedly not a money-making corporation, but a membership organization chartered under the same law of the state of New York as are its social clubs. Is any answer to this amazing riddle possible except that the directors of the Associated Press were afraid to denounce Hearst, that they bowed their knees to his success, his power, his wealth? But if this is the answer, how can the directors of the Associated Press complain if the public's opinion of the whole newspaper profession steadily falls?

This picture goes a long way to explain Hearst's power. But what shall be said of men outside the profession who took and take service under this confuser of ideals? I do not refer, of course, to the rank and file of Hearst's workers who see in his pay only a means to a livelihood. It is the long list of men of distinction who have accepted the shilling of this king of sensational journalism that comes to mind. What shall be said, for example, of Charles H. Parkhurst? Long a preacher of Christian morals in New York and a tower of strength in the fight against municipal misgovernment, he used Hearst's columns to address the multitudes who scanned his pages. Obviously this noted divine took Hearst's pay either because he was in need of money or because he laid the flattering unction to his soul that his ethical teachings could offset some of the evil done by those selfsame publications.

Ambrose Bierce once wrote: "If asked to justify my long service to journals with whose policies I was not in agreement and whose character I loathed I should confess that possibly the easy nature of the service had something to do with it. As to the point of honor (as that is understood in the profession), the editors and managers always assured me that there was commercial profit in employing my rebellious pen, and I, O well, I persuaded myself that I could do more good by addressing those who had greatest need of me — the millions of readers for whom Mr. Hearst was a misleading light." It is, of course, the old, old ethical fallacy that the end justifies the means. You abhor this man Hearst and then this Mephistopheles comes to you and says: "See, I shall turn over to you part of the garden in which I work. You shall spade it as you please and draw golden ducats for doing so," and, behold, Faust yields as readily as ever a Faust did. So the minister of the Gospel preached his sermon between the sex appeals and murder "mysteries," the cheap gossip and tales of the beautiful maiden lured to her destruction, that sold the paper to multitudes.

Thus man after man found himself called to offset the teachings of his employer while accepting the employer's base metal. "Of course, I don't believe in Hearst, but one must get some straight thinking over to the masses." "There are no strings tied to me, so I can say what I please; besides, I don't have to come into contact with the man himself." "Isn't it well that somebody should give a moral viewpoint to those deluded readers?" The language of compromise is always the same; there is the same jargon in the pulpits whose occupants have forgotten Christ to serve Mammon, who take the conscienceless rich man's dollar in order to help him into the kingdom of heaven. Ethically, there was no justification whatever for an alliance like that of Parkhurst with Hearst. Some pitiful excuse may perhaps be made for the petty politicians who go hat in hand to this man to ask his support when in their hearts they loathe and despise him. But for teachers of ethics to wear his uniform was to do the terrible disservice of further confusing the moral values of multitudes. Hearst cared not a snap of his fingers for their views or whether they uplifted or depressed the souls of his readers. These men become Hearst's veil, his camouflage, his garment of respectability, the coiners of more pennies. But the ignorant asked: "How can Hearst be so bad if so saintly a person as Dr. Parkhurst writes for him?"

Well, as to just what kind of character Mr. Hearst is, let us again call in Ambrose Bierce as an expert witness. Here is his summary of his former employer of so many years:

With many amiable and alluring qualities, among which is, or used to be, a personal modesty amounting to bashfulness, the man has not a friend in the world. Nor does he merit one, for either congenitally or by induced perversity, he is inaccessible to the conception of an unselfish attachment or a disinterested motive. Silent and smiling he moves among men, the loneliest man. Nobody but God loves him and he knows it; and God's love he values only in so far as he fancies that it may promote his amusing ambition to darken the doors of the

White House. As to that, I think that he would be about the kind of President that the country — daft with democracy and sick with sin — is beginning to deserve.

As for his writing ability, Bierce said: "As to Mr. Hearst's own public writings, I fancy there are none: he could not write an advertisement for a lost dog. . . . Well, if a man of brains is one who knows how to use the brains of others this amusing demagogue is nobody's dunce."

The problem becomes more complex and difficult when one leaves the Hearst newspapers and considers his magazines. What of the late Norman Hapgood? Mr. Hearst gave him a wonderful opportunity for his exceptional editorial talents by conferring upon him the editorship of *Hearst's International Magazine.* If my information is correct, Hearst had the business wisdom to give Hapgood a free hand. What was wrong in such an arrangement? Well, primarily it was Hapgood himself, who, when editor of *Collier's,* exposed the moral turpitude of Hearst in selling the editorial page of the *Evening Journal* in return for those $1,000 theatrical advertisements and in other ways. Hence it was impossible to reconcile oneself to the spectacle of Hapgood in Hearst's pay, or to the similar acceptance by Fremont Older of a job upon Hearst's San Francisco *Call and Post.* Doubtless both were as free as the air and really believed that their editorial souls were their own, but any union of such men with Hearst was confusing, misleading, and morally discouraging. There was no argument to be advanced for them that was not an excuse, and it is the excuse that accuses, as the French say.

In the political field we are, of course, accustomed to the somersaults of the politicians who seek only their own advantage. But none was more surprising than David Lloyd George's becoming a contributor to Hearst's daily. This was the Lloyd George who ordered Hearst representatives expelled from England during the first World War because of what was called their persistent pro-Germanism, lying, and misrepresentations — offenses deemed to be so serious that the mere possession of a copy of a Hearst paper was made a prison offense in Canada during that war. Hearst must have read with entirely cynical amusement the advertisements in his newspapers in which after the war he set forth the virtues of his distinguished English contributor, whom for years he had abused so roundly, and he must smile as he recalls the breakfast given to him in London at which the hatchet was buried. What would you? The war was over; business was business. "L. G." openly declared he needed the money — and Hearst needed features to advertise. So the "Savior of England" lent his prestige to whitewashing Hearst and thus helped the public on both sides of the ocean to forget what Hearst's record was. The more men of prominence bowed before the flattery of Hearst's offers and the lure of his money, the stronger Hearst was, and the muddier the public thinking about him became.

In London's Fleet Street it is already said that all trace of Lord Northcliffe the man has disappeared, and that the influence of the foremost of British press lords had about been dissipated before the coming of the second World War. Hearst's decrease in influence and power has gone on under his own eyes. As he looks back upon the past, it must come to him that with all the power of his press, with all its ability to speak to millions, it never achieved any of the greater causes for which his newspapers stood. Thus, the railroads are still privately owned, and many of the water powers, too; if more and more cities are owning and operating their traction lines, not even he can assert that it is due to him. If he has stood for home rule for cities, for the initiative, the referendum and recall, for direct primaries, an eight-hour day, a minimum wage, and some of these are now embodied in law, the historian might well ask whether they did not come in spite of Hearst rather than because of his advocacy of them. For at the very moment when he was crying out most loudly for the people's rights he never hesitated to strike hands with the worst of the politicians who robbed the people of those rights at the behest of big business, their real master. There could be no better illustration of this than Hearst's picturing Murphy, the Boss of Tammany Hall, in prison stripes for months, and then making a bargain with him to turn over New York to Tammany at its worst, for personal and selfish reasons.

Hearst was always virtuously against the use of great sums of money to obtain public office — but he spent half a million dollars nonchalantly in his own campaign against Charles E. Hughes for the governorship of New York. And the sincerity of all that he did avowedly for the public welfare was tarnished by obvious self-interest and self-seeking and his efforts to obtain public office. As a politician he was a total failure. In Congress, where he sat from a safely Democratic district by grace of Tammany, he had an excellent opportunity to show what political talents he possessed, but he was an indifferent, colorless Congressman who impressed nobody, neglected his duties, and left absolutely no mark behind him. In addition, he was handicapped by his cold, unattractive, and, from the public point of view, rather mysterious personality. He was once dubbed "a monster of publicity" and a specialist in the psychology of crowds. But however much he might pose in his editorial pages as a St. George to rescue the people from the sinister dragon of business and privilege, in the open he seemed to fool no one. His personal stature shrunk steadily, however much the circulations of his newspapers and magazine grew. It is the old story that in the long run it is character and a reputation for honor and decency that carry men to lasting success.

As a matter of fact, if anyone should make a careful study of the varying attitudes of Hearst and his press, it would soon appear that, like so many politicians, Hearst has been on about every side of every question. This would prove to be especially true in all matters concerning our foreign affairs. There his influence has often been at its worst. There is not space to rehearse once more the role that Hearst and his rival, Joseph Pulitzer, played in bringing on the war with Spain. But there has been no more shameful chapter in Hearst's career than his attitude toward Mexico, in which country he once had enormous land holdings and is a proprietor of mines that have contributed so much to his great wealth. On May 3, 1916 he wrote in his dailies over his own name: "Our flag should wave over Mexico as the symbol of the rehabilitation of that unhappy country, and its redemption to 'humanity' and civilization. Our right in Mexico is the right of humanity. If we have no right in Mexico then we have no right in California or in Texas, which we redeemed from Mexico. . . ." Only six years later, on February 7, 1922, he asked plaintively: "Every human interest that appeals to a nation calls on us to do justice to Mexico — politics, diplomacy, business, national defense. . . . Why inflict conspiracies and injuries on a government that is trying to be friendly and from whose friendship we can derive only benefit?" Plainly someone

in 1922 pulled the strings and told him that his Mexican properties were in jeopardy if he did not change his attitude.

So there at San Simeon in the smaller house in which he has
taken refuge sits this once sinister and powerful figure. If the
ghosts of his past keep him company, his last years must be unhappy indeed. It was within his power to have made himself not
only the greatest, but the most beloved of American journalists.
With his vast wealth he could have served the American people
nobly and achieved lasting reforms for them, had he himself
but been sincere and a patriot. Today he is a wonderful subject
for the moralist in or outside of the pulpit. Almost everything
has turned to ashes in his hands, and the sale at relatively small
prices of the great collections he amassed, while doubtless in part
due to a desire to avoid great inheritance taxes, was probably
also forced in some degree by the relative impairment of his fortune. He still goes through the motions of directing his newspapers; there still appear occasional messages from him to his
public. They only emphasize how far this man of eighty has
fallen. It was long said of him that at the outset of his career
"the sage of San Simeon" hesitated as to whether he should
establish in New York City the best or the worst of newspapers.
He chose the latter. That decision, plus his lack of character,
fixed his place in the history of American journalism. It is hard
to believe that he is today envied by anyone.*

* In 1943 the Hearst magazines comprised the following: *Hearst's International-
Cosmopolitan; Good Housekeeping; Harper's Bazaar; Motor; Motor-Boating; Town
and Country; The American Druggist; House Beautiful* (with *Home and Field*);
Connoisseur (with *International Studio*).

CHAPTER XXI

The FORWARD – a Non-Profit-Making Daily

THE JEWISH DAILY *Vorwärts,* founded in New York in 1897, has made money plentifully, but no individual has profited thereby. It is literally a daily without an owner, and its surplus is distributed to causes and organizations in which the Forward Association, which controls it, is interested. In the last twenty years its profits have totaled $3,000,000, but not one cent went to an individual. Of this great sum, $500,000 was contributed to philanthropies or to the labor movement, more than $400,000 was invested in its radio station, WEVD, and the balance was placed in a reserve fund for just such an emergency as it is facing in this war. The Forward Association comprises some two hundred or more men who receive not one cent for their services, but are profoundly interested in proving that a newspaper carried on in the interest of a great group of people, and to advance the Socialist cause, can make money without being inspired by the private-profit motive and also be able, up to date and progressive. They serve as a council, hold the titles to the properties, supervise along general lines, but leave the details of management to the editor and a special board of management.

It is a genuine cause for regret that the same experiment has not been tried with a powerful English-language daily to see whether in this manner the present crass materialism of the bulk of the American press, and its domination by those who profit most by our economic system, can be offset. The *Forward* has long proved the value of co-operative enterprise. True, it has appealed to a special group in our national life and has had the benefit of a really remarkable editor — Abraham Cahan is still at the helm although eighty-four years of age. None the less, the *Forward* has faced sharp competition in its own field, and now that Jewish immigration has practically ceased, it is hardly surprising that the circulation has declined slightly to about 185,000 copies, still a more than respectable figure, and one certain to produce a fine advertising revenue in ordinary times. There has been a tremendous drop in its advertising income because of the war, so that the *Forward* may show heavy deficits as long as the

war lasts, but it has refused so far to join the other Jewish dailies
in raising its price from three to four cents. Fortunately for it,
WEVD, so long in need of capital, is now able to contribute to
the joint treasury; hence the *Forward* of late has been able to
distribute $20,000 annually among various philanthropic and
labor enterprises.

To carry on a philanthropic business and yet make money —
that is a most unusual happening and one not at all in accord
with the general rule. Those actuated by the impulse to labor
for others, or to serve and advance certain causes, are often poor
business men or are inclined to subordinate business considerations to their real objectives. Probably they are not hard-hearted
enough to pinch the penny adequately. At any rate, the men
who have sponsored the *Forward* have kept clearly in view their
main purpose, which is to publish a successful daily for a mass
clientele in the interest of the Socialist cause and for the advancement of their Jewish readers. They have resisted all temptation
to pay large salaries; for many years Mr. Cahan not only was
content with pay that would have been scorned by a high-grade
reporter on any English-language daily, but actually opposed the
efforts of those who insisted upon increasing it and finally had
their way. Today, however, Mr. Cahan is reported to draw a salary of $20,000 a year, which is but one sign of the serious changes
that have taken place in the *Forward* with the passage of years
of prosperity.

But for a long time the dollar motive could not be attributed
to the *Forward's* conductors. I have heard them bitterly criticized, and sometimes with justice, as once when they made an
utterly unjust attack upon the Friends of Soviet Russia, but
never on the ground of their being swayed by the personal-
profit motive. In an inquiry during the last war into our foreign
press, an official investigator testified that the *Forward* was the
only foreign-language daily in America which could not be
bought. There have been cases of foreigners of great ability coming to this country without means who were placed on its salary
roll at once and then were told that there was no compulsion
upon them to write. Genius, in their case, did not have to labor
at all seasons; its product came when the spirit moved, and it
produced much because genius is warmed and touched when the

hand of fellowship is held forth and the fear of actual want vanishes by one wave of a golden wand.

Yet the *Forward* was long attacked upon the East Side as an enemy to Jewish culture and to racial advancement. Why? First because of the colloquial style in which it is written and what is called its "vulgarizing" of Yiddish, as well as because it is a sensational journal. Its editor-in-chief frankly admits that it writes down to its public. Abraham Cahan was long a writer of brilliant humorous and pathetic sketches of the Jewish East Side for the old *Sun,* the *Evening Post,* and the magazines. For some time he was a remarkable reporter on the *Commercial Advertiser* (later the *Globe*). He has been a novelist with a rare understanding of his race and of all human nature, and finally an American who was the only one of the group which founded the *Forward* in 1897 who was able to speak English. Created in order to combat the views of one Daniel De Leon and his Socialist newspaper, the *Abendblatt,* whose dream of the coming of Socialism visioned its being imposed from above and not as coming through a democratic mass movement, in a couple of years the *Forward* forced De Leon's paper to the wall. But it progressed slowly until the idea of a purely Socialist propaganda organ was abandoned. Then Mr. Cahan came to the front and made it a newspaper first, and only secondarily a political propagandist, though he is always a partisan, and the *Forward,* like many another, colors its news and ignores what it does not like. It is biased, partial, and partisan. Fortunately for Mr. Cahan and his daily, his accession to the editorship was followed in 1903 by a vast increase in the Russian-Jewish immigration to the United States in consequence of the Kishinev pogroms, by which immigration the *Forward* greatly profited.

Although not out to make money for himself or his associates, Abraham Cahan headed first for popularity and decided to make the writing in his journal so simple that the least intelligent on the East Side could understand it. He not only adopted the colloquialisms of the Yiddish of New York, showing no hostility whatever to the introduction of English words, but employed editors to substitute in the news manuscripts the shortest words possible for the more learned ones. In his editorials he dealt with topics of the widest appeal, whenever possible a direct *argumentum ad hominem.* A famous editorial of his, urging every mother who read the *Forward* to see that her child took a clean handkerchief to school with him or her, illustrates his policy. Over this editorial there raged a storm; East Side intellectuals denounced it as insulting to their people, who, they insist, not only need no counsel as to handkerchiefs but are quite capable of understanding and appreciating the best language, the purest form of Yiddish.

But Mr. Cahan felt that the learning of the learned orthodox Jews was of the narrowest. Often great Talmudic scholars are grossly ignorant of things of general knowledge and daily life which every child ought to know and his staff insisted that there were many thousands of people, of the younger generation particularly, who needed precisely the rudimentary education which the *Forward* gave. Wherever the whole truth lies, Mr. Cahan long ago declared that he had completely demonstrated the success of his policy. He and his associates were proud of the fact that for years they swung 65,000 votes at every municipal election, and that for a time the Jewish community declared that Mr. Cahan edited all of the Jewish newspapers, so profoundly did he influence them.

It is unfortunately true that Mr. Cahan in stooping to conquer imitated some of the worst English-language journals, so that his rivals and critics have accused him not only of vulgarity but of going to the very edge of the salacious in some of the *Forward's* news-matter and fiction. In other words, he freely followed in the footsteps of Hearst and other American contemporaries who for a time had won the largest circulations. If it is true that the *Forward* has opposed and vulgarized every spiritual attempt at readjustment of the Jews in America, then its critics, who include many of the East Side intellectuals, are justified in raising the question as to whether its rise has helped or hindered its Jewish clientele, which extends far beyond New York City, and it may well be asked whether its philanthropies can have offset the evil that it has done.

In the two decades that have passed since I first published a study of the *Forward* because of its uniqueness as a non-profit-making daily, the years have taken a toll of Mr. Cahan and his associates. The *Forward* can no longer be accused of being radical, and in 1936 its editors left the Socialist Party. Incredible as it seems to those of us who have long memories, Abraham Cahan is actually charged today with being "a typical rich, bourgeois renegade." Striking workmen have even smashed the windows of the *Forward* building. The young radicals of the 1890s have become the conservatives — as has so often happened in the course of our social evolution. George Seldes quotes Mr. Cahan as saying now: "We are working for a change to a better organized economic system. But we are willing to work at a reasonable rate. We aren't damned fools. We don't think the whole building can be pulled down and changed overnight." Of course Cahan and his paper always represented a conservative Right-wing Socialism, but what has offended the modern generation of Socialists of late years, with the exception of the followers of Norman Thomas, is that they have persistently attacked Stalin and Soviet Russia for their cruelties and the wholesale murders of the Soviet regime. They are taunted by the Communists with taking the same attitude as the most narrow-minded, capitalistic Red-baiters of the daily press. It is true that Mr. Cahan's denunciation of the Communists has been in such sweeping terms, at times without full regard for facts, that he actually has invoked some sympathy for the Soviets. Besides losing some of his belief in Socialism, he has undergone a radical sea-change, largely because of his success and power, and he has become intolerant and domineering.

The unhappiest development within the *Forward* office was Mr. Cahan's breaking off his personal relations with B. C. Vladeck, long the business manager, who had the respect and regard of everyone who met him. His was a rare personality. His mind was keen, his vision wide, his sympathies unbounded, his understanding and love of America complete. Hence he made his mark upon the life of the metropolis. At his too early death he was a councilman and the minority leader of the City Council. It was but right and proper, especially as he was a member of the Mayor's Housing Board, that a block of model homes built by the city at Corlear's Hook, the tip of the East Side, should be named after him. Indeed, the extraordinary outpouring at his funeral of men and women representing almost every phase of the city's life was a tribute not only to him personally, but to some of the journalistic achievements which he so largely helped to accomplish. Certainly no newspaper could ask for a finer or wiser business manager; no one in trouble ever came to Vladeck without receiving aid or comfort, and he and the *Forward* together were warm protagonists of every civic reform and every movement for better government.

Cahan and Vladeck both saw the circulation value of making their daily of personal service to its readers. Once the *Forward* printed fourteen columns of the names of Jews in America who were being sought by their kin abroad. It offers no more striking feature than its letters from readers, often regarding their personal problems. It has been charged in the past that these letters are sometimes suggestive in character and a lure rather than inspired by the desire for aid; but aid these letters often obtain for their writers. Thus a girl suffering from tuberculosis of the throat received $3,000 in quarters, half-dollars, and dollars from sympathetic readers of her letter to the *Forward* asking where she could go for a cure and how she could live during the treatment. Again, there have appeared from time to time extraordinary symposia bearing upon some of the vital problems of the East Side, such as the tragedy of the growing apart and estrangement of immigrant parents and their rapidly Americanized children. When there is suffering on the East Side, or when there have been strikes affecting masses of the population, such as those in the needle trades, it is the *Forward* to which multitudes have looked for guidance and financial aid.

"It is run," says one associated with it, "like a department store. There are all sorts of columns for all sorts of people — headlines for the man who wants to read as he runs, stories, novels, novelettes, and a few columns for the solid citizen who wants his information and an opinion placed before him." Its ten pages of eight columns each (twenty-eight and thirty-two pages on Sunday) offer, therefore, a more variegated bill of fare than the ordinary English-language daily. Pictures, of course; cartoons; relatively little of crime because space forbids more; often sensational matter, at times in questionable taste; extraordinarily valuable foreign letters and correspondence when the condition of the world permits, together with a great deal of Jewish and labor news, with Hearst-like headlines. In one week in peacetime it carried forty-two columns of exclusive letters and cablegrams from its own correspondents in Russia, Germany, Poland, Palestine, Austria, Hungary, and Rumania. Throughout the

first World War it printed much news not to be found anywhere else, among its distinguished correspondents being such
men as Longuet in Paris, Breitscheid, Eduard Bernstein, and
Kautsky in Germany, and the leading British labor men. In
that same week cited above the *Forward* carried 154 columns
of serious reading matter and 137 columns of what may be
termed "light matter," though this does not adequately describe
it, for the extraordinary fact is that while the *Forward* on principle writes down to its readers, it has often printed by far the
best fiction and belles-lettres of any newspaper in America. This
was Mr. Cahan's second striking conception for his journal. He
has employed an amazing array of remarkable writers whose
names are totally unknown to the English-reading public, yet
they have contributed real literature to the columns of this East
Side newspaper.

When I visited Poland in June 1922, I traveled from Warsaw
to Vilna in the company of a staff writer of the *Forward* and I
felt as if I were motoring with royalty. For whenever we
stopped in a town, if only for a few minutes to get a cup of coffee, someone recognized the man who sat on the front seat with
the chauffeur and in no time at all a crowd had gathered to
gaze upon one whom I soon dubbed the uncrowned king of
Poland. Sholem Asch, the novelist and playwright, has a following wherever Yiddish is spoken, and he has now become known
in some degree to English-language readers. In several of the
half-wrecked Polish towns we passed through his plays were
being given; before Hitler's rise he was known from one end of
Germany to the other as a great American writer — he was even
then an American citizen. But Asch is only one of a group of
poets and writers who, like Jonah Rosenfeld, Solomon Levine,
and Z. Libin, have contributed their sketches and studies of
human life, their psychological stories, or their humor to the
Forward and have added to its luster. Of late years, new and
equally important writers have been added to the staff, notably
J. J. Singer, the author of *Yoshe Kalb, The Brothers Ashkenazi,*
and *East of Eden;* his works are now being translated into various languages. Just as in the case of Sholem Asch, Cahan discovered this man's unusual talents in a novel of his that appeared
in a provincial Polish-Jewish newspaper some years ago. And
still another man of achievement and promise is Z. Schneyer.

There is always an opening in the *Forward* for the talented writers of the race.

Best of all, the whole spirit of the paper, though printed in a foreign language, is imbued by a true Americanism. By that, of course, I don't mean the base metal which goes by the name of hundred-per-cent patriotism. It is really actuated by the old American ideals of liberty and justice. Hence it was hounded by the government during the first World War and harassed at every possible opportunity by the secret service. It was not fooled by the slogans of that war for a single second, nor by the false cries that it was a war for democracy and to end war. But it is wholeheartedly behind the President and the second World War, upon the outcome of which depends whether or not there will be a Jew left in Europe. The *Forward* is, of course, not working to keep alive a foreign language in America or to delay the assimilation into our body politic of those who support it. Its editors and backers have never been worried by the thought that some day they may have to publish their journal in English for lack of Yiddish readers; indeed, they do everything in their power to make their readers acquire the English language. Long ago the *Forward* printed fifty articles on learning English and bound them into a book for general sale, and it has awarded prizes for the best essays in English by those between the ages of fifteen and sixteen years.

The board of management of the larger Forward Association comprises nine men, two of them being the editor and the manager, who are elected yearly. Usually the editor's complete control is never questioned. Matters of policy, however, do come before the Association and ordinarily the opinion of the small managing group prevails. It is a democratic procedure, yet the editor and manager must needs conform to the policy of the managerial group. But Mr. Cahan wields a controlling, his enemies say a despotic, influence. The *Forward* is really New York's most interesting newspaper experiment and one of the most challenging in the whole United States since it is far more than just a New York daily. It has a large office in Chicago for its special Chicago edition, and it also is published in Philadelphia, Boston, Detroit, Cleveland, Baltimore, and Newark; for each issue there is provided at least a couple of pages of local news.

In short, the *Vorwärts* is a striking American newspaper in the Yiddish language. The men who write it are members of no Rotary Club and no Chamber of Commerce, and they belong to no social organization on Fifth Avenue. But whatever their faults, and however changed their points of view, they are Americans to the core; they have taught great masses of our working men how to stay organized and how to lift themselves up and thereby to lift up the whole standard of American living. To multitudes they have brought hope and inspiration and courage in times that are the worst possible for men and women of their faith. And these men who are giving this unselfish, loyal service to their people and to the country are Jews.

CHAPTER XXII

Cyrus H. K. Curtis, a Total Failure

CYRUS H. K. CURTIS is a most striking example of the rich man who, having made a great success in one line of business, thinks that he has the necessary wisdom, experience, and fitness to publish newspapers and then makes a total failure of his ventures. Having made millions by catering to the mass mind with the *Country Gentleman,* the *Saturday Evening Post,* and the *Ladies' Home Journal,* Curtis deemed himself entirely fitted to make an additional fortune in the newspaper field. He was entirely mistaken; he was totally unfit to conduct daily journals. As a result he, and his estate after his death, lost many millions of dollars. It was a most lamentable failure. Not so much because of the millions wasted, but because he laid the hand of death upon some fine and historic newspapers — the Philadelphia *Press, North American, Evening Telegraph,* and the *Public Ledger,* a public institution — and he very nearly extinguished the New York *Evening Post.*

In the first place, his was a dull and colorless mentality and personality. He was without intellectual vigor, and without deep convictions beyond those of the ordinary American business man who discovers that he has beliefs only when his "pocket-nerve" is threatened. Next, he had no news sense. The secret of his magazine success was that he guessed correctly the mind and hearts of what abroad would be called the "lower middle class," that he furnished cheap "literary" entertainment and much good fiction for a fabulously small sum; that he made his *Ladies' Home Journal* a composite of good recipes, excellent advice as to home-making and home-keeping, plus good fiction in large doses. He probably did more to mechanize and standardize the mind of America than any other man, yet he often did improve the public taste. With business courage, skill and luck in picking able executives, he built up his two popular magazines until their circulations broke all records, their advertising rates were the highest ever known, and his income was believed to be as much of ten million dollars a year as the income tax permitted him to retain.

Had Curtis been content with this unprecedented success, his fame as the Henry Ford of the magazine industry would today be untarnished. But he longed for new fields to conquer, unaware that he was, like Henry Ford, Munsey, and many another American who has amassed riches by talent in one line or business, without the breadth or the vision or the mental power to master the difficulties of so intricate a business as the modern newspaper. He could deliver to millions every week a magazine that would satisfy their thirst for the weekly printed page; he was unable to create newspapers which could stand on their own feet, make profits, inspire public confidence, speak with authority, and wield great power. It was for him as for so many others just a business enterprise. That there were moral imponderables involved was beyond Curtis. He was unaware of any public responsibility. He destroyed those historic Philadelphia dailies as ruthlessly and as callously as Munsey put to death so large a percentage of those that fell into his hands. Curtis felt sure that as he had created unique magazines and opened up a great virgin publishing field, if he could just decrease the newspaper competition in Philadelphia sufficiently, he, with his great prestige, could market profitably any kind of journal provided that it was not radical, hurt nobody's feelings, followed the conventional lines, and never offended his associates and cronies in the business world and the Union League Club.

Hence Mr. Curtis naturally decided in 1913 to purchase the *Public Ledger,* for generations one of the staidest of Philadelphia's institutions, a perfect embodiment of the conservatism and propriety of Rittenhouse Square, as well as of its dullness and its sanctimoniousness. Despite its national reputation, it had gradually faded into a state of not shabby but penurious gentility toward the close of the George W. Childs proprietorship and that of George W. Ochs. Here was an event indeed. A past master in the magazine field, with unlimited means, had obtained control of one of the most widely known American dailies. Surely, it was thought, the world will now see a notable journalistic development, the revivifying of a great institution along original lines. The Midas touch must bring forth millions here; all the lessons learned in piloting his twin magazines to unheard-of circulations must, in the shortest time, make over the *Public Ledger* into the most powerful of our dailies. Curtis soon let it be known that his aim was to create a national newspaper and that unlimited sums would be spent to develop the *Ledger*. Later on he founded an evening edition to round out the day.

For fully fifteen years after Curtis made this decision he lavished millions upon the *Ledger* in the hope of making it the greatest American daily. Endlessly it was advertised — even as the *"Manchester Guardian* of America." David Lloyd George, who was as glad to contribute to it as to the Hearst papers or any others which might offer him recompense, declared that the *Public Ledger* was more frequently quoted in England than any other American daily. Indeed, the *Morning Ledger* created a remarkable foreign service which it widely syndicated. Colonel House was one of its political commissioners, William Howard Taft wrote for it for months on end many of the most short-sighted editorials that ever saw the light of day, and many other celebrities contributed to its columns. By sheer force of publicity and unlimited millions, the sales of the *Morning* and *Evening Ledger* reached a total of 315,575 on March 31, 1926, with a very impressive sale of 437,024 for the Sunday edition. Further to advertise it, Curtis built for the *Public Ledger* one of the finest newspaper offices in the country (sold in 1942 for a small sum to a man who began life as a *Ledger* newsboy). But for all that, by 1926 the *Public Ledger* — that is, the morning edition — was beginning to go downhill. Despite its excellent qualities and features, it was without originality or distinction and without a heart. It was unable to rise even with a vulgar comic section, the Sunday pictorial, and the usual spread-headed Sunday features.

This was the more remarkable because Philadelphia is so rigidly conventional a city and has been so much more impervious to new ideas than any other of the five largest American cities that it should have been fertile soil for the kind of newspaper which Curtis tried to build. The *Ledger* contained what most people believed to be an admirable section devoted not merely to the news of Wall Street, but to trade and commerce, with which section it claimed to have pioneered. If that was so, it was the only strikingly original departure under Curtis. The brain that found the brains to build his magazines along new lines that every other similar magazine was forced to imitate could not find the men to build up the *Ledger* as the New York *Times* was built up, nor win similar public friendship. After doing about everything that the ordinarily successful newspaper had resorted to, the two *Ledger* newspapers were only just beginning to make both ends meet before they began to slump.

What is the answer? It is probably to be found in Curtis himself, in his uncertainty as to just what he tried to achieve, and in his own philosophy of life. It never occurred to him that a national newspaper could not be published in Philadelphia, and he never clearly understood just what a national newspaper is and ought to be. If he really wanted the *Ledger* to be the *Manchester Guardian* of America, then either he did not know what the *Guardian* was, or he failed to find another great liberal editor like C. P. Scott and give him complete control. Curtis seemed debarred from appreciating what this particular nation, as apart from the "lower middle class," would desire in a national organ, or from making his daily "popular" in the best sense of the word. He was wisely proud of his rise from lowly beginnings and so he ought to have sympathized with all groups of Americans. But the change in Curtis's financial status had the same effect upon him as it has had upon so many others — it placed him in the society of the rich and privileged and contented. He went daily to the Union League Club, there to meet his friends as a super-giant among giants, and from this Olympian height he deigned to give his fellow Americans the benefit of his own views, to instruct them as to what they ought to have and what they should become.

So the wonder was not that the *Public Ledger's* editorial page was vacillating and contradictory, with undefined aims, but that it was as liberal as it occasionally happened to be. Again, Curtis was handicapped in creating an internationally-minded journal because, despite his frequent trips to Europe, he was amazingly ignorant of the post-Versailles European world — indeed, of much that was commonplace to any well-informed reader of his daily — and so he lost his bearings when it came to dealing with foreign affairs. Yet during the first World War, with men like William C. Bullitt and Lincoln Colcord writing for it, the *Ledger* did make great strides toward becoming a newspaper of wide influence in official, political, and journalistic circles. Its circulation jumped from 59,000 to 82,000 in a year. It began to develop an interesting and, for Philadelphia, a some-what original foreign policy — it even leaned somewhat toward the recognition of Russia and especially toward a humane treat-ment of that great and greatly unfortunate country. For a while it looked as if the *Ledger* were going to follow the lead of its clever and liberal Washington office; it would certainly have been a fine stroke of journalism if it had developed that Russian policy editorially and stuck to it. But apparently the Union League Club was too strong. The time came when the Russian tactics changed; the brilliant, farsighted Washington corre-spondents left its service, and the liberal editorials, which the fraternity attributed to Colcord and Bullitt, disappeared.

During this time and until December 1, 1922 the editor-in-chief was John J. Spurgeon, not a commanding or dominant figure, but a liberal at heart, a clear thinker, a humane man, saddened and rendered rather cynical by his experience of life — like many another journalist. He was, moreover, greater as a newsman than as an editor and formulator of policies. But one day the end came. Perhaps Spurgeon was held responsible for the slump in the circulation of the morning edition; per-haps he slipped in one liberal editorial too many or opposed one of Curtis's pet policies too forcibly. At any rate, Spurgeon had the respect of those who worked with him. Many of them felt that he was attempting the impossible. It was the old story of the newspaper editor, in need of his daily bread, entering the service of a rich owner and compromising here and there in order to remain in a great position — until finally the inevitable impasse was reached.

The two great editorial weaknesses of the *Public Ledger* were the uncertainties of its policies and its lack of editorial under-standing of the hidden motives in the political life of its city and state. Until Curtis purchased it in 1925, its able rival, the *North American,* knew far more about what was really going on. But under Curtis the *Ledger* usually stood against the political ex-ploiters. It upheld Mayor Blankenburg's reform administration of Philadelphia, and it threw its full support to Gifford Pin-chot in his campaign for the governorship. It was independent politically, though it would have hardly supported a Democrat for President, or attacked the Republican tariff — instead of de-nouncing the proposed ship subsidies of its time, it merely called for more study of the problem and greater knowledge. But its unsteadiness was illustrated by its belittling one day the attack upon Attorney General Daugherty as probably unjustified, if not inspired by improper motives, yet a few days later declaring that Daugherty, innocent or guilty, had got to go. It attacked the liberals who wished to amend the Constitution, saying that they were "hungry for the spoils, privileges, and powers of office," but was discreetly silent when President Harding himself demanded two amendments forthwith.

Most extraordinary of all, it printed on November 11, 1922 an editorial showing how completely the promises and hopes of Armistice Day, 1918, had become "ashes and dust"; how entirely the peace had failed — is it, the *Ledger* asked, "because humanity is inherently selfish, sordid, and careless?" By the time the evening edition was out it had had second thoughts, which it embodied in an editorial entitled "The War against War Did Not Wholly Fail." In this it declared that it is worth remembering that "jingoes and jingoism, ancient afflictions of our civilization, passed forever from power and authority when the Armistice was signed"! — this just before the time that certain ultra-jingo Greeks were trying and executing ministers, a general, and an admiral for the unsuccessful jingo venture into Turkey, to say nothing of jingoism in fifty other parts of the globe, or the worse than jingoism which has occurred since. The critic found it hard to take seriously thereafter an editorial page on which such precious nonsense, such downright fabrication, could appear, or to believe that this daily might call itself either a national journal or on a par with a second-rate English daily.

In this feeling one was reinforced by the following reference to the problem of the political prisoners in the column of a staff writer: "What we think of the so-called political prisoners and those who are leading the crusade for their release cannot be printed in a decent, self-respecting journal. It is fit only for the fireside. . . . If the friends of the so-called political prisoners will call at this desk, we'll be delighted to tell them what we think." Surely one who had so little knowledge or understanding of fundamental American principles was hardly a sound American adviser. But it must be admitted that this refined writer voiced the policy of the *Ledger*. Thus, in the fight for free speech and the liberty of the American individual the

Ledger helped not at all, and in its policies in regard to labor it was usually reactionary, as might have been expected. Yet it was characteristic of its wobbling policy that it sympathetically portrayed the denials of free speech in Vintondale, Pennsylvania, and elsewhere and that it at times printed articles showing some appreciation of the aspirations of labor. When the coal strike of 1922 came on, the *Ledger* insisted that the miners' demands were "indefensible and foolish," but it did admit frankly that that industrial war was inevitable because of the conditions in this "half-feudal, chaotic industry." In 1919 the *Ledger* was even more violent, declaring that "under the circumstances, a strike of the miners would be 'treasonable' and should be treated as such." In the steel strike of the same year it wanted to "Rip the Roof off the 'Red' Mystery," and it did everything in its power to make people believe that the strike was revolutionary in its purpose and Bolshevik in its inspiration. But then it warned its capitalistic friends that if "capital intends to continue its fight against unionism as it has a right to do it must abide by the new rules of the game. There is a revolt within its own ranks [the Rockefeller position] that will force it to do so."

The *Ledger* always inclined somewhat toward the League of Nations and did not hesitate to criticize freely our former Allies. Believing at one time that President Harding was planning a general economic conference, it expressed itself thus: "America insists that until Europe begins to disarm, pay its debts and reduce its budget, until outgo falls within income, it is useless to bother us for financial help or to make a beggar's plea in avoiding just debts." It had a very clear idea as to where the French policy that culminated in the invasion of the Ruhr was leading Europe. In order to make the European nations understand more fully what the United States stood for and desired, it did a remarkable thing: it joined with certain of the great newspapers of the Old World in placing before their readers a weekly summary of the current political affairs and national happenings in America. These dispatches were published in England and on the Continent. That was a magnificent conception; had it been continued on a large scale, with adequate cooperation from the foreign press, it would have been a great service indeed to everybody concerned. Throughout Curtis's ownership the *Ledger* made a most praiseworthy effort to give its readers adequate pictures of what was happening abroad, and by the quantity and quality of the dispatches published to make its readers realize the stake that America had in the post-war world, and especially in European affairs.

To Curtis's credit it must be written down that he was a liberal and often an unusually kind employer — though able to discharge editors at times with amazing suddenness and ruthlessness — and he was reputed to pay higher wages than any other Philadelphia publisher of a daily newspaper. Under him the advertising columns of the *Public Ledger* were as clean as a whistle in their contents. But despite his great wealth, the *Ledger* was no more to be trusted in the handling of news unfavorable to a department-store advertiser than the ordinary journal. Philadelphia was for many years one of the worst of our cities in the domination of the press by the great department-store advertisers — some of the newspapers offering themselves for prostitution with complete harlotry, while others, like the *Bulletin,* stood out well against any attempt to limit their freedom of utterance. The *Ledger* should have been free and unmuzzled because even the loss of some important advertising contracts would have added but a trifle to the deficits which Curtis met.

But it made anyone who ever worked in Philadelphia journalism, like myself, smile to look over the *Ledger's* record — it was all so familiar a story. It is well worth recording here so that there shall be in this record the true story of how a rich and powerful newspaper proprietor and his journal thought great advertisers should be treated and favored. There is the Gimbel Brothers' department store, for instance, always a tender subject with Philadelphia dailies. In 1914–15 an alumnæ committee of Bryn Mawr College called attention to the fact that Gimbel's was one of several stores that did not conform to the fire laws. The *Manchester Guardian* of America could find no space for such a trifling item of news. Even when the fire marshal brought suit against the store the *Ledger* could not see that there was any news value in the fact. On February 17, 1915 the *Ledger* suddenly altered its attitude toward the incident, then giving space to a statement from the firm denying the charge which the *Ledger* had never printed. On June 5, 1916 there appeared a news article to the effect that the suit had been stopped, the firm having decided to build the fire walls demanded by the fire marshal.

On May 18, 1920 the Gimbels were indicted for profiteering in certain articles of food. Again the *Public Ledger* was mute, but it found room for a half page of Gimbel advertising; the indictment interested the *Evening Ledger* to the extent of nearly a half column on page two. Curiously enough, however, this story could not be found in the next edition. A month later the *Public Ledger* did report on two occasions the indictment of the New York Gimbel store for profiteering in clothing. Prior to the Curtis ownership, when all the Philadelphia morning dailies were silent about the arrest of a member of the Gimbel family, the *Ledger* was among them. During the Curtis ownership, it is needless to say, the *Ledger* index contains such interesting and vital news items as that a Gimbel was "host to waifs at circus," "host to school friends," or chosen president of this or that club. As for the Wanamaker store, it had a strike of upholstery workers during which the store was rather conspicuously picketed. Thousands who passed the store knew of the strike but not the *Ledger's* readers until October 6, 1917, when a two-inch item (all relating to the entire strike that a search of the files and the *Ledger* index reveals) announced that after four weeks the upholstery workers still refused to go back to a certain store whose name was not mentioned!

During the strike of the Amalgamated Clothing Workers in 1919 the employers, A. B. Kirschbaum & Company, ran a series of advertisements in the *Ledger*. The anti-union *Ledger* then refused to take the three carefully-worded advertisements (from the pen of a prominent Philadelphian) offered to it to present the strikers' side of the case. In 1922 the United Gas Improvement Company, the lighting "octopus" of Philadelphia, was indicted by a Federal grand jury for violation of the criminal section of the anti-trust laws. The New York newspapers carried the news conspicuously on their first pages; so did the *North American* in Philadelphia. The *Public Ledger* gave three quarters of a column to it on the second page, and when the indictment was dismissed the *Ledger* forgot to tell its readers about it, although the New York newspapers again informed their readers by means of important display articles. All of these lapses of the *Ledger* were utterly unworthy of it and a treachery to journalism itself.

The story of Curtis's purchase and control of the New York *Evening Post* is an even sadder story, for under him this venerable newspaper never had even one period of growth and effectiveness. It was always dull, drab, utterly conventional, never reaching out for big news, never originating any important "beats," and always going with the herd. How much this was due to Curtis himself, and how much to the son of his second wife by a previous marriage, John C. Martin, it is difficult to say, but it is clear that Mr. Martin was the evil genius of the Curtis newspaper ventures. It is doubtful if any more bitterly disliked newspaper executive ever controlled a newspaper office. His cast of mind can be fully illustrated by the simple fact that he discharged a pressman after nearly fifty years' service when he was entitled to a pension, because he had taken part in the newspaper strike. It was explained to Mr. Martin that this old man had been frightened by threats of violence into staying away from the shop and that he returned as soon as possible. That made no difference. Mr. Martin thought he ought to be "taught a lesson," the lesson being that he had to be supported by private charity for the rest of his days.

Barring the relationship, such as it was, there was no reason at all for Curtis's selecting Martin so far as any newspaper experience or ability was concerned. But that has happened before. Thomas W. Lamont of J. P. Morgan & Company, for example, himself in his early years an excellent journalist, picked the dean of the Harvard Business School, who knew nothing about newspaper manufacturing, to carry on the *Evening Post* for him. Professor Edwin F. Gay filled several important staff positions with men similarly ignorant of the business, with the result that Mr. Lamont sold the paper in a few years at a very heavy loss. The *Evening Post* cost Curtis and the Curtis estate more than ten million dollars, according to the *Editor and Publisher*. At the last moment of the Curtis ownership Mr. Martin tried the unhappy experiment of making a tabloid of the *Evening Post,* New York's oldest and most historic newspaper. It finally went to J. David Stern for a sum reputed to be not over $300,000 in cash, and probably very much less. Had he not taken it over, the remaining New York evening newspapers stood ready with certified checks to purchase and destroy it.

Curtis's final newspaper enterprise was the purchase in 1930 of the very prosperous Philadelphia *Inquirer*. Again according to the *Editor and Publisher,* Curtis paid $8,000,000 for the stock and $10,000,000 for real estate and other property connected with it. It was repurchased by the previous owners, Raymond Patenotre and his mother, Mrs. Eleanor Elverson Patenotre, six years later. In 1940 the Philadelphia *Evening Ledger,* the last remaining Curtis paper, which had been losing money for a long time and had been managed by Cary W. Bok, a grandson of Curtis and one of the trustees of his estate, was sold, and therewith the chapter ended. The *Evening Ledger* ceased publication January 5, 1942, having been bought by the *Evening Bulletin* to put an end to such competition as it still offered. The morning and Sunday *Public Ledger* had been merged with the *Inquirer* on April 15, 1934. Such is the melancholy tale of the eruption of Cyrus H. K. Curtis into the newspaper field.

The trouble was that it was not possible for Curtis to see that the way to build a truly great paper, to say nothing of a national one, would be to give that newspaper an intellectually honest, consistent, and courageous public-serving personality. The road to success would have been the creation of a daily which sought the truth ardently and earnestly above all rivals, which stood four-square against error wherever made, which was determined to sound the depths of economic wrong, which held a brief for no set of men and no class of men, and above all for no privileged groups. It was to set up a journalistic standard to which men of all faiths and all walks of life might repair, certain that their views would be received with tolerance, appreciation, and sympathy. The Curtis papers perished because the vision was not there.

CHAPTER XXIII

Frank A. Munsey, Destroyer of Dailies

"Let Munsey Kill It" — for many years this was the comment of the newspaper fraternity when report had it that some journal was nearing its end. "Good newspapers when they die go to Munsey," wrote that rare humorist, B. L. T., in the Chicago *Tribune,* while Arthur Brisbane in lamenting the deaths of the Pittsburgh *Dispatch* and *Leader,* asked: "Where was Frank Munsey? His is the original patent on killing newspapers. You say to him as Henry IV said to the bravest man in France: 'Hang yourself, Crillon, you were not there.'" Years ago *Life* printed a cartoon showing a cemetery of newspapers and magazines slain by Munsey. In it were tombstones to the memory of the *Daily News,* the *Sun,* and the *Daily Continent,* the Philadelphia *Times* and the New York *Press;* the *Scrap Book,* the *Quaker,* and the *Puritan.* To this list *Life* should have added *Godey's* and *Peterson's,* two of the oldest American magazines, as well as the Baltimore *Star, Woman,* the *Live Wire, Junior Munsey,* and the *Cavalier.* After the cartoon appeared Munsey merged the *All-Story* magazine with the *Argosy,* gave the *coup de grâce* to the *Railroad Man's Magazine* and the *Evening Sun,* and caused the *Sun* of Charles A. Dana to give forth a feeble light at night. In June 1923 he brutally destroyed the New York *Globe,* then the oldest daily in the city and the newsiest of the metropolitan evening papers. He sold the Boston *Journal* for merger with the Boston *Herald* — that was characterized as a tragedy of journalism — and then he sold the Washington *Times,* the Baltimore *American,* and the Baltimore *News,* all of which have been merged or have totally disappeared. It was common knowledge that he also wanted to buy and chloroform the New York *Evening Post,* whose desperate struggle to keep alive he doubtless watched with the expectant eye of a man-eater awaiting a hapless bather whom he has cut off from the shore. All together Munsey owned eighteen newspapers and killed more than half.

Next in the Munsey mortuary record was the New York *Herald,* for that was amalgamated with the *Sun* only to lead an unhappy, devitalized life until it was merged with the *Tribune* on March 17, 1924, through its purchase by Ogden Reid. Munsey insisted that during his brief ownership of the *Herald* it was "the best in its history, with all that was best of the *Sun* intertwined with it and the whole revitalized." But the truth is that Mr. Munsey never vitalized any paper. They became more or less colorless in his hands; certainly none ever developed a strong character. Indeed, the product of a merger never combines the personalities of both the journals put together. In the case of the *Sun* and the *Herald,* both newspapers had their separate, widely differing identities, and historic traditions; the combination of them was a hybrid that could not last long. As the *World* said at the time (February 1, 1920), the amalgamation gave us neither the *Herald* nor the *Sun,* and the profession was the loser thereby. What has survived out of these changes is merely the evening *Sun,* organ of the tired and hard-boiled business man. Under the ownership of William T. Dewart, long a right-hand man of Munsey, it is a good, conservative newspaper, with excellent financial pages and numerous effective departments, plus an editorial page one is never compelled to read for fear of missing something instructive or interesting or otherwise worth while.

The profession took the disappearance of the two most distinctive New York morning newspapers all the more to heart because most journalists were certain that both newspapers could have been restored to their old prestige even though the *Sun* had only 59,000 readers left and the *Herald* 55,000. Then, Munsey was anything but popular in the profession — it was not hard to understand why. True, he was no more an interloper than other merchants who had made a great success in other lines, like Cyrus H. K. Curtis, for instance. But Munsey was not liked by his employees, who changed jobs so frequently that it used to be asked on the Philadelphia *Times,* as on the *Herald* and *Telegram* under the second Bennett: "Well, who's editor today?" — and there were those who felt that his wealth was always too new with him. More than that, he alienated everyone because he turned adrift ruthlessly the veterans of the dailies that he killed, sometimes without even a week's salary. Again, his newspapers were of the utterly conventional type; they never offended large advertisers; they followed the public; they played their special favorites and never took an original or interesting line. His critics said that he broke every rule of journalism and that he never created a successful daily, but profited only through amalgamations, the suppression of rivals, and by using already established newspaper reputations for his purposes. He was a dull man personally, and he published dull newspapers.

Munsey frankly admitted that his successes resulted from his trying first one style of publication or type of format and then another, rather than beginning with a clear-cut mental conception of what he was after. He was about the first to try a tabloid newspaper in New York, only to fail, where Mr. Patterson of the *Daily News* has created the greatest circulation in the United States, if not the world. Munsey was the first to publish a Sunday afternoon paper, and for a time it succeeded. It cannot be denied that through his publishing enterprises and others in the commercial field Munsey amassed great wealth. It was long believed that a good deal of this came from a fortunate placing of money in steel stocks in Wall Street, when a great many other people who had similar courage and foresight made great sums of money simply by investing in stock of the United States Steel Corporation, locking it up in their strongboxes, and then selling it after a few years, when the phenomenal rise of common, in particular, gave them a tremendous profit.

In his manly and straightforward but characteristically naïve reply, on August 28, 1922, to the published charges that he had made millions out of the war, that he was the worst kind of a war profiteer in munitions-making, Munsey did not deny that he had been a successful investor in Wall Street prior to his entering daily journalism, but he did affirm positively that he owned no share of any Wall Street security and did not at the outbreak of the war, or during the war, and that he "had no connection, directly or indirectly, with any property or interest that lent itself to profiteering during or after the war." "I made no money whatever," he added, "directly or indirectly out of the war or anything associated with the war. On the contrary, my interests, due to the high cost of magazine and newspaper-making and the generally disturbed condition of affairs, suffered a very heavy shrinkage during the war and in the inflation period after the war."

There was no reason to doubt the correctness of his statement.

The great rise in steel stocks took place between 1903 and 1910 and he could easily have made a huge pile and put it away before the war came on. But the truth is that if he had never gone into Wall Street, Munsey would still have been a very rich man. He published his net earnings from his magazine ventures from 1894 to 1907 inclusive.* They aggregated for these fourteen years $8,780,905.70 — a sufficient reward to compensate most mortals for the labor put into them, tremendous as that was. True, Munsey did not state in this extremely interesting and self-revealing address how much money went into his private cemetery of unsuccessful publications, but a man who made more than a million a year from his magazines alone in 1905, 1906, and 1907, before we had the income tax, who had no expensive tastes and no wife or family, could afford a good deal of costly experimentation. More than that, not all the publications which Munsey killed or sold were losing money. He was reported to have said more than once: "That paper is making only ———— a year. That's not worth while. I can't bother with it any longer. Kill it."

This is all the more plausible because Munsey was an autocrat in his business affairs. He never had a partner nor an all-dominant legal adviser nor a real board of directors to hamper him. He never even found himself in the trying position of having to consider minority stockholders, and only those who have been placed in that position can realize the freedom which the Munsey way of doing business brings with it. He had no one but himself to blame if money was lost, and no one else to congratulate if money poured in. The drawback is, however, that this fortunate position tends to make one domineering, arbitrary, and trying to work with in one's shop, and that was one of the charges made against Munsey.

Curiously enough, very few of the many people who have busied themselves with Munsey's money-making have learned where a large portion of his revenue came from. He was one of the most successful grocery men in the country, for he owned the chain of Mohican Stores which are to be found in certain New York and New England cities. Once a Governor of New York appointed a commission to investigate the ever pressing

* *The Story of the Founding and Development of the Munsey Publishing House; a Quarter of a Century Old,* by Frank A. Munsey. December 1907.

question as to why the public is mulcted of such large sums by the middleman who operates between the producer and consumer of foodstuffs. A member of that commission informed me that they found in Frank A. Munsey the ablest merchandiser of all those whom they investigated. That is, his Mohican Stores were run with a maximum of ability and a minimum of waste; in them was the most skillful handling of goods and the greatest marketing efficiency. In every case the stores were exceptionally well placed, as to both trade opportunities and the receipt of freight, and being on the "cash and carry" principle, they were freed from the endless bookkeeping and bad debts which go with the system of charge accounts. No one could really take the measure of Munsey the journalist without knowing of Munsey the merchant, for merchandising was the key to his journalism as it is an explanation of part of his honestly earned wealth.

Then before evaluating Munsey the journalist one must also study Munsey the magazine proprietor. If he took a most ingenuous view of his own success and discussed it freely in public — he explained, in his statement already cited, that he owed his success to two things, "the forty dollars I brought with me from Maine to New York forty years ago, and the capacity God gave me for work" — was he not entitled to do this under all the historic American canons? Is it not the pride of all America, the very life and breath of Main Street, that here in the United States a boy may rise from log cabin or tow path to enormous wealth, or to the White House? Does not the rise of a Munsey or a Cyrus H. K. Curtis or a Charles Schwab or a Carnegie exemplify beyond all else American social freedom, the boundless opportunity before every citizen, the perfection of our social, our political, our moral, and our intellectual order, and of our beloved Constitution — to be defended with one's life-blood against the kickers and the dissatisfied, the ne'er-do-wells who haven't made a killing? From this point of view Munsey was surely entitled to much greater applause and public goodwill than he received. Certainly his story had enough romance in it to make him properly a chief hero of *Success* and the *American Magazine.*

In all seriousness, no one can read his story without being impressed by it. A restless, ambitious manager of the Western Union Telegraph office of Augusta, Maine, he risked his forty dollars and all he could borrow to come to New York to start a juvenile magazine. How he toiled, how he was his own office boy, bookkeeper, clerk, advertising solicitor, manager, editor, serial-story writer and all the rest, he set forth. He had a right to be proud that in the face of incredible obstacles, his total ignorance of all publishing, his lack of training and education for the task, his scant book-knowledge, he succeeded in his aim — to publish and make money. They told me in Maine that he once employed a man to look up the Munsey family tree and to seek to deduce from it why he alone of all the tribe should so have achieved. The answer was his extraordinary pluck and determination — and the absence of embarrassing ideals and standards.

For the striking fact is that in his own narrative Munsey voiced no ideal or aim save to succeed, to publish something, juvenile or adult, daily, weekly, or monthly, and to earn much money by doing so — he felt he could never return to Maine unless he did. There was not a drop of the reformer's blood in him; there was nothing in him that cried out in pain in response to the travail of multitudes. He was never a muckraker. He espoused no cause with fire and enthusiasm — he probably could not have. He sought power to voice no idealism, to plead for no newer or different day. His magazines were slight and ephemeral. No one will ever go to library shelves for them to find out what was their contribution to the literature or politics or science of the country. They were made to entertain and to sell and were perishable stuff. But in justice it must also be added that Munsey seemed to be without personal ambitions. At least, in a position to demand an ambassadorship ("I suppose," said Theodore Roosevelt of one New York editor who desired the London post, "he'll knife me if I do and knife me if I don't"), Munsey asked no political reward. He did not splurge with his wealth nor offend the conventional moralities, nor use his papers to puff himself. He apparently had no hobbies or avocations. He was usually absolutely absorbed in his business, notably in the *Herald,* which was his particular pride, and he was credibly reported to feel that his position as the head of several American dailies was fully as dignified as that of the President of the United States, if not more so. If he occasionally took a trip to Europe, he was nevertheless, it was said, the hardest working man in his offices. He personally directed all his dailies, but he was not one of those unusual newspaper proprietors who are gifted with the news sense and are themselves able directors of news policies.

With this background, Munsey's journalism could only be that of the contented, prosperous, *petite bourgeoisie.* There was no editorial illumination, no vision, no real power, no quest of the millennium, because for the erstwhile manager of the Western Union office in Augusta, Maine, the millennium was pretty well here. Just as his wealth did not go to his head, so it did not betray him into tilting at established social customs. The conventional he supported and upheld because he knew nothing else. In the first World War, for instance, he wanted us to go in before the country did; all his associates did likewise — and nothing ever crept into his dailies to prove that the war was anything else but a glorious success, a one-hundred-per-cent achievement of all the American aims with which our men entered the struggle. True, he early saw the facts in regard to the invasion of the Ruhr, and his *Herald* told more about the truth of that mistaken move than any other daily except the *World,* but not in any way to offend. As a whole, his papers reflected the mind of the average prosperous American and his narrow intellectual range. They were clean and respectable, both in their news columns and in their advertising. No such salacious "stories" as occasionally slipped into the *World* marred the columns of the Munsey papers. They were eminently safe, sane, and wholly undistinguished.

Some of the editorials Munsey wrote himself, and it is interesting to note that as he grew older he now and then became almost excited over some policy which he opposed. Thus, he bravely fought the bonus for our returned soldiers, believing that it would do them no appreciable good and the country much harm. A handsome pamphlet told us that this is *Militant American Journalism* and announced that the fight of the *Herald* was "personally directed by Frank A. Munsey." Another pamphlet recited the *Herald's* most creditable fight against the Fordney tariff and reprinted a number of excellent editorials. Its owner manfully said that he could not "stand for damn fool protectionism and the New York *Herald* will not stand for it" — which illustrated Munsey's willingness to part company now and then with the Republican Party — he did not support Harding in the President's appeal for our entry into the World Court.

In the main, however, Munsey was a regular; he did not go back upon his own order sufficiently to disturb his business friends seriously. He desired plenty of foreign labor because "the wages of labor will never come down until the supply exceeds the demand." What we needed in Washington, he said, was machinery which would "give service." America, he surprisingly found, "has cut loose from the conservatism of our fathers and penetrated deep into the wilderness of radicalism!" Ere we could recover from our amazement, he added: "This is true in our politics, in our statesmanship, in our social life, in our business life, in our point of view in all things." In this same address (before the American Bankers Association) Munsey declared: "America is worth saving. If it is saved, it will be saved by you and by men like you. . . . Nothing succeeds without ownership interest and management." His own philosophy was further apparent from this message: "Public service does not consist solely in holding public office. The organization back of public office is the public service quite the same as the Congressman, or the Governor, or the President, for it is the organization that puts him in office. Service in the organization is fundamental and imperative in the life of a democracy."

If this is the apotheosis of the mechanistic, reform-your-organization-from-within creed of life, it must not be forgotten that Munsey and George W. Perkins were the two men who made it possible for Theodore Roosevelt to bolt from the Republican Party in 1912. He did not do so until they urged him to secede. To their largesse, to their business acumen and skill in organization, the extraordinary "Bull Moose" achievements in the summer of 1912 were considerably due. Munsey was then quite ready to go "off the reservation" and seek to reform the Republican Party from without. He even suspected that the two old parties had had their day and he urged a union of them in order that the country should have the political line-up it desired and deserved — a liberal, or radical, party and a conservative. His interest in Senator Borah, as evidenced by the friendly attitude of his dailies toward the Senator from Idaho (though the Baltimore *American* shortly before he sold it called Borah "an idealist without ideals"), was another sign that Munsey was still unafraid of a man who threatened to kick over the party traces. Munsey also favored one reform: direct election of the President and Vice President, which was not popular with the group of which he saw most.

Finally, no one can study the several positions he took without wishing that Munsey could have put in a couple of profitable years studying European political conditions, reading deeply certain books which he never touched, and meeting all kinds and conditions of men at home and abroad. For there was much that his press knew not of and so much going on right here at home which his reporters never saw and his editors apparently never heard. Some day a Cook's tour into the hearts of plain America ought surely to be organized for a few hundred of our editorial writers. Munsey himself said: "It is clearly more important that the newspapers should study deeply and seriously the needs of the poor, rather than the needs of the rich," but his editors never took his advice. The poor were *terra incognita* to them.

Meanwhile Munsey's dailies remained on the whole as conventional and insular in every phase of life as they were respectable. Yet when I heard them severely criticized I had to confess that if a choice were necessary I should have preferred them to the Chicago *Tribune* and others of this type. Despite their reactionary or stand-pat tendencies, Munsey's papers were surely far less hurtful than Hearst's sensational dailies. I felt we should be thankful that Munsey's conservative press was as good as it was. It was free from hatred and from bitterness; it treated an adversary with respect and it carried on no campaigns against personalities — that was not Munsey's nature. Barring the *Telegram,* it was never sensational. It usually did not straddle; that is, if his papers had no clear opinions about an issue, they kept silent about it. If they were "organs of the Steel Trust," as many declared, and the "apotheosis of Main Street," they were also home papers and they evidently were meant to be reasonably free from propaganda. If they were without the ability of the London *Morning Post,* long foremost of conservative dailies, and without its "punch," they were also without its snobbishness or arrogance. They were class organs, of course, as much so as our class-conscious labor dailies; but their attitude was less a deliberate assumption of policy than a reflection of what Munsey himself was. Had his background, his struggle, and its results been different, they would have been different too. There was no pretense either about him or about them.

The fatal defect of Munsey as a journalist was admirably illustrated by his public declaration of his reasons for destroying the *Globe*. That was a purely commercial and materialistic statement such as might have been made about the consolidation of two boot and shoe stores. It was without the slightest recognition that there are such things as journalistic ideals or public service, or the nobility of a great profession, or that *noblesse oblige* — and wealth as well. Munsey never felt the slightest sense of responsibility to the public as the proprietor of any medium for the printing of the news. He was a dealer in dailies and a destroyer of them — little else and little more. When he died, on December 22, 1925, at the age of seventy-one, he willed the *Telegram* and the *Sun* to the Metropolitan Museum of Art, as he had no family heirs. Mr. Dewart purchased both the newspapers and the Mohican chain of stores from the Metropolitan for about $13,000,000, and announced that the newspaper properties would be mutualized so that the employees could acquire stock. Subsequently the *Telegram* was sold to the Scripps-Howard Syndicate for the sum of $2,500,000.

When Munsey died the bitterest comment on him and his career came from William Allen White. It read thus: "Frank Munsey, the great publisher, is dead. Frank Munsey contributed to the journalism of his day the talent of a meat-packer, the morals of a money-changer, and the manners of an undertaker. He and his kind have about succeeded in transforming a once-noble profession into an 8 percent security. May he rest in trust."

CHAPTER XXIV

Edwin L. Godkin, Master of Comment and Style

To THE SENIOR Samuel Bowles, of the Springfield *Republican,* George Harvey awarded the distinction of being the greatest of American editors. If by that Colonel Harvey meant that he was the greatest of our editorial writers, he erred; that palm belongs rightfully to Edwin Lawrence Godkin, founder of the *Nation* and its editor until its merger, in 1881, with the New York *Evening Post.* Of this newspaper, after two years of rule by a triumvirate consisting of Horace White, Carl Schurz, and himself, he became the directing head, with complete editorial power and freedom. Few men in American journalism have had so untrammeled an opportunity when not owners of the newspapers they directed, and none others have so nobly used it. To his adopted country Godkin, like many another foreign-born citizen, brought an enthusiastic loyalty and devotion, a veritable idealization of its traditions and its possibilities rarely found in native-born Americans, who take their birthright as a matter of course and have no European experience by which to measure the richness of their heritage. But he brought far more than that; a determination to do everything in his power to serve America, to better her, to uplift her standards, and to keep her true to the ideals of the Founders who made their country in their time such a beacon light to all the world.

This he did easily because he was a master of prose style. His English was clear and straightforward, wonderfully powerful, free from all unnecessary verbiage. No one else, no Bowles, or Watterson, or Raymond, has approached that style in our press except occasionally. For one thing, it was the writing of a completely educated man polished by travel and the society of intellectual leaders everywhere, who wrote only with profound conviction, who till the last of his long career burned at injustice with the ardor of youth. To this he added a power of irony and sarcasm never equaled by anyone else, almost too great at times.*

* A writer in the *Atlantic Monthly* for January 1897 declared of Godkin's style that "for lucidity and directness it is unequalled among contemporary writers in this country or in England."

Woe to him who laid himself open to that trenchant attack! But not even those familiar with his style by contact with its daily expression can run over his editorials now without a sense of amazement at their clarity and logic, at their ability to interest at all times, at the way in which he dissected the statement he proposed to attack with the skill of a great surgeon in laying bare the seat of a disease before actually beginning to operate.

That dissecting, or restating in Godkin's words, of the position taken was often in itself enough to refute the fallacies or shams he set out to expose. But to it knowledge, logic, and power added fact after fact and argument after argument, until the column editorial was complete. "Never write without conveying information or expressing an opinion with reasons," was his injunction to me as a youthful writer. That rule was always followed by the office. Indeed, his ordinary style could be imitated — one of his subordinates used to flatter himself that his writings were often mistaken for his chief's. But that mordant humor and that biting irony of Godkin's at his best no one could imitate. Not even Horace White, indubitably for three decades the ablest writer in journalism on questions of currency, finance, and economics, could so clearly analyze and set forth the essentials of an issue, could so strip the clothes from the puppet held up to deceive the public and lay bare its hidden stuffing.

And behind it all lay great cheerfulness, joy of life, and the keenest appreciation of the humor of every situation. It was the custom to picture the most brilliant editor of the *Evening Post* as sour and crabbed, as a continual scold and fault-finder, because he was incessant in his attacks upon evil, unyielding in his return again and again to a subject — no editor has ever more clearly understood the editorial power of constant iteration. Just as it was actually asserted by some that Godkin opened his editorial council every morning with the singing of *God Save the Queen* and the distribution of gold received in the morning's mail from the Cobden Club in London, so it was believed that his council was marked only by pessimism and gloom — exactly as in England Dean Inge for his setting forth truly the darkness and dangers of a given situation or policy earned the sobriquet of the "gloomy Dean." Instead, the editorial council sparkled with wit and good humor and cheer; rounds of laughter were its usual accompaniment. No matter what his political defeats, Godkin's

faith and good cheer never waned save that at the close of his
career, when ill health had come upon him, and the American
plunge into the needless and therefore wicked war with Spain
profoundly depressed him. His prophetic eye visioned then our
subsequent overseas conquests in the Caribbean and elsewhere,
our big-navy mania, and all the other symptoms of that imperialism which in the long run has wrecked more than one rich
and powerful nation.

Godkin, like most reformers, was gifted with unusual political imagination and the ability to look into the future and foresee the results of a given procedure. Like all men whose lives
are steeped in principle and fortified by beliefs held with profoundest conviction, he could not be content to sail with the
wind or to go with the popular passion. Hence he was nearly
always engaged in stemming the tide, with the result that the
superficial newspaper reader — and there are few others in
America — wrote him down for a scold. Was he not perpetually
criticizing? For opposition editors this was, of course, the most
natural opening. They played upon his "un-Americanism";
naturally his English birth was constantly brought out, and the
kindly invitation to go back where he came from, which one
type of American thinks the fitting answer to anyone born
abroad who dares to criticize anything American, was frequently
given to him, always to Godkin's amusement. Where men
thought their arrows would penetrate, they fell harmlessly from
his armor of humor. No one who has not gone over the files of
the New York and Chicago newspapers for the summer of 1884,
during the Cleveland-Blaine campaign, can have any idea of
the lengths to which personal abuse went in those days.

The respectables of that day, only nineteen years after Appo-
mattox, were horrified at the decision of Godkin and the *Evening Post* to support a Democrat for the Presidency. Were the
Times today to declare for Stalin and Communism, its editors
would be subjected to no greater abuse or more emphatic social
pressure. This campaign of 1884 gave Godkin precisely the
opening he was looking for and established his reputation as a
first-class "fightin' man" and a superb political campaigner. But
for Godkin, George William Curtis, Joseph Pulitzer, and Carl
Schurz, Grover Cleveland must have been defeated. As it was,
the press associations insisted that Blaine was elected — it all

turned on a matter of a few thousand votes in New York State, where the efforts of the *Evening Post* were, of course, most felt. Every other newspaper except the *Evening Post* conceded Blaine's success, but, thanks to the excellent work of the *Evening Post* in getting special dispatches of its own from up-state, the tide was turned and perhaps even the danger of another stolen Presidency ended. For Godkin it was not merely a question of fighting against a candidate who was obviously unfit; for him there was a straight-out moral issue at stake and it was his ability to see moral issues more clearly and more often in the complexities of personal politics and the confusion of issues, and his readiness to stand for the ethics of politics, quite as much as his style, that made him the greatest of our daily editorial writers. As Viscount Bryce put it: "It is not for his intellectual gifts that Mr. Godkin was most admired, but for the moral qualities that directed the exercise of those gifts."

For the student the significance of the "Mugwump" movement of 1884, with Godkin as its chief exponent and protagonist, lies in the fact that it marked the beginning of political freethinking in our modern America. Voters had, of course, changed parties before that, notably on the Free-Soil and slavery issues; but this was the first time that the principle of independence in politics had been avowed by a large body of voters who announced their determination thereafter to vote according to convictions and not according to inherited partisan allegiances and party ties. The hidebound Chicago *Tribune* and the New York *Tribune* were justified from their point of view in pouring out the vials of their wrath upon Godkin's head and in waving the "bloody shirt" anew and insisting that the Democrats were still the party of treason and disunion, because the custom of "bolting" thus begun has persisted to this day. In every election since then party ties have sat looser and looser until the average voter has arrogated to himself that right to switch from one party to another which in 1884 filled his father with horror as a species of infidelity to the two-party system and to the country. So with the press; from the day that Blaine was nominated down to the present hour there have always been independent political journals in place of the practically absolute partisans before that time. Of these independent journals the two greatest were unquestionably the Springfield *Republican* under Bowles and the *Evening Post* under Godkin.

From 1884 to 1900 marked the final period of the wielding of great power by the editorial page of the dailies; certainly it is a commonplace that no single daily editor today ranks with Bowles or Greeley or Raymond or Godkin. Had the last-named done nothing else than sponsor the bolt from Blaine, his fame would still be secure; the establishment of party independence and the assuring of an able, independent press, if only for a brief period, were achievements enough, great and constructive as they were. Few, of course, estimated them at their true worth or even recognized their constructive value. Like every other severe critic he was constantly accused of being *de*structive instead of *con*structive.

The reforming editor has no more tiresome or banal critic to meet than he who is forever crying out that the editor who sees many evils to attack is destructive — unless it is the platitudinous and dull person who says to the editor, parrot-like: "I read your paper but I don't always agree with your views" — as if the aim of a true editor were to obtain unanimity of belief and agreement instead of stimulating independent thinking and formulating of opinions. Godkin's constructive services were enormous at all times, but for these he never got credit, nor will any critical editor who aspires to follow in his footsteps. It is the highest constructive service to unveil evils, to castigate wrongdoers, and to insist upon the fundamental moralities in the conduct of public life and the policies of a nation. This Godkin never ceased to render. But far more than that, he championed almost every constructive reform that came within range.

Civil service reform, honest and humane treatment of Negro and Indian, the establishment of a respectable consular and diplomatic service, sound money — but why go on? Almost every one of the reforms in government of our day Godkin championed, and always by going to the root of the thing, by seeking the underlying principle and setting it forth.* The now familiar signs against spitting that one sees everywhere should have his

* The anonymous writer in the January 1897 *Atlantic* says that "there is not a distinctive principle underlying the independent movement of his period for which he [Godkin] has not found its best and most forcible expression, and not an impulse to action that has not received impetus, and in many cases life, from him."

name upon them. When he began his campaign for this great cultural and sanitary reform everyone laughed and said: "Godkin's crankiness again." But with his leadership the crusade was taken up by the health authorities, whence it spread all over the country as the knowledge grew of what spitting meant for the propagation of deadly disease. At last the disgraceful spittoon was banished from private house and public place. But did anybody credit Godkin with leading in the press this great constructive achievement? Oh, dear no. It was merely his crankiness again.

Never one of his critics had a hundredth part of the constructive record to disclose that lay to Godkin's credit. But that made no difference. Were he to live his life over again now, the shallow-pates would once more be lamenting Godkin's total lack of any constructive suggestion. Indeed, his views on war and peace — he went through the Crimean and witnessed our own Civil War — would have subjected him to endless abuse if not prosecution had he lived through the World Wars. Certainly he would not have been permitted to print again in the *Evening Post* his bold prophecy that some day the soldier would find himself properly ranked next after the hangman. In fact, the whole trend of daily journalism is entirely away from the Godkin type; and if there are men of his stamp available they will not take service with owners who run great business institutions and give to no editor the complete and unhampered control of a great daily which Mr. and Mrs. Henry Villard bestowed upon Edwin L. Godkin; such as he cannot under modern conditions give vent to their constructive ideas.

It was, of course, constructive service of highest moment to tear off the mask from Tammany Hall and to be the first editor to reveal clearly that Tammany was itself but a mask for great and crooked corporations and those malefactors of wealth who profited by them. In this field Godkin's labor was enormous. His ridicule of the leaders of Tammany was as scorching as it was eminently useful. For all the discouragements, New York and our American cities have since progressed enormously in the science of government — everybody would recognize that if we were to have re-established overnight the New York and Philadelphia of 1881. We should, for once, face a revolution if we were to go back to the dirty, ill-paved, unlighted, foul-smelling, "wide-open" towns with all the open, coarse immoralities which that term signifies. No civic worker in this field but owes a debt to the unconstructive Godkin. No city but has profited by his labors.

To the masses he was unknown — the *Evening Post's* net circulation under him never reached 25,000; it was to leaders of thought that he appealed. To a secretary Governor David B. Hill once remarked during the Maynard campaign (in which the reformers, Godkin again leading in the press, waged a successful, though at first apparently hopeless fight against the efforts of Hill's machine to elect a totally unfit man to high judicial office): "I don't care anything about the handful of Mugwumps who read it [the *Evening Post*] in New York. The trouble with the damned sheet is that every editor in New York State reads it."

So did every public man. For Grover Cleveland it was a daily Bible until Godkin broke with him over the still utterly inexplicable bringing of the United States to the verge of war with Great Britain over the little-known Venezuelan boundary issue; then Cleveland, with the politician's characteristic gratitude, went out of his way to sneer at the *Evening Post* by saying publicly that he daily read one portion of its editorial page — the newspaper jokes in the lower right-hand corner. The politicians who felt Godkin's lash were naturally the ones to echo that brilliant but shallow woman who declared that Godkin made virtue odious. What he did was to make the *Evening Post* an extremely unpalatable daily diet for those who wanted things left as they were, or were fattening because of their ownership of certain public privileges; for those who, being dulled or tainted of conscience, were resentful of being made to think, or to feel their own guilt, or were merely disturbed in taking their ease on the fat of the land.

Within the journalistic profession Godkin never stood well; he was far too aloof. If he ever went to gatherings of journalists, it was in his earlier years. He was unknown personally to most of the profession, which neither liked nor appreciated him and was only too happy to join in the hue and cry against him. For one thing there was a not inexplicable touch of intellectual snobbery about him. His training, his antecedents, his friendship for the great minds of his day who were devoted readers of

him in the *Nation* and the *Evening Post,* men like the two
Jameses, Charles Eliot Norton, Charles W. Eliot, Ruskin, Morley, Bryce — in brief, the intellectual élite of two worlds —
made Godkin find his happiness with them. Few if any other
American daily journalists entered that sphere.

Then, Godkin was, quite beyond question, never a great
editor, but a noble and unsurpassed editorial writer. He was no
Bennett to build a great daily and to guide its news editors and
reporters. He was no directing head of a great news-gathering
institution; had he been, the *Evening Post's* story would have
been quite different. True, he supervised the style of its writings,
laid down the principles upon which it should be conducted, and
often suggested notable articles and striking and far-reaching
campaigns in the news columns. There was much truth in his
laughing statement that he had one editorial rule: "I see no one
before one, and at one I go home." He not only, as his biogra-
pher, Rollo Ogden, wrote, "more and more threw off the drudgery of an editor's work," but in his later years thought his work
done just as soon as his leader was written and all the editorial
proofs were read. The financial and business progress of the
newspaper interested him scarcely at all, although he was himself, by the bravery and independence of his pen and his fiery
championship of unpopular causes, the chief reason for the failure of the *Evening Post* to have other than occasional years of
great prosperity.

That in the main was as it should be and the owners welcomed this price of his service. Yet the often sorely tried business manager did feel much upset, and the owners a little
disgruntled, when Godkin's magnificent assault upon the hundred-dollar tariff exemption for travelers abroad and the bar-
barous customs methods on our wharves was so marked by bitter personal attacks upon New York merchants as to result in
1897 in a boycott of the *Evening Post* from which it never wholly
recovered during the Villard ownership. This cost it hundreds
of thousands of dollars and for years made dividends impossible.
Had Godkin's demand that the American traveler be freed
from any financial limitation upon his personal importations
been differently phrased, it would have made some friends and
not bitter enemies. In his subordinates Godkin was little interested; many of them he did not know by name — the reporters

often not by sight. Such a thing as getting the whole staff together for a meal never occurred to him. Yet he did inspire the
editorial staff and set the standards. Hard as he was upon the
shortcomings of his subordinates, I, for one, can record with unending gratitude that for a brief time I sat at this master's feet
— even though that master at times thought too much of himself and too little of the others whose daily toil or whose large
financial sacrifices made possible the great medium in which he
for twenty-one years enjoyed complete freedom of utterance
without a financial care or responsibility.

Why was it, then, that a man and a journal, the one so brilliant and incisive, the other so free and untrammeled, failed
after twenty-one years of this editorship and thirty-seven years
of this ownership to ensure for this daily a permanent place in
journalism? The conjunction seems so ideal, so precisely what
the public today cries for in our daily press, that an analysis of
the failure is certain to be of value. Indeed, this deduction of the
moral of this unique episode in American journalism in order to
see what lesson it has for the student of modern journalistic
problems must be the excuse for putting into a volume chiefly
composed of contemporary journalistic figures this analysis of
one who today is merely a memory or a tradition even to the
teachers in our schools of journalism, which seem unitedly to
ignore the great moral leaders in our journalism of the past.
As to that ownership, the assaying of its shortcomings must be
left to other hands since I was so long a part of it. As to the
editorship of Godkin and that of Rollo Ogden which succeeded
it, after a brief control by Horace White, one of the purest and
most lovable of characters, there can be no question that its failure to make a wide appeal is not merely to be explained on the
ground of its high intellectual quality and the severity of a journalism which clung to lofty standards, eschewed cheap cartoons
and every appeal to the groundlings, and followed the best English models of propriety, taste, and style.

The truth is that in addition to these things Godkin, for all
his constructive achievements, was not a thoroughgoing democrat. He fought magnificently for the higher education of
women, but he failed utterly to see that the day they turned the
leaves of the textbooks in the high schools made inevitable the
victory of the movement for their admission to the suffrage. He

felt deeply sympathetic for the plight of the colored people and
steadily opposed every discrimination against them, but the
working-class movement he did not understand and the evils
of labor unions with him far outweighed the good they accomplished. Godkin was a devoted adherent of the Manchester
School; the lofty idealism of Cobden and Bright had made him
its own. But their laissez-faire theory went steadily into eclipse
during Godkin's lifetime. When the first factory-inspection acts
were passed in England, the entering wedge for government
supervision of industry and business was driven in. The simple
fact is that, theoretically ideal as the Manchester theory is, human nature cannot live up to it. The exploitation of the worker
under our intense modern industrial competition was such that
as one restrictive legislative step followed another, one organization of workingmen arose after another until we have today
unions of intellectuals for mutual defense and advancement.
The follower of Manchester could not look upon this steady advance toward State control (and State Socialism) without dis-
may.

Even so Godkin, though he fought for political ideals and
sound economic theories like free trade which would benefit the
workingman most of all, never had that deep personal sympathy for and understanding of the toiler, that infinite and loving
pity for all who struggle, which would have given a much wider
appeal to the *Evening Post*. Thoroughly convinced theoretical
democrat that he was, and staunch believer in the republican
theory, he yet had an instinctive shrinking from men without
intellectual power or achievement. Theoretically he was with
Lincoln in trusting the common sense of the people; he honestly believed that the cure for a stumbling democracy was more
democracy. Yet when it came down to the concrete, he was an
aristocrat in taste and concept. His fault-finding with our shirt-
sleeve diplomatic service was less that the men were intellectually out of place than that they were without polish and social
manners. The commonness, not to say vulgarity, of the Tammany crowd irked him as much as their venality. From the
English bourgeoisie he did bring with him one trying inheritance — prejudice against the small tradesman. In his attack on
the personal baggage restriction he gave his greatest offense because he ridiculed the merchants' association responsible for

the hundred-dollar exemption limit as little tailors of Tooley Street, as haberdashers, "miserable shirt-makers," and boot-makers.

Again, the fundamental economic background of many issues wholly escaped him. A profound anti-imperialist, utterly opposed to our overseas conquests as destructive of the character and the idealism of our American democracy, he yet did not realize the connection between the exportation of capital and political conquest. How profoundly economic forces have molded national policies and national destiny escaped him. He was like James Bryce in that it was the political phases of life and our political institutions that interested him, and in them he became expert. Under him and his successors the real significance of the Theodore Roosevelt cult was quite overlooked; they saw with justice just how shallow the man was, how lacking in true statesmanship, how barbaric and Prussian in his views as to armaments, how untrustworthy even to his friends and adorers — as witness his deliberate killing of the Progressive Party when it had served his own personal purposes. But the *Evening Post's* editors failed to realize and to interpret the great surge for more democracy of which Theodore Roosevelt took advantage and upon which he rode into office in 1904 and became the idol of great masses who excused every bit of wrongdoing because they thought he was *their* Teddy.

Above all, the editors of the *Evening Post* had too few social contacts beyond their own circles. They had little or no personal knowledge of the sufferings of the poor, of that laboring class who are without any margin between a bare existence and starvation. Perhaps they lacked heart somewhat, perhaps social imagination. The fact remains that they never brought the *Evening Post* to the position occupied by the *Manchester Guardian* in its city and that, whatever the cause, Godkin could make his paper respected and admired the world over but not beloved by many. It never seemed the champion of the plain people that it really was — yes, infinitely more so than many another which mulcted the people of their pennies by posing — for profit only — as the protagonist of the multitude. The *World,* in the latter years of Joseph Pulitzer's regime, much more nearly approximated the ideal of a great public defender than the *Evening Post.* Of course, there will be many to say, like the land reformers, that it is because Godkin did not espouse their particular pet reform that he failed to become the great popular leader and force his talents should have led him to be.

Perhaps it was because some fundamental economic truths escaped him; perhaps the hard function of critic, of censor of public morals, is not to be combined with leadership. To be absolutely independent and detached as an editor, to spare not even one's friends when they merit castigation, is to serve the State well, but usually not to raise up multitudes to call one blessed. Yet one can but wonder if at some time in Godkin's life there had been hard places, if he could have lived in the Middle West and seen for himself the pure, sound gold that lies underneath the commonness of exterior, the commonplaceness of much of the thinking of our rural and small-town multitudes, there might have come that fuller understanding and appreciation of American democracy which even this noble defender of it lacked.

Whatever his faults, what would we not give for such another? In all the field of American daily journalism there is not one today to measure up to him as critic, writer, or scientific student of politics — nor one pen so brilliant, so brave, so free, and so unrestricted.

CHAPTER XXV

Joseph Pulitzer and His Journals

WHEN THE NEW YORK *World* came to its untimely and unnecessary end in 1931, the American newspaper world suffered a shattering blow. It is of little avail now to discuss why it failed, but it would be wrong not to put on record the facts lest anyone be misled into believing that the *World* died because there was no field for a great liberal journal. The truth is that while Joseph Pulitzer provided in his will that nothing in it "shall be taken to authorize or empower the sale or disposition by the trustees of any stock of the Press Publishing Company, publisher of the New York *World* newspaper," the Surrogate's Court of New York set aside this prohibition and permitted the sale of the newspaper to which Mr. Pulitzer had given so much of his life. He went further than that in his will in saying: "I particularly enjoin upon my sons and my descendants the duty of preserving, perfecting and perpetuating the *World* newspaper in the same spirit in which I have striven to create and conduct it as a public institution for motives higher than mere gain."

Unfortunately two of Pulitzer's sons were not endowed with either his ability or his sense of public duty. As he once bitterly complained to me, they were not newspapermen, though he would today be proud of the fact that under his son and namesake, Joseph, the St. Louis *Post-Dispatch* has kept its high standards of public service. Under the other sons the New York *World* ran down from 1925 on. The last editor in charge of its editorial page, Walter Lippmann, was a failure as the successor of the brilliant Frank I. Cobb. However great his talents as an analyzer of the passing scene and a commentator upon it, he was without the fighting edge, without the passion needed in the editor of a militant liberal journal; perhaps his roots were not deep enough in our American soil. Certainly his changing opinions ever since his departure from the *World* have been proof enough that he had not sufficiently found himself or discovered what he really believed to enable him to be the crusading type of editorial director which this newspaper needed.

Its versatile managing editor, Herbert Bayard Swope, also shares the responsibility for the disaster. He was not the man to be tied down to regular executive duties; his forte lay in being the newspaper's representative before the public, with his talent for friendship and his unusual "nose for news." The business management also had its part in the collapse.

But the real responsibility rested with Ralph and Herbert Pulitzer, chiefly the former since Herbert was very young when his father died and was relatively briefly connected with the newspaper. Sincere, well-meaning, but with nothing of his father's force and vigor and without writing ability, Ralph Pulitzer was not the man to deal with so difficult a situation. The staff broke up into cliques. The circulation of the *Morning World* decreased slightly, but that of the *Sunday World* fell from 571,181 in 1928 to 491,796 in 1931. The *Evening World* decreased by 38,000 during the same period, and it is a heinous offense in the eyes of advertisers for a daily to lose ground. When the three sons of Joseph Pulitzer appeared on February 24, 1931 to ask permission to break their father's will and sell the *World,* they and their lawyers explained to the surrogate that their plight was due to the increasing success of the high-class newspapers on the one hand and tabloids on the other, while the *World* had always sought middle ground. They maintained that they had discovered that it is not advisable to publish a morning and evening edition of the same newspaper, and, finally, they averred that New York had too many newspapers anyway. Herbert Pulitzer testified that the cash assets of the *Morning World* were then only $400,000, and that at the existing rate of loss it could only continue for ninety days longer. Since 1926 its annual loss had averaged $811,000, and in 1930 was $1,970,000. The paper, he said, had been offered to Adolph S. Ochs, to Ogden Reid, to Cyrus H. K. Curtis, and to Bernard M. Baruch but only the Scripps-Howard managers were interested. Mr. Howard was in court with an offer to buy the "intangibles" of the newspaper for $5,000,000.

On February 26, 1931, 2,800 employees of the *Morning* and *Evening World* pledged $650,000 in a last desperate effort to prevent the tragedy, but on the next day the surrogate authorized the sale, the edition of the *Morning World* which appeared that morning was the last appearance of that great newspaper, and the nearly 3,000 employees were without jobs; the $500,000 that Roy Howard paid as cash down gave them two weeks' additional pay. The *Evening World* was merged with the *Telegram* and within a year the *World-Telegram* had obtained a circulation of 413,178, compared with the *Telegram's* 236,581 in 1931 before its purchase of the two *Worlds*. Mr. Howard stated that: "The thought uppermost in the minds of our associates, Robert P. Scripps and myself, is that the consolidation means not the death of the New York *World,* but its rebirth." Alas, there is little in the successor to suggest the fearless courage, the vigor, the independence, especially of advertisers, that marked the New York *World* when Joseph Pulitzer controlled its destinies. The liberalism of the Scripps-Howard papers is no longer something of which to boast.

But the achievements of Joseph Pulitzer ought never to fade out of the records of the American press, for, despite weaknesses and a period of repulsive and sensational yellow journalism in the *World* and other New York papers, they constitute one of its most brilliant episodes. Like many another immigrant from central Europe, Pulitzer brought to America a devotion to its ideals and institutions quite unsurpassed by any native-born. True, Pulitzer was not a product of the Revolution of 1848 like three others who left their mark upon American journalism — Carl Schurz, Oswald Ottendorfer, and Henry Villard. He belonged to a later generation of immigrants and did not cross the ocean as a result of that idealistic uprising which would have liberalized Germany and probably spared the world its greatest agonies had it succeeded. Nevertheless New York owed what was for a time its most liberal English-language daily to a simple Jewish-Hungarian immigrant of humblest origin, who came to this country friendless and unknown. Indeed, he came over here only with the aid of recruiting officers for the Union Army, in which he enlisted at once — the Civil War was going on. He remained to make a very great journalistic contribution to the country which adopted him.

This does not mean that the *Morning World* at any time achieved what it might have. It was always a creature of compromise. It wanted to be popular in its appeal, and especially to be known as the organ of workingmen. Yet its editorial pages made their appeal to intellectuals, to liberals, to patriots who were steeped in the traditions and the records of this Republic. Nothing could have been finer, however, than the vision of its purpose, which Joseph Pulitzer published when he purchased it in 1883, which it carried under its masthead on the editorial page until its death — it still appears on the editorial page of the St. Louis *Post-Dispatch*. Here it is:

An institution that should always fight for progress and reform, never tolerate injustice or corruption, always fight demagogues of all parties, never belong to any party, always oppose privileged classes and public plunderers, never lack sympathy with the poor, always remain devoted to the public welfare, never be satisfied with merely printing news, always be drastically independent, never be afraid to attack wrong, whether by predatory plutocracy or predatory poverty.

His platform, dubbed radical, demagogic, socialistic, and altogether upsetting (in the lack then of the easy epithet of "bolshevist"), called for the taxation of luxuries, inheritances, large incomes, and monopolies, the abolition of all the special privileges of corporations, as well as a tariff for revenue only, and the reform of the civil service. Most of the taxation proposals are now law.

At the beginning of Pulitzer's ownership the *World* (which was originally founded as a one-cent religious daily!) proceeded to touch even lower depths of journalism than had the *Herald* under the elder James Gordon Bennett. Pulitzer played far more directly to the base passions of the multitude than Bennett, yet his objective was a great daily of the working masses among which he had himself toiled, suffered, and almost starved until his feet reached the road to renown and to riches. It was by this appeal to the crowd that Pulitzer succeeded; like many another he deliberately stooped for success, and then, having achieved it, slowly put on garments of righteousness. I am old enough to remember that fifty years ago in New York it was impossible to find the *World* in any refined home; it was regarded much as Hearst's *Evening Journal* was at a later period.

It was the *World* as well as the *Journal* that Godkin had in mind when he wrote in the *Evening Post* that "a yellow journal office is probably the nearest approach, in atmosphere, to hell existing in any Christian state, for in gambling houses, brothels, and even in brigands' caves there is a constant exhibition of fear of the police, which is in itself a sort of homage to morality or acknowledgment of its existence." If this language seems preposterously strong today, it was pretty well justified at the time by the devilish work done by both the *World* and the Hearst press in bringing on the war with Spain. Then Pulitzer was willing to outdo Hearst in shameless and unwarranted sensationalism lest Hearst inflict on his papers irrevocable injury. That chapter in the *World's* history was not one to be read with satisfaction by anyone connected with it.

But like Bennett's *Herald.,* the *World* grew more conservative with time, because its permanence was established, because Pulitzer himself grew older, and because he and his family came to a social prominence in which a more sober appearance and less sensationalism in their chief newspaper had merits. It is undoubtedly true also that the change lies in part in our own altered vision. A first page which horrified New York in 1898 would seem tame and commonplace today. As Pulitzer outdid Bennett, so did Hearst's yellowness make the *World's* seem merely a sickly pallor. Nevertheless the *World* was for decades under the spell of Pulitzer's constant admonition to his editors to hold its popular following. In modern slang, he wanted a "highbrow" editorial page embodied in a "low-brow" newspaper. This Pulitzer policy long exerted an unfavorable influence upon the *World* and caused it to lose the great opportunity of becoming the newspaper of the thoughtful middle-classes which Ochs and his *Times* seized — to the community's loss, for the liberal editorial page of the *World* would have accomplished great good in thousands of homes in which the dull reactions of the *Times's* editorial writers did harm. For decades, and long, long after the *World* was rich enough to buy the best of paper and ink, it kept to its poor ink and newsprint apparently in craven fear lest, if it presented a front page as clear and typographically handsome as that of the *Times* or the *Evening Post,* the toiling masses who rush downtown in the subways or surge across the bridges would abandon it. Only within its last years did the *World* make a slight effort to improve its appearance. One hesitates to put one's own opinions against those of the able business men who builded with Pulitzer the newspaper's success, yet I had for years a very strong feeling that, as the *Manchester Guardian* in England had a large labor following, so the *World*

could have improved its appearance and yet held its labor con-
stituency if its editors and owners had had the vision and the
necessary courage. After all, workers would have been best
drawn to the *World* by a friendly, understanding, appreciative,
and just editorial attitude toward the aspirations of labor, together with frank and honest and intelligent reporting of its
actions and achievements, rather than by typographical cheapness.

This unhappy duality of editorial aims was everywhere in evidence in the *World*. Alongside excellent and worth-while reporting, there were occasional vulgarities, often lapses of omission, and much poor recording of events, as in labor matters;
next to admirable foreign correspondence, notably in the Sunday issues, there appeared crude and sensational articles to make
a "wide appeal" and keep up the Sunday sales. The *Times* was
then selling 600,000 copies on Sunday without having to turn to
a comic supplement as a circulation-getter; to the last the *World*
stuck to its distinctly inferior and often vulgar supplement of this
type. But the most striking illustration of the duality of the *World*
was to be found in the other daily published under the same
roof and owned by the same person, which hid behind the
reputation of the *Morning World*. The *Evening World* was the
black sheep of the family, about whose whereabouts and mode
of life one does not inquire too carefully. Like others of questionable repute, this denizen of Park Row lived for the moment
and the hour. It was of the earth earthy, although it, too, grew
more respectable as dissolution neared. For many years it was
supposed to be the money-maker and to have kept the more
respectable member of the family in funds. It played down to
the masses; the *Morning World* tried hard to do this, yet worm
its way into the politest society and the classes.

This it sought to do by calling into its service distinguished
writers in the United States and elsewhere in the world, men like
H. G. Wells, A. G. Gardiner, Joseph Caillaux, André Tardieu,
George N. Barnes, Frank A. Vanderlip, Maximilian Harden,
Henry W. Nevinson and many others of world-wide fame. For
a time its foreign correspondence ranked with that of the *Christian Science Monitor* as of the best. Its readers were certain that
the paper's correspondents wrote what they thought, untrammeled either by editorial inhibitions or by subconscious con-

sciousness of the paper's prejudices and policies. Like the Baltimore *Sun,* the *World* gave great attention to the reporting of the Washington Conference on the Limitation of Armaments by many distinguished writers from all countries and all points of view — it brought over H. G. Wells. Yet it did not profit by this as much as it should have, again because of its appearance. The ordinary city reporting on the *World* was probably done as well as on any other New York daily, if not better, but its editors were known to bewail, quite as if they could not check it if they would, the shocking decadence of the modern reporter. It was not the reporters' fault that every now and then there appeared crime "stories" in the *World* which were not fit for print and helped to bar it from many a breakfast table upon which it should have been. The freedom of the news columns from control by advertisers was admirably complete and highly to its credit.

Independence was the *World's* stock in trade. To its honor be it said that it was among the first to become, with the New York *Evening Post* and the Springfield *Republican,* really independent politically. That, too, was Joseph Pulitzer's policy, and right nobly did the paper cling to it despite its natural leanings to the Democratic Party. Its championship of Grover Cleveland and its espousal of the cause of Woodrow Wilson were of enormous benefit to those two Democratic Presidents — Cleveland almost directly attributed his first victory to its support. Its refusal to accept the specious and superficial Bryan went a long way to ensure that gentleman's defeats. In the local politics of New York City it never faltered in well-doing; yet after years of battling for reform it paid its share of the price the whole press pays for loss of public confidence by seeing the candidates it, like every other reputable newspaper, opposed overwhelmingly elected and re-elected. Despite Joseph Pulitzer's admonition to its editors "never to lack sympathy with the poor," despite the great hold it had upon the laboring classes, the *World* did not wholly escape the wide criticism of New York's dailies that they are of the "kept press" and that they reflect primarily the views of the great capitalists.

Yet it waged some tremendous fights for the people against those capitalists. It at times, for instance, wanted to abate the Stock Exchange, as occurred under Franklin Roosevelt. It at-

tacked its own hero, Grover Cleveland, in the matter of a national bond issue which he sold to the House of Morgan at a
greater profit to them than was earned by all the bankers combined who floated the loans of the Civil War. It compelled him
to convert the next issue into a popular one, thus giving the public a chance to subscribe and saving a high commission for the
government. There never was a secret bond issue after that. It
fought nobly against special privilege in the form of tariffs, subsidies, grabs, bonuses, and all sorts of raids upon the Treasury.
It opposed the government in many of its overseas ventures,
such as the Venezuela policy of Cleveland. Nobody forgets like
the American public and it forgets nothing so rapidly as a newspaper's good deeds. Indeed, the daily is usually judged every
day afresh, and a single stumble today will bring down a tor-
rent of abuse no matter how white the record may have been
for years before. So it was a fact that the *World* did not stand so
well as a champion of the people toward its end as it had two
or three decades earlier, and that it became the object of widespread suspicion among people who ought to have been its
friends and admirers.

But blame for that is by no means wholly to be laid at the
door of the public; the newspaper was itself at fault because its
liberalism had grave lapses, because it was not always consistent,
and because it curiously lacked driving force in its efforts to ram
home its views. This occasional inconsistency was doubtless
partly due to the mechanics of the editorial page; it seemed as
if the editor on duty evenings was sometimes overruled the next
day. Joseph Pulitzer, in praising to me the alertness and prompt-
ness of expression of editorial opinion of the *Evening Post,* complained bitterly that he could not get his "editorial gentlemen"
to write on events the day they occurred. In connection with
its failure to win for its usually sound, wise, and admirably expressed views the attention and influence they deserved, it is to
be noted that Henry Watterson did Frank I. Cobb, long the
World's chief editor, the disservice to characterize him as the
greatest editorial writer of his generation. Clear, cool, able,
forceful in the presentation of his views, excellent user of English, Cobb never equaled Rollo Ogden at his best in the *Evening Post* before the World War gravely tarnished his liberal-

ism and he took the plunge into the senescence of the *Times's* editorial page.

Once Ogden wrote with a passion for justice and righteousness which no one equaled after the retirement of his exemplar, Edwin L. Godkin. It was Ogden's fiery pen as much as anyone's that made the McKinley Cabinet deliberate one morning during the Spanish War whether it should not have the editors of the *Evening Post* and the Springfield *Republican* indicted for treason; it was his pen which with a single stroke punctured the dangerous Hearst boom for the Presidency in 1904. That particular quality of passion Cobb lacked as well as Walter Lippmann; nor did he somehow use as effectively as he might have the weapon of reiteration, which was one of the deadliest in Godkin's arsenal. There was, in other words, often a failure to follow through the stroke.

Perhaps the point can best be illustrated by a really great editorial which Cobb published, double-leaded, in the *World* on December 5, 1920, entitled "An Antiquated Machine." To it was devoted the entire editorial page of that issue. Had it appeared in one of the weeklies which are called radical, it would have been denounced as dangerously revolutionary. Had it been printed in the conservative *Tribune* or *Times* it would have created a national sensation. For it declared that our Constitution is outworn, our scheme of government hopelessly antiquated and inefficient, our Congressional system as if planned to exclude the best minds of the country "except by accident." "The cold inexorable fact," Cobb wrote, is that "the Congressional system is no longer adequate to the political necessities of 105,-000,000 people. The failure of government is largely the failure of that system, and until the legislative machinery is modernized the affairs of government are bound to go from bad to worse no matter what party is in power or what its policies or promises may be. An ox-cart cannot do the work of an automobile truck, and an ox-cart does not cease to be an ox-cart when it is incorporated into the Constitution of the United States." But Cobb did not stop there. "We talk much of representative government in the United States, but we have no representative government." The political, social, and economic conditions of 1920, he pointed out, "bear little relation to the political, the social, and the economic conditions of 1787, yet the American people are trying to make a governmental machine which was constructed under the conditions of 1787 function under the complex conditions of 1920 and are bitterly complaining because they do not get better results." Then followed this dangerous iconoclasm:

During the first half of the nineteenth century the United States remained the model of all nations seeking self-government. It is no longer the model. Of all the new republics that came into existence as a result of the Great War, not one of them has fashioned its machinery of government after that of the United States. All of them have adopted the British parliamentary system as adapted to the uses of a republic by the French. All of them have rejected congressional government in favour of parliamentary government. All of them have made their government directly and immediately responsible to the people whenever an issue arises about which the will of the majority is in doubt or in dispute. In consequence all these governments have become more democratic than that of the United States, more responsible to public opinion and more responsive to public opinion than that of the United States, and more closely in touch with the general political sentiment of the country than that of the United States.

Instead of remaining the leaders in the development of democratic institutions, the American people have lagged behind. They cling obstinately to most of the anachronisms of their Constitution although they are wholly indifferent to the great guaranties of human liberties embodied in the Bill of Rights. They retain a legislative system that time has made obsolete; but they have forgotten all about the principles of local self-government which was at the foundation of the republic, and they have equally forgotten all about the rights of the minority which are at the foundation of all freedom. While holding to the letter of their Constitution, they have so far perverted its spirit that the United States is now the one country among the great civilized nations in which the will of the people can never be definitely ascertained, in which it can never definitely be put into effect, and in which it can be successfully overruled whenever a political cabal is organized for that purpose.

Every intelligent American citizen knows that the machinery of government is breaking down. He knows that the public confidence in government is at the lowest ebb. He knows that government has ceased to function in harmony with either the political or economic necessities of the people, that it is rapidly becoming a thing apart from the actual life of the country and in a great degree indifferent to the life of the country. It is a huge, clumsy machine that requires a maximum of energy to produce a minimum of results, and those results are often worse than no results at all.

Surely an editorial so startling and revolutionary — the only one in more than two years to which the *World* devoted its entire editorial page in one issue — ought to have brought down on the *World* the wrath of hundred-per-cent patriots, of every one of the multitude of worshippers of things as they are. The society for the preservation of the Constitution, whose head-quarters were in Washington, ought to have solemnly resolved that the *World* was a traitor to its country. The American Legion ought to have risen in its wrath to point out the truth that if the *World* had published such an editorial during the war, Cobb and Ralph Pulitzer would have gone to jail — many went for saying less. Wall Street ought to have removed all its financial advertising from the *World,* and the New York State Chamber of Commerce should at least have demanded that Cobb be fingerprinted. None of these things happened; indeed, so far as it was possible to ascertain without having subscribed to the clipping bureaus, the editorial attracted surprisingly little atten-tion. Was it due to the absence in the editorial of the passionate ring of the reformer who must be heard no matter what the price? Certain it is that the Constitution and our legislative sys-tem did not rock as they should have and that that remarkable editorial did not produce the effects it should have. The *World* did not follow up this blast in a way to carry its message to large numbers of people. Yet the truths it told are clearer and even more needed today than twenty-four years ago.

But there was still another reason why the *World* toward its end did not lead as it once had. The *World's* editors were of those liberals who failed utterly to see that when liberalism strikes hands with war, liberalism withers if it does not die. The *World* supported Woodrow Wilson because he proclaimed in his "New Freedom" largely the *World's* own gospel of social and political reform. After the first World War the progressive movement in America, which looked so hopeful in the first three years of Wilson's Administration, was flat on its back, and every reform cause was checked. The "New Freedom" read like a travesty, or like a note out of a long dead past. It bore no relation whatever to current political action, and no one more than the *World* bewailed the political reaction of the hour — a reaction which was as inevitable after the war as the following of night upon day — which the *World* itself had done its full share to create. Farsighted editors truly steeped in democratic liberalism would have foreseen this; Joseph Pulitzer would certainly never have been taken in by such phrases as the "war to end war" and "make the world safe for democracy" and the rest of the war humbug whose falsity and hypocrisy were later so clearly evident and led so directly to the second world catastrophe. In vain in the sight of so experienced a bird would those nets have been spread.

But the *World* and Cobb in this case followed the ordinary run of dailies and editors. They were silent or mildly protested while liberalism was done to death; while every right guaranteed to American citizens was trampled underfoot with the consent and approval of the great prophet of liberalism, Woodrow Wilson. During the greater part of the war the *World* ran with the herd and was as rabid and poisonous as the rest. Only long after the mischief was done and all danger to the protestant was over did Cobb speak — bravely, eloquently, ably, persuasively, effectively. The *World* suffered rightly for assenting to the eclipse of political independence, the muzzling of the press, the denial of the famed historic American right to one's conscience at any and all times.

How can the masses be expected to rise to a leader who falters and keeps silence when the enemy is most powerful and in control? To its blind faith, too, in its idol, Woodrow Wilson, must be attributed some of the *World's* vagaries in regard to the League of Nations. It seems incredible that it really swallowed so many of the pro-League arguments, because, democratic methods being its specialty, it ought to have resented most strongly the undemocratic character of the League. Last of all American newspapers should the *World* have given currency to the idea that, if we had entered the League, the whole history of Europe would have been different, that all would have gone as happily as a marriage bell. For that totally ignored European economic conditions and the fact that the infamous Treaty of Versailles was at the bottom of the steady collapse of Europe, and that the League was hopelessly woven into the texture of the treaty. Far more defensible is the contrary belief that if the United States had been in the League, under a Harding and a Hughes, this country would have thrown its weight on the side of the imperialists of Europe, especially to the French. Surely, if Lloyd George could make no headway against the French policies, there is little to make one believe that the United States could or would have done so. The World War of 1939 was the final answer to those who took the *World's* position.

None the less, whatever its shortcomings, the *World* at the day of its death was, with the *Post-Dispatch,* the nearest approach to a great liberal daily we had in America, and its loss caused deep grief wherever newspapermen came together. For all knew that it was honest; that its reporters and editors could write the truth as they saw it; that, as when Theodore Roosevelt's Administration attacked it, it was unafraid even of the government in Washington; that no advertiser could control its news or editorial columns; that on the whole it lived up well to the instructions of Joseph Pulitzer, and that no more patriotic daily ever left the presses. Surely it is but right that the memory of its great services should endure.

CHAPTER XXVI

Henry Watterson and His COURIER-JOURNAL

FOR HENRY WATTERSON geographical location did much. To be the leader of the press for a section of the country is to speak with much authority and influence, and after the death of Henry W. Grady of the Atlanta *Constitution* there was no one to challenge Watterson's pre-eminence in the South. His death, indeed, left the old Confederacy without a single editor whose pen had made itself known outside the confines of his state. Whether Watterson would have been as large a frog in the Northern puddle is open to much question; he, at least, was clear in his mind that he belonged to Louisville. There he typified the opinion of the Border States, if not of the entire South, in the minds of most Northern editors. It was his opinion that was sought and quoted as the representative one of his part of the country.

He held this position because of unusual gifts. He had a rich, picturesque, and powerful, though usually verbose and often bombastic style, a style so characteristic that everybody recognized in it the man, with all his rich and human qualities, and understood that the picturesqueness was as potent in the editor himself as in his expression of his thoughts. He wrote at great length, as was the habit of his teachers and predecessors and many of his generation, like Carl Schurz, of whom Watterson once said: "His is immeasurably the best intellect which has appeared in this country since Calhoun." Indeed, Watterson never yielded to the modern demand for "brief, pungent paragraphs" and to the end did not hesitate to write not only two- and three-column, but nine-column editorials, spread over three successive editorial pages, often signed, often initialed, just as if it were necessary to label what could never be concealed or by any chance attributed to anyone else.

The older he grew, the richer, of course, became the vein of his reminiscence and his historical background. If his historical interpretations were by no means always sound, he could at least fortify them with a wealth of detail; *quorum pars fui* was a phrase he could justly quote as to himself in connection with many an episode of national political importance in which he played a part behind the scenes — notably the ill-starred Greeley campaign. Undoubtedly he was the last survivor of his genus, and this he sensed himself, for he wrote in his *Marse Henry* * of the newspaper of today: "Neither its individuality, nor its self-exploitation, scarcely its grandiose pretension, remains. . . . There continues to be printed in large type an amount of shallow stuff that would not be missed if it were omitted altogether. But, except as a bulletin of yesterday's doings, limited, the daily newspaper counts for little, the single advantage of the editor — in case there is an editor — that is, one clothed with supervising authority who 'edits' — being that he reaches the public with his lucubrations first, the sanctity that once hedged the editorial 'we' long since departed."

It is not only that the public is wearied of long editorial fulminations. It is no longer interested in the same degree in political events and political machinations. Once of absorbing interest to the newspaper public, they no longer arouse the enthusiasms, the bitter sectional antagonisms, or the intense loyalties of the seventies, eighties, and nineties. The emphasis in national life thereafter shifted to matters industrial and economic, which Watterson barely sensed and perhaps never plumbed until the first World War came. True, he was an ardent and enthusiastic tariff reformer, a never failing champion of tariffs for revenue only. Yet his main interests were in the political game. There, he was shrewd enough to see, an editor can only wield great influence if he himself refrains from political office. He put it: "Disinterestedness being the soul of successful journalism, unselfish devotion to every noble purpose in public and private life, he should say to preferment, as to bribers, 'get behind me, Satan.' . . ." His reminiscences clearly show his appreciation of the weakening effect of the political career of Whitelaw Reid. Yet Watterson himself often ventured too deep into practical politics, as the episode of his clash with Woodrow Wilson shows; the safest course for the editor is after all to let the politicians come to him and to sit as an independent judge upon them and their actions.

But wherever the Colonel went he took deep feeling and in-

* *Marse Henry, an Autobiography,* by Henry Watterson. New York: George H. Doran; 1919.

tense emotions with him. Sooner or later he quarreled with almost every President. Of Grover Cleveland he once declared at a Kentucky Democratic Convention that if he should be a candidate in 1892: "I will not vote for his nomination, if his be the only name presented, because I firmly believe that his nomination will mean the marching through a slaughter house to an open grave and I refuse to be a party to such a folly." Of Theodore Roosevelt he wrote that he was "as sweet a gentleman as ever scuttled a ship or cut a throat," and much more of the same character, which, however, did not prevent their dining together after Roosevelt had returned to a dissatisfied and restless private life. Watterson found in Grant an easy target for his diatribes, and it is certain that if Horace Greeley, whom he profoundly admired and ardently supported, had been elected, their friendly relationship would not have lasted long.

But these and other eccentricities and his offenses against taste, like his long list of unfulfilled prophecies, were readily forgiven by the audience which hung upon his words. For them he was a licensed editorial libertine; his lapses were laughed aside as just one of "Marse Henry's" pleasant idiosyncrasies. What other editor could so have abused a President as popular as Theodore Roosevelt and escaped unscathed? The truth is that the South took a pride in him as in any other noted Southern institution and the Haldeman family, with him the owners of the *Courier-Journal,* were wise enough to agree to complete editorial autonomy as his share in the publication and were shrewd enough to realize that he was their greatest asset and a national one. They soon found that educated Kentuckians who moved to other parts of the United States usually subscribed for the *Courier-Journal* to read what the Colonel was saying. He lifted the *Courier-Journal* out of the position of a purely local or sectional paper. Together owners and editor produced a daily which in its ability, its cleanness, and its dignity, its excellent display of news, and its varied and informing correspondence was a credit to the country.

His unique position Watterson fully realized; it is only natural that he should have played up to his part. How could he help knowing that whenever he appeared on a Southern platform men and women beheld the "Lost Cause" and identified him with the romance with which the South has sanctified and glossed over its memory of the abortive effort to break up the Union? Yet, Southerner that he was, he could swim counter to the stream of public opinion. It is related of a poor white in Watterson's section that in defending his wayward son after atrocious misbehavior he sought to palliate the boy's offense by assuring an eyewitness that, whatever else might be said of his scion, his son had "never cussed his ma at the table." Watterson never cussed his Southern motherland in a way to offend the prejudices of his friends and neighbors. But he was not a hidebound partisan, as his advocacy of the Greeley Liberal Republican ticket showed; he was politically truly independent.

He was not, therefore, to be classed politically with the "professional Southerners"; there were distinct streaks of liberalism in him. Booker T. Washington wrote of him: "If there is anywhere a man who has broader or more liberal ideas concerning the Negro, or any undeveloped, I have not met him"; and the great colored orator gratefully recalled Watterson's going on short telegraphic notice to speak in New York on behalf of Tuskegee, although the death of one of his children had led him to forswear all public appearances. Watterson came to speak extremely well of the Abolitionists, and could write in 1910 with considerable detachment and much discernment of the puzzling character of John Brown.

It is a fact that the Colonel drifted almost accidentally, largely because of social ties, into the Confederacy and entered its service without enthusiasm. Hence he never shared the bitterness of many and was early in the field for the restoration of the old feeling of goodwill between the sections. The very fact, however, that he was a conventional Southerner in aspect and bearing and often in mode of thought made it easy for him to say things and to take positions which would in others have aroused fierce antagonisms. He could advocate changes which, when they came from the pen of a Northerner, gave rise to coarse abuse and anger. Indeed, Watterson must have appreciated the unique character of his position; he could differ with almost every administration without being called a fault-finding, carping critic or a pessimistic or un-American one, or one never satisfied, or a holier-than-thou person, or any other of the epithets applied, for instance, to Carl Schurz, George William Curtis, Samuel Bowles, and other editors of the Mugwump school, as the early independents were called. In another man in another place this going scatheless might have been set down as proof of the fact that he could be safely ignored. No one could suggest that in Watterson's case.

Yet when the measure of the man is taken, it cannot be said that, for all his extraordinary knowledge and range of writing, he left a profound impress upon his time. Undoubtedly he suffered from the lack of a more complete intellectual and cultural training in his youth, and was, perhaps, not wholly beyond a familiar fault of the successful orator or editorial preacher of being himself the victim of his alliterations and his swelling periods. He once wrote thus pessimistically of his tribe: "The editor dies even as the actor, and leaves no copy. Editorial reputations have been as ephemeral as the publications which gave them contemporary importance."

It will always be difficult to assay Watterson the editor apart from Watterson the darling of his Southern gods. Yet his limitations as editor were marked. No one need quarrel with him because he was a sharp critic and therefore ever disappointed in the politicians he helped to make and unmake. By that critical faculty he served well. But at bottom his professional philosophy was faulty. The editor, he thought, "should keep to the middle of the road, and well *in rear* of the moving columns; loving his art — for such it is — for art's sake; getting his sufficiency, along with its independence, in the public approval and patronage, seeking never anything for himself." Naturally, with this code it is not surprising that, for all his liberalism, for all his anti-imperialism and anti-militarism, there was little love lost between him and men of the type of Samuel Bowles, Edwin L. Godkin, and Horace White.

Curiously enough, he never even mentions Godkin in his memoirs, and finds in Godkin's newspaper antithesis, Charles A. Dana of the New York *Sun,* his editorial ideal — which is perhaps one reason why in the indexes to the New York *Nation* from 1870 to 1900 there is only one reference to the Kentucky Colonel. Dana, "Marse Henry" declared, was "the most scholarly and accomplished of American journalists, he made the *Sun* shine for all. . . . I never knew a more efficient journalist, what he did not know about a newspaper was scarcely worth knowing" — a correct estimate in some respects, but one which leaves out all moral valuation and touches not at all upon the moot question of Dana's cynicism and the character of his contributions to American political and cultural life and its advancement. Dana, however, surely did not believe in keeping "well *in rear* of the moving columns." Perhaps it is due to that principle as well as to some human weaknesses and the lack of a closer political reasoning that Watterson failed to leave as rich a heritage as his talents would have warranted. Toward the end of his life he, like all of his generation, was more and more apart from the deep underlying economic currents of our national life; he wrote some of the bitterest, sharpest, and most prejudiced editorials of his career when the first World War came on.

Probably Henry Watterson will be best remembered in the years to come by what he did to bring North and South together when to be a liberal Republican and politically independent in the latter section took courage and character; by his efforts for real reconstruction, by his realization that even after emancipation it is true that this nation cannot exist half slave and half free. With great individualities all but gone from the American press, it is a melancholy reflection that there is no editor remaining south of Mason and Dixon's Line — indeed, anywhere — whose written or spoken word can deeply influence so many people, or voice the aspirations of a group, or any editor who can be so freely a law unto himself.

Even before Henry Watterson's retirement from active editorial service a great change had come over the *Courier-Journal.* A conflict — over Prohibition, it is said — between the members of the Haldeman family paved the way to a sale in 1918 of this historic daily and its evening edition, the Louisville *Times,* to a "rank outsider," Judge Robert Worth Bingham, who by his marriage had acquired great wealth and after his purchase figured as "the editor" of both newspapers. This connection made it possible for him to obtain his appointment as American Ambassador to Great Britain. Watterson himself wholly severed his connection with the *Courier-Journal* after a year in retirement as editor emeritus, because Bingham swung it to the support of the League of Nations. Under Bingham the *Courier-Journal* had the aim, the vision, and the weaknesses of a metropolitan daily. "Watterson loved the Irish, the South, the Negro, the valiant, the oppressed, and the unequal," wrote a prominent citizen of

Louisville at that time; "today the *Courier-Journal* has no loves." In other words, the paper was no longer the vehicle of a personality, but became more like the New York *Times* and *Sun* and others which were once distinguished by powerful editors, but later largely known as business institutions.

In writing of the retirement from the *Courier-Journal* of Arthur Krock, long its able Washington correspondent and managing editor, and now the brilliant Washington representative of the New York *Times,* the Louisville *Herald,* a morning rival, declared that that left no one on the *Courier-Journal* with similar journalistic knowledge and experience. It then made the following extremely pertinent and interesting comment upon the problem presented by the *Courier-Journal* of Bingham:

It is the singular fate of newspapers which become the property of men of large wealth, which are brought to satisfy and to subserve an ambition, that they have a tendency to become separated from the newspaper world as such and to plane in an orbit of their own. It does not matter whether the new owners are bitten by political ambitions or not. It does not signify whether their purposes are of a lofty beneficence or inspired by some generous ideal. The story is the same. Its progress follows a regular course. The newcomers are convinced that money will buy anything, a fallacy which in the newspaper world has been proved time and time again. They are convinced that all they have to do is to open wide the purse, to distribute largesse broadcast, and victory will perch on their banners and the blessings of a grateful people reward their efforts. But we do not recall a case where that desired result has been achieved. And we have in mind a great many where an ancient prestige has been lost, a solid reputation imperiled, a great influence squandered and nothing has been left but a plant and a staff.

But while the Louisville *Herald* was right as to what happens in most cases when a rich man buys a newspaper, it was not correct in its forecast that nothing would be left of its rival except a plant and a staff. Actually the *Courier-Journal* has evolved into a vital and powerful daily which has attracted to itself such interesting personalities as Barry Bingham, the son of Judge Bingham (the judge died December 18, 1937), Mark Ethridge, the publisher, and Herbert Agar, who resigned to enter the navy in 1942. Both Mr. Agar and Mr. Ethridge have carried on the tradition of Watterson's friendly interest in the Negro to an extent most unusual for men living in the South. Mr. Ethridge served on President Roosevelt's ill-fated Committee on Fair Employment Practices, but resigned in protest when it became apparent that Paul McNutt, under whose authority it was placed, did not intend really to play fair with the committee or the Negro. Today the *Courier-Journal,* with its evening associate, stresses the fact that, although it is published only four blocks south of the Mason and Dixon Line, it is still profoundly interested in the "deeper South" and desires to be considered Southern, but it insists that it is not sectional in its interests. It has published the following statement as to the composition of its staff:

The owner and president of the *Courier Journal* and its affiliated newspaper, the *Louisville Times,* has been one of the leaders of the fight on poll taxes and is the author of one of the most comprehensive pamphlets on the subject. (He is now serving abroad in the Navy.) Another member of the staff formerly headed the Farm Security Administration in a deep Southern state and is as familiar with the problems of Southern agriculture, particularly tenancy, as anybody in the country. Another member of the staff ranks as one of the best authorities in the section on discriminatory freight rates, which so much handicap this section. (Northerners would do well to learn something about them, if they are interested in justice.) Another member of the staff follows Southern politics and writes and orders stories about them. Another is an authority on the race problem in the Southern states. At least four of our staff members are thoroughly familiar with the whole T.V.A. area.

It cannot be said that the *Courier-Journal* is wholly free from the usual aspects of the rich man's daily. It is rather conventional in its make-up and its features. It has a strong reader appeal and is an excellent collector and publisher of news, though one good judge writes that he would not grade it as better than B for news accuracy. The staff creates an interesting and provocative editorial page, but it is criticized as being more of a discussion forum than the expression of a strong newspaper personality fighting vigorously for clear-cut ideals. It is an interesting fact that the editorial page frequently contains articles written and signed by responsible members of the staff and disagreeing with each other. This is certainly all to the good, if only because it proves that the Bingham ownership does not desire to make the editors write what they do not believe. It is a rare thing to

CHAPTER XXVII

The James Gordon Bennetts and Their Newspaper

It would be easy to moralize about James Gordon Bennett and to dwell upon his frailties, for the lesson of his career is obvious. As a young man there came to him a wonderful opportunity to serve his country through a great newspaper then near the zenith of its prosperity and power. The end of his life of self-imposed exile and absentee ownership found his newspaper but a shadow of its former self, with so little to distinguish it that newspapermen frequently forgot to glance at it on their way to work — overlooked the New York *Herald* with its international reputation of yesteryear unsurpassed by any journal in the world, the New York *Herald* with more great "beats" to its credit than any other newspaper! There were years and years when no rival journalists dared to go to bed before seeing a copy of the early edition of the *Herald,* which they picked up in fear and trembling lest they find in it one of those record-breaking "stories" which made its name as famous as that of "The Thunderer" in every capital of the globe. Who could forget the thrills that ran through the world when the *Herald's* "special commissioner," Henry M. Stanley, reported the discovery and rescue of Livingstone in darkest Africa, when out of the forlorn Lena Delta came the story of the stark tragedy of the *Jeannette,* sent to the Arctic by the *Herald?* No one who experienced them.

The truth is that if the Bennetts, father and son, were short of some of the ordinary moralities, they were the most remarkable newsmen this country has ever produced. The father revolutionized the whole science of news-getting, and the son outdid him by creating exclusive news. He would invest thousands of dollars in a news story, knowing that it might be two years before he could get any return. There must have been many thousands spent without any result, but the younger Bennett had learned in his father's school that nothing pays like news. The father began his career as a rank sensationalist, a muckraker, a

purveyor of scandal. People read his sheet — as so many thousands once read Hearst's — "to see what the demagogue is saying," and lamented that so great a scourge could come to harry
staid and respectable New York. From having to write the whole
sheet himself, the father was soon able to hire many to write
for him — it was his boast that he sent sixty-three special correspondents into the field during the Civil War, to some of whom
he guaranteed and gave complete freedom of utterance un-
checked by any blue pencil. Gradually what we should today
call the "yellowness" of the early *Herald* began to fade away.
It always had a penchant for personalities and gossip, but it became a remarkably accurate news sheet. Take up its files for
1858 and 1859 — printed on a splendid rag paper which is white
and strong to this hour — and you will find it mild indeed compared to the conservative dailies of 1918, and, what is more interesting, you will find that it reported local news with an accuracy
nowhere equaled today. Anyone who has had occasion to test
those files of the *Herald* knows that they are remarkable historical material, whereas no historian would care to rely upon the
daily journalistic records of today — woe to future generations
if they should trust the contemporary press accounts for the
true story of the great wars of the nations!

Not that the morals of the *Herald* of 1850–60 were what they
should have been. The first James Gordon Bennett was pro-
slavery, pro-Tammany, and pro-everything which we should
say today "made against good government." "Intercourse with
him indeed quickly revealed his cold, hard, utterly selfish nature
and incapacity to appreciate high and noble aims," wrote one
of his war correspondents. When the Civil War broke out, he
was in much the same plight as his modern imitator, Hearst, in
1917; people denounced him as disloyal and unpatriotic and
threats of a mob compelled a radical change of front. At once he
became a loyalist of the loyalists; he gave a yacht to the government, his son became a volunteer officer in the navy, and he
saved the day by redoubling his news efforts. Politicians still
had to reckon with the *Herald's* influence. Count Gurowski
wrote in his diary in August 1861 that it was generally believed
that Lincoln read only the *Herald*. John Bright at the same time
blamed the "reckless tone of your New York *Herald*," which,
according to Rhodes, "spoke for a potent public sentiment out-

side of New England." The best news from the front was in either the *Herald* or the *Tribune*. For decades the special foreign service of the former was unsurpassed; even though it carried trivialities and scandal, one had to read it if one would be posted as to events and political personalities in Europe.

To this service the younger Bennett gave his personal attention when events took him to Paris to live. There is no doubt of his ability, and no doubt that he had it in him also to play a great part in his country's history had he desired to live another life than he chose. To have guided the destinies of his newspapers by cable — he founded both the *Telegram* and the Paris *Herald* — is evidence in itself of his power, for he was always in closest touch with the smallest details and constantly upsetting this or that for some freakish reason as his eccentricities grew upon him. There was much of the pioneer in him. As his father speedily recognized the news possibilities in the cable, the son became one of the owners of the Commercial Cables in order that the *Herald* might profit thereby. When the automobile appeared, it was Bennett who saw the news and business value of being first in this field, and the same was true of the airplane, as it had been of the bicycle. He liked the novel and the bizarre and he did not mind if people ridiculed him and the *Herald;* what he dreaded was their not talking about his papers. Until late in life he kept the faculty of looking far ahead; it was not by accident that a correspondent of the *Herald* stood beside Dewey on that memorable morning in Manila Bay when he said to Gridley: "You may fire when you are ready."

Again, the second Bennett had the great good sense to make himself supreme in several fields, realizing the value of specialties to a daily. Thus the *Herald* was for generations the great shipping medium because it spent thousands in special dispatches from all over the world reporting ship arrivals and departures. In the theatrical field, as in that of sports, it was long without a rival. Every naval officer, yachtsman, and lover of horses read it, as did every sporting man, the latter tempted for years by a class of immoral advertisements to which the Department of Justice, in the person of one Henry L. Stimson, put an end, the famous proprietor himself being fined $25,000 — a remarkable public achievement on which the press of New York was silent — to its shame. Moreover, the *Herald* succeeded without a strong editorial page. Outside of Bennett's own name, there is hardly that of a virile journalist to be recalled in connection with his properties. This may have been because many men may not have wished to be associated with one whose whims were so apt to terminate careers without warning. In his last years Bennett apparently lost all faith in the uses of an editorial page, and the *Herald's* influence, unlike that of the *Tribune* and the *Times,* rested exclusively upon its presentation of the news. Gradually, as Bennett grew older, his grip relaxed, his visits to this side became fewer and fewer, and the *Herald's* star began to wane. Its circulation rapidly fell off until he was compelled to drop the price to one cent in order to achieve 100,000 readers where once there had been 500,000. On April 1, 1918 it swore to 128,814; in 1916 to only 92,853; years previously its finances had compelled the dropping of its costly special dispatches from every quarter of the globe.

Whereas for years the *Herald* had met the deficits of the *Telegram,* that pink drab of lowest journalism kept its elder sister afloat during the last years of the Bennett ownership, despite the fact that during the war it was the soul of mendacity, killing off in a few months of the war more Germans than were ever in the Kaiser's Empire and preaching the worst kind of bitterness and hate. Incidentally, the *Telegram* knew itself how it feels to be killed because, in one of his unaccounted-for moods, Bennett, on November 21, 1897, thus took the public into his confidence and notified his advertisers by the following editorial in the *Herald* that he had been deceiving them:

The *Evening Telegram* ceases to appear from yesterday for the time being, in accordance with Abraham Lincoln's wise saying that "you can fool all the people some of the time and some of the people all the time, but you can't fool all the people all the time."

And he was right. The public also can fool publishers all the time and advertisers can fool publishers some of the time and they seem to be continuing to fool them all the time. But the *Evening Telegram* doesn't propose to be fooled all the time.

An up-to-date evening newspaper at one cent doesn't pay. Therefore those who are publishing evening newspapers at one cent are either fooling the public or fooling themselves.

As the *Evening Telegram* doesn't intend either to fool itself or fool the public it has ceased publication until the time becomes ripe when it can stop being fooled and stops fooling.

This was on a Sunday, and the entire newspaper world was agog the next day to see if Bennett would really slay his journalistic child. Whether on sober thought he came to it himself, or whether he was persuaded by cablegrams from New York, the *Telegram* was granted a stay of its execution by the following announcement in the *Herald:*

In view of its many outstanding advertising contracts and large circulation and for other considerations, the several editions of the *Evening Telegram* will continue to appear as usual every day, with all the latest news and the numerous bright features that have made the *Telegram* the favorite evening paper of Greater New York.

The death of Bennett on May 14, 1918 revealed the fact that his fortune had been rapidly shrinking and that there were not available the means to carry on the newspapers. For years the faithful men of long service, who had kept the Bennett properties alive, had been assured by their employer that these properties would be left to them to conduct as a co-operative experiment. These pledges were broken in the will and the executors directed to continue to publish the papers. This being impossible for several reasons, they passed in January of 1920 into the hands of Frank A. Munsey, whereby there ended one of the most brilliant chapters in American journalism and the *Herald* became a hybrid, part *Sun* and part *Herald,* without the great characteristics of either.

CHAPTER XXVIII

William Lloyd Garrison, Editor; "The Good Old Days"

A FIVE-THOUSAND-DOLLAR reward for him, "dead or alive," offered by the legislature of a sovereign American state after a single year of editorial activity — this would seem to be a striking enough achievement for an American journalist in what history and civilized opinion everywhere have since proclaimed to be a holy cause, the freeing of the slave. It certainly entitles William Lloyd Garrison to a position as an editor as well as a reformer, for I do not know of any other to whom quite such a handsome tribute has been paid as that reward constitutes. This and other protests from the South induced the Mayor of Boston to send around some of his minions to investigate the firebrand whose weekly journal was being publicly burned, barred from Southern post offices, denounced wherever it penetrated — precisely as if it were what is called a "Red" journal of today — and was generally throwing a half of the United States of that day into spasms of rage and fear. What Mayor Otis's agents found James Russell Lowell described as follows:

> In a small chamber, friendless and unseen,
> Toiled o'er his types one poor, unlearned young man;
> The place was dark, unfurnitured, and mean;
> Yet there the freedom of a race began.

There is no poet's license in this description of Garrison's beginning. He had not a single dollar to his name nor a single subscriber secured in advance. The first paper he used was obtained on credit. On the floor of the attic he and his partner, Isaac Knapp, slept, eating what they could get from a near-by bakery, and in that attic they set and distributed every bit of type, made up the forms, put them on their little press, printed from them, and wrapped, addressed, and mailed the copies. Theirs was a workshop, office, and home in one. For a year and a half Garrison lived thus in what Mayor Otis's men declared to be "an obscure hole, his only visible auxiliary a Negro boy, and his supporters a few insignificant persons of all colors."

[278]

This editor had had to go to work as soon as his common school-
ing ended; his passion for justice, his love of humanity, were his
high school and his university. Of friends he had but a few, of
influence none. How preposterous that he should attack an evil
so firmly entrenched in American life, customs, and laws! How
absurd that the state of Georgia should think his dead body
worth $5,000 or that the Vigilance Association of Columbia,
South Carolina, composed of "gentlemen of the first respectability," should offer a reward of $1,500 for the "apprehension
and prosecution to conviction" of any white person caught dis-
tributing or circulating the *Liberator*! Why should Church and
State tremble before the attack of a youth so utterly ridiculous?

It was, of course, because he had "a faith so absolute in the
sacredness and power of moral principles, a trust in God so firm
and immovable," and because the hideous institution he attacked
was rotten to its core and bound to tremble before the blasts of
any honest and fearless man. But, aside from any spiritual or
moral reasons, Garrison was to be dreaded because the press was
free to all men. It was not the enormously costly, commercialized undertaking of today, and it took no large circulation for
a newspaper to make itself felt. There was, moreover, time in
the newspaper offices of that day for the editor to read his ex-
changes, in consequence of which editors knew well the characteristics of their rivals, their power and their weakness. Garrison
was not unknown in the profession; he had worked on several
other papers before starting his own and there were a few cordial greetings from Northern associates when he began. It was
soon seen that he could not be ignored. To attack him was a regular duty; at best one deprecated his "harshness of language,"
the "bitterness of his tone," and was shocked at his refusal to
spare the Northern respectables who coined so many dollars out
of the bodies of the slaves.

The point is that he had a self-created weapon and that none
could wrest it from him. Whereas it takes hundreds of thousands of dollars to carry on a little political weekly today, he produced his with a few hundred. Whereas one must now build
circulation in order to succeed, he cared little whether subscribers came or not. In his Valedictory when he voluntarily, in December 1865, ended the life of the paper that had been his life,
he wrote: "I have never consulted either the subscription list of

the paper or public sentiment in printing or omitting to print any article touching any matter whatever. Personally, I have never asked any one to become a subscriber nor any one to contribute to its support, nor presented its claims for a better circulation in any lecture or speech or at any one of the multitudinous anti-slavery gatherings in the land. Had I done so no doubt its subscription list might have been much enlarged."

A hopeless editor, indeed; but the freest and happiest of all the profession! Indifferent to subscribers and advertisers and unfavorable public opinion; bent only upon giving forth the deepest and best he felt — how many such are there today? Two, or three, or half a dozen? Surely his was the golden age of American journalism, for in it any man of similar or lesser parts and similar industry who burned with similar fire could also have the rare privilege of complete and fearless self-expression. Many another such an anti-slavery paper found its way to the hearts of men, able, keen, often inspired; the smallest community might have its *Clarion* or its *Standard,* which likewise were content with a few hundred dollars of revenue.

That was the joy of those days, that was one explanation of the thoroughness with which public opinion was educated up to supporting Lincoln when the day of emancipation came. It was a time of teeming intellectual life, enormously stimulated by the fact that the Stowes, Whittiers, Lowells, and Emersons had behind them a small but virile and outspoken press to give them aid, comfort, support, and an avenue of expression. Fortunate the country which finds itself and its press in such a situation!

It was a day of small things in journalism, if you please, in comparison with our huge dailies and monster circulations of today, and things then were cheap — notably the pay of wage-earners who stood at the fonts or composed more or less laboriously in the sanctums of the editorial quarters. Garrison's pay was probably never much over a thousand dollars a year. The subscription price was but two dollars a year. In the first year he found 500 adherents and readers. Only a similarly embattled editor can possibly know what it meant when, after the start, one subscriber in Philadelphia sent fifty-four dollars for twenty-seven subscriptions; what a vision of vast success that check must have aroused! By the third year this editor had won 1,000 to his banner, and by the fourth 1,400 when someone for him begged for 600 more. Of his two dollars for each subscription, fifty cents, he reported, had to go for postage, agents' fees, free copies, and distribution costs. The other dollar and a half had to pay all wages, including the editor's, who in time had a wife and five children to support, but for years the deficit ranged from only $700 to $1,700 a year. It was a day of low costs and self-denying. Efficient management did not begin in this century! Never did the circulation go far beyond 3,000 copies; yet they counted in the political life of the country as if they were a full 300,000. It seems, too, as if every copy must have been preserved, for New England attics still give up their treasures of scattered copies, which make possible the putting together now and then of fairly complete files.

As for advertising in the *Liberator,* hardly ever did it run over three columns, and usually two columns sufficed to contain it. It seems as if a wide-awake advertising manager could have overcome the deficit, but such a one there was not. Then the sad truth must be told that much of the advertising was of patent medicines, for which the editor himself had a weakness. Frequently the editor endorsed an advertiser, as in the case of a dentist who illustrated his announcement with a cut of himself applying a huge instrument to a resigned patient's mouth, while setting forth that the rates were reasonable — twenty-five cents for pulling a tooth, a dollar for a filling and two dollars for a false molar. Surely this dentist was as modest in his charges as the editor who endorsed him. The very last issue carried a patent-medicine card urging the merits of Ayer's Ague Cure, which was quite fitting and as it should be, but not as touching as a little inch announcement that all the furniture and type of the *Liberator* were now for sale — it had had its own printing office and press for all the thirty-five years during which this comet took its fiery way through the constellation of journalism.

A "Free Labor Dry Goods Store" in Philadelphia was one of the most faithful advertisers; no article in that store, it boasted, was the product of slaves, and nothing, we venture to say, that Garrison ever said or did — no lengths to which he went — could ever make that particular advertiser take his announcement out in indignation. "Stop-my-paper" subscribers even this most fortunate of editors must have had; but surely no adver-

tiser ever complained that the rates were too high, or the returns
unsatisfactory, or asked for rebates, or begged for a free reading
notice to go with his advertisement. The menace and the tribu-
lation of advertising were here reduced to a minimum; all the
advertising must have been unsolicited, like one notice from a
distracted mother of color asking for the return of her little boy
who had run off once more and — wayward, indeed — was
likely again to impose upon Abolitionists by representing himself as a fugitive slave! Not much resemblance in all this to the
Saturday Evening Post with its rate of $7,000 and more a page!
Which will live longer in history, one wonders; which bulk
larger in the history of American ethics and reform?

Well, though the editor boasted that he never solicited subscriptions, his friends did it for him. Frequently one finds notices from a friendly committee that four or five hundred subscribers are in default, coupled with a stern demand that they
pay up promptly. Frequently there were cash or other gifts to
the paper. The anti-slavery fairs took notice of its needs and
there were plenty to see that neither it nor its editor perished
from starvation. No journal ever had warmer friends or more
devoted contributors, and when the editor stated at the death of
the *Liberator* that he ended it "without a farthing as the pe-
cuniary result of the patronage extended to it during thirty-five
years of unremitted labor" the fact was not forgotten. A national
subscription resulted in a small fund which kept him free to use
his pen as he saw fit for the rest of his life. The more he was, as
one of his staunch adherents said, "taunted, ridiculed, carica-
tured, misrepresented and denounced by the vulgar and treated
with contemptuous scorn by the rich and great," the more his
friends rallied to him.

For one thing, Garrison was of those rare editors who never
fail to let their readers see the worst that is said about them. The
more atrocious the calumny of himself, the more ready he was to
print it. Some of the unending threats to assassinate him he
cheerfully reproduced in his columns, which were not too pure
for those beginning: "You damned rascal." That was part of
his original conception of what a journal ought to be, and that
conception varied very little during the thirty-five years of the
Liberator's existence — there is but little difference between
the first and last numbers in editorial policy and execution. The

editor always maintained a department of poetry — in which, among others, John G. Whittier's poems first saw the light of day — and there was plenty of verse in the final issue. Like many modern editors, he believed in departments and "stock" heads. The back page, like the back page of many a daily of today, was meant to be of feuilleton quality, and Garrison anticipated the editors of today with their bedtime stories by a department entitled "Juvenile," by which the children were surely edified and enlightened, but hardly amused or entertained, as the effort was to bend the twig that the tree might incline in the desired direction. Besides "Poetry" and "Literary" and "Miscellany" one finds "Philanthropy," columns or half columns devoted to foreign news, "Non-Resistance" (to which, like woman suffrage, the editor was ever devoted), and "Moral"; and valuable above all there were for years a "Refuge of Oppression" and a "Slavery Record," in which latter not only appeared some of the most telling blows at slavery, but many a horrifying or enlightening item culled from the enemy's own Southern press.

What is today the most convincing argument against American slavery and the clearest proof that it was not the kindly beneficent institution which our Thomas Nelson Pages and other latter-day romancers portray it is a solid pamphlet entitled *American Slavery As It Is; Testimony of a Thousand Witnesses.* This contains hundreds of extracts from the Southern press telling of lynchings, beheadings, brandings, flogging to death, and all the minor tortures of the system — the inevitable outrages which happen in every clime in which white men, be they Germans, English, Spaniards, French, or Americans, have possession of the bodies and souls of men and women of another race. Many of these thousand testimonies were clipped in the *Liberator* office and appeared originally in its columns. Indeed, the editor was a master of the shears; his "Refuge of Oppression" never lacked material to stir the slaveholders to mighty wrath.

Undoubtedly from our modern standpoint the *Liberator* could have been much improved journalistically. We certainly should hardly expect a journalist of today to do what Garrison once did — supply his readers with one whole page and a column of texts from the Bible with which to confound the upholders of slavery. The sameness of its headlines and of its make-up would pall now. The dispute whether its editor should have abandoned it when he did, just when the freedmen were so profoundly in need of help and support and safeguarding, will doubtless go on indefinitely, exactly like the controversy as to whether Garrison's vigor of language was or was not justifiable and whether effective reform is or is not furthered by such violence of assault upon the other side. The dispute as to whether one reforms best by the uncompromising spirit or by compromise goes back to the ancients and will continue as long as there are reforms to be achieved. But the fact remains that for all its heavy moral caliber, its Biblical language, its ponderousness, and what seems today its stiltedness and flowery writing, the *Liberator* achieved its purpose with the middle-class, bourgeois Americans at whom it was directed and in whose keeping there rested the conscience of the United States. Crude as the weapon seems to us of today, it accomplished its aim of a moral regeneration of America regarding the question of freedom. To this Lincoln attested when he received its editor in the White House.

To not many editors has it been or will it be given to achieve in the space of forty years so much. But that others shall have a similar opportunity to do their jobs as well as Garrison or better is the great need of our journalism of today. American journalism of the first half of the nineteenth century was crude, narrow, and perhaps entirely too self-centered, but its freedom was boundless, its open avenues vistas of patriotic usefulness which no republic ought to be without. The cry of today that the period of the great editors is gone is directly connected with the commercialization of the press and its domination by the owners for whom the editors are but hired men. Greeley, Garrison, Bowen, Godkin, Bowles, and others, the journalists who have profoundly stirred the conscience of America, either owned their own journals or were given complete freedom of expression. That they were also profoundly engrossed in moral causes helps to explain their power.

With the world in the mess that it is in today, it is obvious that the need of moral leadership in the press was never greater, if only because of the extension of American influence in world affairs. Everyone is crying for a program of reconstruction, moral issues through which to rebuild a broken-down society, guidance toward a world without fratricidal strife. As yet no man is in sight, no large enough prophet, no editor burning with Garrisonian vigor to lead the way, even if it were possible for such a man to command the sums of money necessary to support even the simplest of weeklies. Nor can one today, however trenchant one's pen, be in a garret and expect to reach the conscience of a public by ninety millions larger than the America of Garrison and Lincoln and at least two hundred years remote from them in its failure to comprehend and apply the fundamental, basic principles of American liberty. Yet somehow the prophet of the future will make his message heard, if not by a daily, then by a weekly; if not by a weekly, then by pamphleteering in the manner of Alexander Hamilton; if not by pamphleteering, then by speech in the market-place. However it shall be, the truth must out.

Index

Abbot, Willis J., 117

Accuracy, loss of, 13

Addams, Jane, 90

Adler, General Julius Ochs, 78, 85

Advertising, 3; absence of, from *PM,* 155; and news presentation, 86; danger in, 19; dependence on, 26; influence on news treatment, 23, 225–7, 257; national, and local, 4; omission of, 4, 155

Agar, Herbert, 270

Agencies, news, 173–4. *See also* News agencies, foreign; *and names of agencies*

Agriculturist, 159

Albany *Knickerbocker Press* and *News,* 158, 164, 165

Allds, Jotham P., 44

Allen, Frederick Lewis, 78, 80

Allotment of space, 14

Amalgamated Clothing Workers' strike, 226

"American Century," of Luce, 134

American news in Europe, 224

American Newspaper Guild, 48, 146; and the Associated Press, 56

American Newspaper Publishers Association, 10, 23, 27

Anderson, Paul Y., 43, 44, 120–2

Armistice, fake (1918), 173

Asch, Sholem, 215

Associated Press, 6, 19, 40–69, 153, 172, 173, 201–3; activities and influence, 67–8; and the American Newspaper Guild, 56; and the government, 53, 55, 60–9; as a "monopoly," 60–9; bias in presenting news, 41–50; co-operative character, 67; criticisms of, 57; disciplining of members, 50; domestic news, 54; feature stories, 54–6; foreign news, 53–4, 57; investigation of, 51–2; membership requirement, 60; misrepresentation of news, 91; picture service, 55–6, 65; Washington column, 55

Atlanta *Constitution,* 202, 264

Atlanta *Georgian,* 199

Authority, fear of, 20

Ayer, F. Wayland, Cup, for typography, 117–18

Baillie, Hugh, 172

Baker, Elbert H., 202

Baldwin, Hanson W., 74, 81

Baltimore *American,* 236

Baltimore *Sun,* 32, 39, 180, 186, 187, 257

Barriers Down, by Kent Cooper, 53–4

Baruch, Bernard M., 252

Beard, Charles A., 90–1

Bender, Robert J., 172

Bennett, James Gordon, Sr., 97, 230, 246, 254, 255

Bennett, James Gordon, Sr. and Jr., 273–7

Better Times, 80

Bickel, Karl, 172, 173

Biddle, Francis, 69

Bierce, Ambrose, 203; on Hearst, 204–5

Bingham, Barry, 270

Bingham, Robert Worth, 269–70

Binghamton *Press,* 166

Blaine, James G., 241–2

Blanding, Rear Admiral W. H. P., 147

Bok, Cary W., 228

[i]

PRINTER'S NOTE

This book is set on the Linotype in GRANJON, *a type named in compliment to Robert Granjon, type-cutter and printer — 1523 to 1590, Antwerp, Lyons, Rome, Paris. Granjon, the boldest and most original designer of his time, was one of the first to practice the trade of typefounder apart from that of printer.*

Linotype GRANJON *was designed by George W. Jones, who based his drawings upon a face used by Claude Garamond (1510–1561) in his beautiful French books.* GRANJON *more closely resembles Garamond's own type than do any of the various modern faces that bear his name.*

The book was composed, printed, and bound by The Plimpton Press, Norwood, Massachusetts. The typography and binding are by W. A. Dwiggins.